What Is Cultural Translation?

Bloomsbury Advances in Translation Series

Series Editor: Jeremy Munday, Centre for Translation Studies, University of Leeds, UK

Bloomsbury Advances in Translation Studies publishes cutting-edge research in the fields of translation studies. This field has grown in importance in the modern, globalized world, with international translation between languages a daily occurrence. Research into the practices, processes and theory of translation is essential and this series aims to showcase the best in international academic and professional output.

Other titles in the series:

Community Translation
Mustapha Taibi and Uldis Ozolins
Corpus-Based Translation Studies
Edited by Alet Kruger, Kim Wallmach & Jeremy Munday
Global Trends in Translator and Interpreter Training
Edited by Séverine Hubscher-Davidson & Michał Borodo
Music, Text and Translation
Edited by Helen Julia Minors
Quality In Professional Translation
Joanna Drugan
Retranslation
Sharon Deane-Cox
The Pragmatic Translator
Massimiliano Morini
Translation, Adaptation and Transformation
Edited by Laurence Raw
Translation and Translation Studies in the Japanese Context
Edited by Nana Sato-Rossberg & Judy Wakabayashi
Translation as Cognitive Activity
Fabio Alves & Amparo Hurtado Albir
Translating For Singing
Mark Herman & Ronnie Apter
Translation, Humour and Literature
Edited by Delia Chiaro
Translation, Humour and the Media
Edited by Delia Chiaro
Translating the Poetry of the Holocaust
Jean Boase-Beier

What Is Cultural Translation?

SARAH MAITLAND

Bloomsbury Academic
An imprint of Bloomsbury Publishing Plc

BLOOMSBURY
LONDON • OXFORD • NEW YORK • NEW DELHI • SYDNEY

Bloomsbury Academic
An imprint of Bloomsbury Publishing Plc

50 Bedford Square	1385 Broadway
London	New York
WC1B 3DP	NY 10018
UK	USA

www.bloomsbury.com

BLOOMSBURY and the Diana logo are trademarks of Bloomsbury Publishing Plc

First published 2017

© Sarah Maitland, 2017

Sarah Maitland has asserted her right under the Copyright, Designs and Patents Act, 1988, to be identified as the Author of this work.

All rights reserved. No part of this publication may be reproduced or transmitted in any form or by any means, electronic or mechanical, including photocopying, recording, or any information storage or retrieval system, without prior permission in writing from the publishers.

No responsibility for loss caused to any individual or organization acting on or refraining from action as a result of the material in this publication can be accepted by Bloomsbury or the author.

British Library Cataloguing-in-Publication Data
A catalogue record for this book is available from the British Library.

ISBN: HB: 978-1-4725-2686-1
PB: 978-1-4725-2627-4
ePDF: 978-1-4725-3045-5
ePub: 978-1-4725-3091-2

Library of Congress Cataloging-in-Publication Data
A catalog record for this book is available from the Library of Congress.

Series: Bloomsbury Advances in Translation Studies

Image © Brankica Vlaskovic / Alamy

Typeset by Newgen Knowledge Works (P) Ltd., Chennai, India

Contents

Preface vii

    Introduction: The urgency of cultural translation 1
1. Interpretation: Translation and the quest for understanding 31
2. Distanciation: Translation and the space-time continuum 55
3. Incorporation: Objects in translation appear closer than they are! On the cartographies of interpretation 83
4. Transformation: Translation as revolution 105
5. Emancipation: Translation as a critique of ideology 131

    Conclusion: Cultural translation: Saving us from ourselves? 159

Bibliography 163
Index 173

Preface

My intention in this book is twofold: to develop the first in-depth definition of the evocative and yet frustratingly abstruse concept of cultural translation, and with it, to advance an argument for the relevance of translation thinking to our understanding of how we live and work in globalized societies confronted increasingly with the presence of difference in all its forms – different ideologies, different modes of being and different modes of living and acting in the world. In a more specific sense, my aim is to demonstrate the critical dimension inherent in my approach to cultural translation – that is, its capacity to serve as a vehicle for new ways of seeing and being that enable us to question the received ideas that structure the worlds in which we live. My argument is that it is through 'text' in its broadest understanding – through the traditions, inscriptions and institutions of culture and society – that we communicate our being in the world. In a hermeneutic sense, to 'read' the world as if it were a text is to understand something of how our being is constructed and what this implies about being alive. By looking to the practice of interlingual translation, as the purposeful means by which a text written originally in one language is made meaningful in a new time and place to an audience that speaks another, we discover complementary attitudes of explanation and understanding, interpretation and transformation analogous to the act of reading. My model thus construes translation both as the means for exploring the sociocultural phenomena of the world around us and, in turn, as a route to understanding in the world.

Over the course of five chapters I have attempted to trace cultural translation processes at work in a wide range of everyday social and cultural contexts, from the production and reception of Internet memes in Chapter 1, to acts of memorialization in Chapter 2 and mapping strategies in Chapter 3. In Chapter 4, I tackle political satire and resistance movements and in Chapter 5 my concern is to explore how cultural translation can be operationalized for emancipatory purposes in the critique of ideology. Across each of these chapters, the interpretive framework behind the process of interlingual translation provides the critical lens through which to examine processes of understanding between different ideologies, different modes of being and different modes of living and acting in the world, where 'translation' serves as the means both to advance *and* to contest meaning.

Introduction

The urgency of cultural translation

To say that Europe is in a perpetual state of crisis appears to make light of the successive horrors of war, genocide, terrorism, ethnic cleansing and economic collapse. But it is simply to observe that despite the economic union of states that emerged from the Second World War, we do not, in our present configuration, enjoy a sense of political or social union. Although battles between European member states are now fought across boardroom tables, between diplomats, civil servants and heads of government, ideological division appears to be more prevalent now than ever. As I write this, the battle lines have once again been drawn and this time division in Europe is over the question of immigration. Of course, this is a question that has divided European member states for some time, not least following the outbreak of civil war in Syria and military intervention in Iraq, Afghanistan and Libya. According to the UNHCR, the majority of the 137,000 people who crossed the Mediterranean Sea into Europe during the first six months of 2015 were fleeing from war, conflict or persecution. One-third of the people who arrived safely by sea to the shores of Italy or Greece during this period were from Syria; the second and third most common countries of origin are Afghanistan and Eritrea (UNHCR, 2015). But the harrowing spectacle of mutilated bodies washed up on the shores of the Aegean and the Mediterranean, capsized dinghies, the erection of razor-wire fences, changes to border policy and refugees sewing their lips shut in protest gives the impression of nothing short of a crisis. In our debating chambers, in our newspapers, on our radios, on social media and on our television screens, some of the most urgent questions of our time are now being asked. To what extent do European member states have a responsibility towards refugees and, if so, how should this responsibility be enacted? How should the economic and social cost of responsibility be shared out more equally among the countries of Europe so that the greatest burden is not borne by only the countries of first arrival? How many refugees should each country take? By what criteria should these numbers be reached? What standards of care should states provide to refugees while their cases are being processed? The questions go on and on. But while state organs grapple with these questions and the fourth and fifth estates of the media and Internet become the battleground of debate, for the thousands of refugees who have reached Europe safely, only to find themselves stranded without access either to asylum procedures or to basic humanitarian services as a result of new border controls, the *real* debate is about how we imagine other people, the extent of their suffering and our duty to act upon it.

Somewhere in the acres of column inches filled by this public debate we witness the attempt to conjoin two mutually antithetical orientations that Rorty identified with regard to writing: those who write in the pursuit of self-created private perfection and autonomous human life such as Kierkegaard, Nietzsche and Heidegger and those writing in favour of the shared, social effort to make our institutions and practices more just and less cruel, as exemplified by Marx, Habermas and Rawls. Rorty believed fervently that there is no way in which philosophy or any other theoretical discipline can ever let us create a more comprehensive philosophical outlook that would somehow combine within a single vision self-creation and private perfection with justice and human solidarity. We can certainly attempt to create just and free societies where citizens are free to be as *privatistic* as possible, as long as they do so on their own time and cause no harm to others by depleting important resources. But at the level of theory he saw no real way to bring justice and self-creation together, for the vocabulary of self-creation is private and, by necessity, unsuited to argument, while the vocabulary of justice is necessarily public, a medium for argumentative exchange (Rorty, 1989, p. xiv).

If we could accept the fact that no theory can synthesize Heidegger with Habermas, he wrote, we might start to see the relationship between writers on autonomy and writers on justice as something similar to the relationship between different kinds of work tools – as little in need of synthesis as a paintbrush and a crowbar. Instead, Rorty's project in *Contingency, Irony and Solidarity* (1989) was to show how things would look if we dropped the demand for a single unifying theory of the public and the private and instead contented ourselves to view self-creation and human solidarity as equally valid but forever incommensurable ideals. He sketches the figure of the 'liberal ironist', where 'liberal' refers, as in Shklar's conceptualization, to those people who think that cruelty is the worst thing that we do, and 'ironist' to the people who face up to the contingency of their beliefs and desires – people who know, with historicists, that beliefs and desires are not transcendental but situated socially, culturally and historically:

> Liberal ironists are people who include among these ungroundable desires their own hope that suffering will be diminished, that the humiliation of human beings by other human beings may cease. For liberal ironists, there is no answer to the question 'Why not be cruel?' – no noncircular theoretical backup for the belief that cruelty is horrible. Nor is there an answer to the question 'How do you decide when to struggle against injustice and when to devote yourself to private projects of self-creation?' This question strikes liberal ironists as just as hopeless as the questions 'Is it right to deliver *n* innocents over to be tortured to save the lives of *m* x *n* other innocents?' or the question 'When may one favor members of one's family, or one's community, over other, randomly chosen, human beings?' Anybody who thinks that there are well-grounded theoretical answers to this sort of question – algorithms for resolving moral dilemmas of this sort – is still, in his heart, a theologian or a metaphysician. He believes in an order beyond time and change which both determines the point of human existence and establishes a hierarchy of responsibilities. (Rorty, 1989, p. xv)

In Rorty's liberal utopia, ironism is universal and post-metaphysical, where human solidarity is construed not as a fact to be perceived once prejudice has somehow been abolished or by drilling down into previously hidden depths of human interconnectedness:

> It is to be achieved not by inquiry but by imagination, the imaginative ability to see strange people as fellow sufferers. Solidarity is not discovered by reflection but created. It is created by increasing our sensitivity to the particular details of the pain and humiliation of other, unfamiliar sorts of people. Such increased sensitivity makes it more difficult to marginalize people from ourselves by thinking, 'They do not feel it as *we* would,' or 'There must always be suffering, so why not let *them* suffer?' This process of coming to see other human beings as 'one of us' rather than as 'them' is a matter of detailed descriptions of what unfamiliar people are like and of redescription of what we ourselves are like. This is a task not for theory but for genres such as ethnography, the journalist's report, the comic book, the docudrama, and, especially, the novel. (p. xvi, original emphasis)

In the sort of historicizing culture Rorty envisages, the sermon and the treatise are replaced with the novel, the film and the television programme as the principal vehicles of moral change, rejecting theorization that would signal all sides of life within a single vision and vocabulary in favour of *narratives* that simultaneously connect the present with the past and with the possibility of different futures. I dwell on this utopian vision – in which the drive to better imagine the suffering of the other is fulfilled by treating the exigencies of private autonomy and human solidarity as coequal incommensurables, where solidarity is not a state to be 'achieved' in the sense of an end to be arrived at through better theory, and in which, as one assumes is the project of all theorization, the desire to achieve better reflection is a deliberate stance to be taken – because it is a vision that animates the definition of cultural translation I elaborate over the course of this book. Its guiding principle is the belief that no form of communication – whether word *or* deed – exists outside the spatiotemporally constructed domain of human creation. As Rorty maintains, we need to make a distinction between the claim that the world is out there and the claim that the 'truth' is out there. To say that the world is out there is to affirm the existence of many things in space and time that are the effects of causes other than human mental states. Not all of the world results from human creation. But to describe the world, to put the world around us into sentences, is to enter into something other than truth, for while descriptions of the world can be verified as true or false, the world itself cannot. The world does not speak, *people* do.

If the communication of the contents of the mind is contextually contingent – if, in other words, the things we say and do communicate only our unique construction of the particular time and space in which we find ourselves – then when human beings communicate with one another, whether directly or indirectly, we participate in mutually assured regimes of constructedness by which nothing in the world can be spoken of and nothing can be said that does not already exist outside of our own modes of construction. Communication is not the transmission of 'meaning', in this sense, but its very creation. To understand one another is to enter into forms of dialogue that result in some form of mutually satisfactory agreement as to the 'meaning' of what is said. It is to step outside the safety of our spatiotemporally contingent domain of understanding in which the world makes sense *to me* and to acknowledge the way in which the world appears *to someone else*. This realization, that others exist and that they construct the world differently, serves to repudiate not just the continuity of meaning from one context to another but, more important, the assumption that the world of others is either the same as or can be subsumed to my own. To recognize that others construct the world differently is to recognize the existence of difference in others and myself, both as a bearer of difference and as another 'other' myself. By acknowledging the constructedness of the world of human descriptions, to employ Rorty's vocabulary, I simultaneously valorize the others around me as bearers of constructedness of their own and I rid myself of some of the self-confidence with which I might presume to know the truth of the world.

If every being constructs the world according to their own experience of it, then in interacting with the other beings of the world we cannot assume that communication will result in our seeing the world in precisely the same way. We imagine one another through a glass, darkly, not between boundaries of difference, but across them, constantly imagining others and the world around us while others do the same to us and to the world around them. Within this infinite Venn diagram of interconnected imaginations, we start not from the assumption of separate cultural contexts from which we speak and into which we retreat after we have done so, but from a position of constant and mutual construction. In other words, we understand the world not directly but through our understanding of other people. We exist not in separate contexts but from a place in which our relation with others secures our very existence. If we are constructing-beings in a world of constructing-others, then the worldview that we hold is simply one worldview among many. If it is always in the penumbra that we understand others, then by exposing ourselves to the perceptual lacunae that separate us from the world and the others within it, we escape the limits of the familiar, the confines of our own subjectivity, and are required to open ourselves up to unfamiliar others, to alien worlds and unknown ideas. By reaching outwards to revisit what we think we know and understand about the world around us we are also required to revisit what we think we know and understand about ourselves.

This was the sense in which Ricoeur looked to translation as an ethical model for the hospitality of otherness in a European context. He wrote that to translate a foreign culture into the categories peculiar to one's own presupposes one's prior transference into the cultural milieu governed by the ethical and spiritual categories of the other. In other words, for successful translation to the local, we must place ourselves in the foreign other's shoes, acknowledging the other's existence as a thinking, feeling, constructing being and, simultaneously, our inability to understand these constructions. Through this empathetic gesture, not by which we would claim to 'understand' the other, but by which we would acknowledge them precisely as bearers of that which we do *not* understand, Ricoeur maintained that we could start to view the identity of groups, cultures, people and nations not as immutable substances or as fixed structures to be accepted *or* rejected, but instead as 'recounted stories' from which we would receive a sense of 'narrative' identity which is at base, mobile:

> If each of us receives a certain narrative identity from the stories which are told to him or her, or from those that we tell about ourselves, this identity is mingled with that of others in such a way as to engender second order stories which are themselves intersections between numerous stories. Thus, the story of my life is a segment of the story of your life; of the story

of my parents, of my friends, of my enemies, and of countless strangers. (Ricoeur, 1996, p. 6)

By remembering that our 'story' – our identity, what we say and do – is an amalgam and is neither original, nor primary, we renounce the idea of a fixed 'truth' and with it the implacability of the ideologies by which we organize our realities, for it is through stories revolving around others and around ourselves that we articulate and shape our own temporality. Behind Ricoeur's approach lies a lesson on the suspension of judgement about what we can understand of the world through direct perception, requiring of us instead to explore indirect routes of understanding:

> To communicate at the level where we have already conducted the work of translation, with its art of transference and its ethics of linguistic hospitality, calls for this further step: that of taking responsibility, in imagination and in sympathy, for the story of the other, through the life narratives which concern that other. This is what we learn to do in our dealings with fictional characters with whom we provisionally identify through reading. These mobile identifications contribute to the reconfiguration of our own past and that of the past of others, by an incessant restructuring of stories that we tell, some of them about others. But a more profound engagement is required by the transition from the level of fiction to that of historical reality. It is not of course a matter of actually reliving the events that happened to others; the inalienable character of life experiences renders this chimerical 'intropathy' impossible. More modestly, but also more energetically, it is a matter of exchanging memories at the narrative level where they are presented for comprehension. A new ethos is born of the understanding applied to the complex intertwining of new stories which structure and configure the crossroads between memories. (pp. 6–7)

Importantly, however, storytelling is above all an act of interpretation, for as Benjamin reminds us, the storyteller frames the stories she tells according to her understanding of them, 'amplifying' the information she conveys through the narrative she unfolds: 'It does not aim to convey the pure essence of the thing, like information or a report. It sinks the thing into the life of the storyteller, in order to bring it out of him again. Thus traces of the storyteller cling to the story the way the handprints of the potter cling to the clay vessel' (Benjamin, 1999, p. 91). Every understanding in the world is thus actively interpretive, in the sense that everything we write and say about the world means more *or* less something other than it says. Life is not one continuous story, recounted teleologically from one point to another and exegesis, whether within one language or between several, is both embodied and historical.

We cannot stand outside the subjectivity of our embodiment and we cannot remove ourselves from our own historicity when we speak, write and interpret. The model of translation which so fascinated Ricoeur simultaneously recognizes *and* articulates difference, for it is not just about the perception of difference, the cognitive negotiation into which one enters in one's mind; it is the importation of this difference, the articulation of it from one's own perspective, for at base, translation subsumes the difference of the *alien* into the *own*. With this comes the possibility of failure. By necessity the articulation of another's experience in one's own words requires the importation of *other* ideas, *other* viewpoints, *other* worldviews. But we always transform irrevocably that which we perceive, because we must necessarily reframe it from our own point of view. To identify with another is to 'assimilate' them – to make *similar* that which is other to us. The point is that we do so in the knowledge both that the other is also doing the same to us and that our articulations can never grasp the other wholesale. This is enough to unseat us from the implacability of our worldview. Through translation, we exchange memories and confront traditions different from our own and so imagine the other with empathy for their story. Or, to put it another way, difference is what refuses translation, but it is also that which makes translation possible.

Hermeneutics, as elaborated by Ricoeur, is the 'art' of interpretation that questions the limits of our interpretation, a form of understanding that is not simply a way of knowing or a method of analysis but an ontological imperative: to understand who we are and where we stand before the object-for-interpretation. We speak of hermeneutic 'enquiry' precisely because understanding is not a given. Understanding is only a possibility; it is not something we achieve but a journey we undertake and it is one that does not leave us unchanged. As we enter into thoughtful encounter with another, interpretation is a high-risk, high-yield strategy, because we transform something of ourselves along the way. As Simms observes:

> To read, then, is to do hermeneutics, and to do hermeneutics is to understand ourselves – to understand, among other things, that our being is such that it can only be fulfilled by doing hermeneutics. This circular argument is yet another variation of the hermeneutic circle, but its circularity does not make it pointless, unless we want to say that life is pointless – it is what we do in life, insofar as we are constantly interpreting the world around us in order to understand that our *raison d'être* is to interpret the world around us in order to understand it. It is the constant renewal of this circular journey, with all its imaginative variations on the theme, that makes life worthwhile. (Simms, 2003, p. 42)

We exist insofar as we interpret; we gain life by engaging in the conflict of interpretations. Consciousness, a sense of self-awareness, a sense of being in the world, is thus not the first reality we achieve but the last. For these reasons, interpretation is the first step towards critique – of the beliefs and actions of others and our own:

> We see immediately how translation constitutes a model which is suited to the specific problem that the construction of Europe poses. First, at the institutional level, it leads us to encourage the teaching of at least two living languages throughout the whole of Europe in order to secure an audience for each of the languages which is not in a dominant position at the level of communication. But, above all, at a truly spiritual level, it leads us to extend the spirit of translation to the relationship between the cultures themselves, that is to say, to the content of meaning conveyed by the translation. It is here that there is need of translators from culture to culture, of cultural bilingualists capable of attending to this process of transference to the mental universe of another culture, having taken account of its customs, fundamental beliefs and deepest convictions; in short of the totality of its significant features. In this sense we can speak of a translation ethics whose goal would be to repeat at the cultural and spiritual level the gesture of linguistic hospitality mentioned above. (Ricoeur, 1996, p. 5)

The act of translation, by necessity, broadens our horizons; it means living *with* difference and living with *failure*. It means acknowledging the co-equal incommensurables that separate us. But because it also enables us to envisage and embrace that which we did not previously imagine, translation is about self-transformation. As with Rorty's warning about the paintbrush and the crowbar, this does not mean that foreign practices, other ideas, beliefs, traditions and ideologies can always be integrated successfully into the familiar. But perhaps it is enough to acknowledge their incommensurability and to place our focus firmly on the relationship it opens up between us. We take *responsibility* in life precisely when we recognize both that understanding is always partial and that it is only through reflection – by imagining outwards towards that which we do not understand – that we learn something about ourselves. Translation is as much about recognizing the limits of our own understanding as it is about overcoming them, for implied in the translational gesture of reaching outwards is the simultaneous recognition of the fallibility of our knowledge and our *need* to reach outwards anyway. To 'imagine' the other is to recognize that they are the bearer of positions potentially antithetical to our own; that these are co-equal with our own and the two are incommensurable. What appears to be a translational cul-de-sac in Ricoeur's conceptualization, therefore, is in fact precisely what is needed. As Nancy notes,

> 'To be exposed', means to be 'posed' in exteriority, according to an exteriority, having to do with an outside *in the very intimacy* of an inside. Or again: having

access to what is *proper* to existence, and therefore, of course, to the proper of *one's own* existence, only through an 'expropriation' whose exemplary reality is that of 'my' face always exposed to others, always turned toward an other and faced by him or her, never facing myself. (Nancy, 1991, pp. xxxvii–xxxviii, original emphasis)

When construed as social practice, the describing activities of human beings, as Rorty would say, become constructions to be read and engaged with. In this conceptualization 'translation' is so much more than that which we produce when we undertake to communicate the contents of a text written in one language for the benefit of an audience that speaks another. Translation is the social practice of embracing the existence of the other. We understand the world from the self outwards; one self among many others, human existence but the interaction of myriad selves across borders of difference. In the sense that it is both essential and prior to the communication of meaning, translation is in fact primary to that effort – it is quite simply what we do in social life and it is in translation, in other words, that we live.

It is with this foundation in hermeneutic philosophy that I sketch my definition of cultural translation, both the process by which we disclaim the notion that understanding is intrinsic and the means by which we contest ideology. My aim here will be to trace the contours of Ricoeur's philosophical hermeneutics and to discuss some of the questions it raises, with particular reference to what we think we know and understand of the practice of translation and the realization of resistance in the world. In this vein, I will neglect many of Ricoeur's other philosophical contributions on discourse, narrative and metaphor and so forth in the hope that the broad availability of his material in a range of different languages vitiates the need for an introductory overview here. Hermeneutics in Ricoeur's theory concerns the rules required for the interpretation of the written documents and human actions of our culture and construes the communication of the contents of the mind as a process analogous to the reading of a text. By 'reading' human action as we would a text we reveal something about how meaning is constructed and how we communicate ourselves as beings in the world.

My first principle with regard to defining cultural translation is that as a hermeneutic enterprise par excellence the translational model represents the practical outworking of Ricoeur's theorization. By this I mean that a translator is, in the first instance, a reader of a text. And, as such, is engaged in the complex process of understanding something that, by definition, refuses to be understood. This 'something' is a text written in another language, in another time, in another place and for the benefit of another audience. It is the translator's job to understand this text and write it in yet another language, for another audience, in another time and in another place. But the text does not speak. The translator must read at a remove, for the text-for-translation has been written by an author now deceased or inaccessible. The author's 'intention' for the text now no longer animates its meaning in the here and now of reading. Even where the author remains and is accessible to the translator, the inherent plurivocity a text enjoys as soon as it is released into the interpretive wild means that 'meaning' always remains something *other* than what the author intended. It cannot be found by seeking out the author. It must be 'guessed'. Translation is based primarily on a translator's cognitive engagement with a piece of writing, on the one hand, and with the needs, knowledges, expectations and perceptual lacunae of an audience who will receive the translation, on the other. To understand the hermeneutics of translation, therefore, is to understand that the primary dialectics at work in translation are those between the translator-*qua*-reader and the text-for-translation and the translator-*qua*-writer and an audience. My definition of cultural translation is therefore concerned as much with interpreting the objects of the world as 'source texts' with which we each can and should engage as it is with the *communication* of this interpretation towards an eventual audience.

Within this model, the process of cultural translation comprises five broad dimensions mapped to each of the five chapters of this book: the interpretation of a plurivocal 'text' to be understood; an act of reading across a distance of time and space; the incorporation of the text within the sociocultural context of the translator; the transformation of meaning for a purpose; the emancipation of the translator as a reader. For Ricoeur, the textual model of interpretation was only just the beginning. By highlighting the moral and political character of our decision-making in the social sphere, Ricoeur created a framework for the interpretation, analysis and criticism of social action and institutions based on the lessons of textual interpretation and aimed at bringing about a democratic society. As with Ricoeur, who saw philosophical reflection, critique and liberation as inseparable, and whose critical theory was aimed at personal and social transformation, my approach to cultural translation is imagined as *critical* – in the sense that it seeks both to identify the limits of human understanding and to uncover and oppose domination, exploitation and oppression. With Ricoeur, my approach to cultural translation is interested in the ethical dilemmas posed when texts, human actions and human productions exercise power over people. *If, at base, hermeneutics is what we do in life, cultural translation is the purposeful orientation of the hermeneutic dimension of life towards meaningful action and the transformation of the interpreting self.* This book represents the first attempt to locate cultural translation at the heart of human communication, as the means by which we produce and engage with cultural, political and social production in a globalized, multicultural world, and, as such, it views cultural translation as the site of such contestations. By uncovering processes of interpretation, distanciation, incorporation, transformation and emancipation most closely associated with the translation of texts behind the cultural phenomena of everyday life, we find a means for putting Ricoeur's theories into practice – making 'translation' not just a touchstone for what we see, do and say in public life, but also who we are.

Cultural translation: The story so far

The place cultural translation holds in the popular imaginary is undeniable. Enter the Internet search string 'cultural translation' and the results are astonishing: over 150,000 hits returned in Google alone – newspaper articles, blog posts, YouTube videos, SlideShare and Prezi presentations, translation agency mission statements, city and town councils, third sector organisations, research projects, summer schools and academic conferences. The website for the only MA degree in cultural translation even advertises that according to a recent panel of the Modern Language Association cultural translation is 'the most important concept in cultural theory today' (American University of Paris, n.d.).

Cultural translation made its academic debut in 1985 in an article by Roger Keesing for the *Journal of Anthropological Research* entitled 'Conventional Metaphors and Anthropological Metaphysics: The Problematic of Cultural Translation'. Keesing criticized the way in which anthropologists working in tribal societies tended to repackage unconnected examples of ritual practice using methodologies familiar to their academic readers but which no native informants used themselves. This localizing practice made disparate modes of living appear coherent and concealed the real-life differences between tribal peoples and the dominant Western philosophies of the cultural anthropologists charged with studying them. Keesing argued that without the capacity for self-criticism in the application of conceptual tools designed to understand the unique cultural character of the different peoples of the world and the attendant acknowledgement of the ways in which anthropology apprehends the reality of others, we run the risk of what he termed cultural translation, that is, recreating our objects of study in our own image. The next year, Talal Asad published a chapter in James Clifford's landmark collection *Writing Culture* (1986) entitled 'The Concept of Cultural Translation in British Social Anthropology' in which he argued that cultural translation was an institutionalized practice that resulted from the differentials of power that separate societies. His project was to draw attention to the critical distance between the anthropologist and the people written about. Viewed from this vantage point of privilege, the attribution of 'meaning' to other languages and cultures is: 'an operation the anthropologist alone controls, from field notebook to printed ethnography. In other words, it is the privileged position of someone who does not, and can afford not to, engage in a genuine dialogue with those he or she once lived with and now *writes* about' (Asad, 1986, p. 155, original emphasis). In the context of British social anthropology, he showed how a powerful academic game was established in the 1950s by which anthropologists' translation strategies with regard to non-Western societies were driven largely by the needs of the Western academy waiting to read about them back home. Although the overarching aim was to understand modes of living different to their own, when it came to writing up the results of their research the work of anthropologists was always geared towards fulfilling particular audience-directed objectives. Writing about others is never innocent, Asad maintained, and entirely enmeshed within global flows of power. The people and practices at the basis of their work, in other words, were treated as texts, subject to regimes of representation dominated by the norms of the academic readership.

In 1987 the *Journal of Anthropological Research* once again returned to the topic of cultural translation, in an article by Todd Larsen entitled 'Action, Morality, and Cultural Translation', in which he called for the capacity for 'self-criticism' in the application of anthropology, in a bid to better acknowledge that while the aim might be to understand others on their own terms, the terms and conceptual tools that are used to do so are themselves not culturally neutral. I will not dwell on these contributions, for this ground has already been well covered, except to note that while Keesing and Asad were the first to write of cultural translation as a discrete phenomenon of which we can talk, they tap into a longer-running ethical debate surrounding the perceived neutrality with which anthropologists mediate cultural difference when they attempt to reproduce the complex cultural worlds of foreign others for the consumption of local academic audiences. As early as 1954 Lienhardt equated the problem of interlingual translation with the problem of describing to other people how the members of a remote tribe think, 'of making the coherence primitive thought has in the languages it really lives in, as clear as possible in our own' (quoted in Asad, 1986, p. 142).

Since Asad, and outside of anthropology, interest in cultural translation has gone from strength to strength. In an interview published in 1990, in which he discussed notions of cultural difference and the presumption of incommensurability, Bhabha spoke of cultural translation, following Benjamin's own observations on translation and the task of the translator, to suggest that: 'all forms of culture are in some way related to each other, because culture is a signifying or symbolic activity. The articulation of cultures is possible not because of the familiarity or similarity of contents, but because all cultures are symbol-forming and subject-constituting, interpellative practices' (Bhabha,

1990, pp. 209–10). He later followed this in 1994 with *The Location of Culture*, in which he related cultural translation to the 'insurgent' acts of renewal that occur in the colonial encounter with cultural difference. He looks to Salman Rushdie's *The Satanic Verses* (1988), in which a disembodied voice asks 'How does newness come into the world? How is it born?' (quoted in Bhabha, 1994, p. 8). Bhabha identifies this newness with those who have migrated from the Indian subcontinent to 'the West'. The migrant faces a challenge: either to remain unchanged by the migration process or, through a process of integration, to become transformed. With the arrival of 'newness', the past and present, own and other, known and unknown, come into contact, such that the past is refigured, 'as a contingent "in-between" space, that innovates and interrupts the performance of the present' (p. 10). This continuum is disrupted primarily by the encounter with cultural difference, which brings with it the possibility of cultural contestation, 'the ability to shift the ground of knowledges, or to engage in the "war of position" ' (p. 233). Cultural identity and the ways in which it is expressed and inscribed are therefore always in a state of flux – necessarily incomplete and open to cultural translation. Through the transnational dimension of migration, diaspora, displacement and relocation the unifying discourses of our time – 'nation', 'peoples', 'community', 'us' – cannot be easily specified for the global space of cultural difference is above all one of constant negotiation (p. 318). It is this space of negotiation that Bhabha names cultural translation, for it is transgressive, blasphemous and contestatory. It challenges received authorities and places them within a context of cultural relativism, where other possibilities and other 'enunciatory positions' are available. Thus, he writes: 'Cultural translation desacralizes the transparent assumptions of cultural supremacy, and in that very act, demands a contextual specificity, a historical differentiation within minority positions' (p. 327).

In the years since Bhabha a handful of articles and book chapters mentioning the concept followed, but it was not until the dawn of the new century that cultural translation really exploded onto the academic stage, with the majority of journal articles, books and book chapters dealing in any way with cultural translation as a discrete term published in the last ten years alone. Across the humanities, in fields as diverse as cultural studies, postcolonial theory, travel writing, history, intercultural communication, heritage tourism and social semiotics, cultural translation has been invoked in discussions ranging from nineteenth-century photography; intercultural thinking; Cuban-American identity development; women's fashion; accented writing; the history of popular music in South Korea and Taiwan; West African drama; news production; Chinese diaspora; and subtitling, to name but a few. It has been described variously as: the 'cultural encounters' that ensue when one side tries to make sense of the other, a 'double process of decontextualization and recontextualization, first reaching out to appropriate something alien and then domesticating it' (Burke, 1997, p. 8 and p. 10); 'an anti-essentialist and anti-holistic metaphor that aims to uncover counter-discourses, discursive forms and resistant actions *within* a culture, heterogeneous discursive spaces within a society' (Bachmann-Medick, 2006, p. 37, original emphasis); the construction of a source text and its transference into a different language (Sturge, 2007, p. 6); and the 'interpretive acts' that draw from different sources of information in order to describe a culture (Conway, 2010a, p. 189). As a topic of academic study in the twenty-first century, cultural translation is clearly here to stay. But what do these claims actually mean? Despite this current of epistemological excitement, the notion of cultural translation remains as diffuse as it is tantalizing.

On one level, widespread under-theorization has left the majority of accounts of cultural translation, and the assumptions that underpin them, necessarily incomplete (Ha, 2010, p. 359). In the majority of the literature in which it is invoked as a discrete concept, for example, cultural translation appears in the title of a text, in paragraph subheadings, journal abstracts or keywords; but beyond one or two oblique references in the body of the text its meaning is taken largely as self-evident, leaving it to readers to construct a definition for themselves. Thus in an intervention by Spivak published on the website for the European Institute for Progressive Cultural Policies, cultural translation is referred to as a 'special task', something one can 'assign' oneself or 'plot', a 'problem', 'an extremely complicated thing', yet without an explanation of what she means with these assignations, what her understanding of cultural translation is or how it bears on her overall argument (2008). Even in works where cultural translation maintains a more substantive presence, quotations from Asad and Bhabha – presumably viewed as authoritative because of the sense of authenticity and legitimacy that surrounds their names – take the place of making an actual case for the validity of the particular stance on cultural translation being taken. What is meant by cultural translation, the rationale for choosing the scholarship that is invoked, how one writer's usage differs from that of others or how this usage differs more generally from any other brand of translation that we know of, must be simply intuited. This has contributed to a sense in much of the literature that this thing we call cultural translation already exists empirically, that it does not need to be defined or questioned, and worst of all, that we do not actually need to prove that it takes place (Young, 2010). A consequence of the sheer popularity of cultural translation is that discussions go round in circles because writers do not make clear what they mean and presume that others share their implied paradigm of cultural translation even when they do not (Conway, 2012). As Pratt identifies, in the growing literature on cultural translation, the dearth of examples is a symptom that often nags. The thing is referred to as if we already know what we are talking about; our scholarly ruminations retain a vagueness that the ungenerous could take for intellectual impoverishment, or languor. When specific examples are introduced, they are often cited as self-evident instances of a self-evident practice called cultural translation, not analyzed so as to demonstrate how that concept actually works, what kind of understanding it enables, what it misses or obscures. (Pratt, 2010, p. 94)

The confusion this creates can be seen most clearly in a seminal intervention on cultural translation that was published in the *Translation Studies* journal in 2009. As part of a newly introduced forum for interdisciplinary debate on cultural translation, Buden and Nowotny published a provocation entitled 'Cultural Translation: An Introduction to the Problem' and invited responses to their theory of cultural translation, which was based on the notion of the German citizenship test and the ways in which migrants must conform to culturally framed constructions of race, identity and ethnicity in order to pass. The uptake of their invitation was so strong that in 2010 two subsequent volumes of the forum were published. As the editors note in their introduction to the forum:

> 'Cultural translation' is a term currently much used in a range of disciplines both inside and, perhaps especially, outside translation studies itself and in very different ways. Many of these approaches seem to promise valuable insights into cultural practices of transfer, yet the precise use of the term 'cultural translation' remains controversial. It is also as yet unclear how the concept will impact on some of the fundamental assumptions of translation studies. This Forum aims to explore and evaluate the potential of the concept both for translation studies and for its neighbouring disciplines. (Buden and Nowotny, 2009, p. 196)

Yet in their twelve-page 'position paper', Buden and Nowotny devote just over six hundred words to the concept of cultural translation itself, which they say is linked to Benjamin's rejection of the primacy of the original text in translation and Bhabha's emancipatory politics of resistance through cultural production. Their central case study of the German citizenship test – and the ways in which migrants must conform to a culturally framed construction of border politics if they are to pass – does not explain how questions of national identity and citizenship link either to Benjamin or to Bhabha. Indeed, as Young observes in his response to the paper, away from the context of borders, migrancy and supra-, inter- and transnationalism, Buden and Nowotny do not convince the reader that the taking of a citizenship test is an example of cultural translation since migrants navigate the many statutory interrogations to which they must learn the right answer or tailor their response to what is expected – this does not necessarily prove or explain that they have been 'translated' (2010, p. 357). Tymoczko (2010) likewise criticizes their choice of case study because it lacks transferable knowledge, since it is not the case that all states require certain group identities to be silenced or assimilated in order for citizenship to be acquired. Here, as elsewhere, cultural translation is supposed to name by itself the state of affairs to which it speaks. In a piece entitled 'On Empiricism and Bad Philosophy in Translation Studies' (2010) – and this should give some idea of the writer's position – Pym reveals that a copy of Buden and Nowotny's text had been sent to him for comment prior to publication:

> I declined to comment because, to be honest, I had no idea what the text was about. Now that I see it has been published alongside no less than eight responses, I do not feel so ashamed – most of the respondents simply talk about their own ideas, perhaps as a polite way of avoiding the embarrassing confusion about 'cultural translation'. I have nevertheless now read the piece several times, carefully, and I'm afraid I still have no clear idea of what 'cultural translation' is. Is that the problem the text introduces? (Pym, 2010, p. 6)

In what Conway (2012) terms the 'messy' theorization of cultural translation it is no exaggeration to say that it is now nothing short of a heated *debate*. Cultural translation's detractors are right to signal the lack of examples, distinctions or definitions as evidence of a poorly developed – and at times, poorly articulated – paradigm. Critics cite the ambiguity and the lack of precision and clarity when scholars write about cultural translation (Conway, 2012; Chesterman, 2010; Pratt, 2010; Bery, 2009). If theorization about cultural translation is to result in relevant, specific and transferable knowledge that can help us better understand and analyze the way in which we live – if, in other words, it is more than a flash in the discursive pan – then we must do a better job of convincing readers that cultural translation not only exists, but that it can be defined, evidenced and exemplified in new, interesting and concrete ways. This requires us to be very clear about what cultural translation is, where it can be applied, what it can help us understand and, perhaps more important, what its limitations are. Of any academic theory that claims to speak to the challenges of the human condition in a globalized, interconnected world, we should demand nothing less.

This is not to say that attempts have not been made. Both the *Routledge Encyclopedia of Translation Studies* (2009) and the *Handbook of Translation Studies* (2012) carry entries on cultural translation, and recent interventions by

Pym (2009) and Conway (2012) have attempted to catalogue the dizzying array of existing contributions. As Sturge observes in the *Routledge Encyclopedia*, the term is used in many different ways and in diverse circumstances. In some of these it is a metaphor that challenges received conceptualizations of the 'translation' paradigm (that 'source' and 'target' languages and cultures exist as discreet and mutually coherent categories) and in others it refers to the work of intercultural mediation and representation at the heart of literary translation. Cultural translation, in this context, is not a translation strategy per se 'but rather a *perspective* on translations that focuses on their emergence and impact as components in the ideological traffic between language groups' (2009, p. 67, original emphasis). In the broadest uses of the term, she writes, cultural translation signals not the interlingual transfer of meaning between cultural and linguistic monads but the transformation of the very fabric of culture itself.

As Pym notes in his own survey, cultural translation in this non-linguistic, non-grammatical sense differs from its textual counterpart because it assumes no fixed source from which to translate and no clear target audience to whom the translation is directed. At base, therefore, the category of 'translation' referenced within the term cultural translation implies something other than linguistic or cultural production and instead the more general process of communication between different cultural groups (2009, p. 143). As bearers of culture, in this sense, cultural translation is something that we simply *do*. In the face of the 'frequently messy collection of ideas' such a perspective has produced, Conway's survey, meanwhile, attempts to provide 'an initial map of the terrain' by classifying existing contributions according to the differential way in which 'culture' and 'translation' are employed (2012, p. 264). This enables him to create a conceptual map demonstrating that although scholars do not necessarily delineate between meanings of cultural translation, invocations of the term fall largely into one of two camps: those that view translation as a form of rewriting (of an anthropological, symbolic or cultural community) and those that view it as a form of 'transposition' (in which foreign interpretive horizons, artefacts, texts and people are relocated into a new locale (p. 266).

All four surveys do a good job of tracing the broad contours of the cultural translation literature as it has developed thus far. It is not my intention to reproduce such an exercise for three principal reasons. First, each survey makes clear that despite the immense popularity cultural translation enjoys, the concept itself remains paradoxically ill defined. Current efforts should most usefully be orientated towards the production of an in-depth definition that can be tested, contested, engaged with and developed, contributing to the evolution of the concept as a whole. Second, each survey makes explicit reference to the fear that in a bid to promote translation in its broadest metaphorical understanding, the interlingual practice of those charged with solving the communicative challenges linguistic difference creates – translators – will eventually be marginalized. There is thus an immediate need to articulate the relevance of cultural translation as a discrete concept and to outline its position vis-à-vis interlingual translation. Third, and perhaps most important, by relying on only two broad conceptualizations of cultural translation, as epitomized in the work of Asad and Bhabha, the surveys themselves continue to circulate what remains an oversimplified epistemology reflected throughout the cultural translation literature as a whole. Of course, from one perspective, the surveys are themselves simply reflecting a disproportionate reliance on Asad and Bhabha already present in the bulk of the literature. But we should be careful not to limit our theorization. With Rorty, rather than attempt to unify what are at base disparate perspectives, the definition of cultural translation I advance in this book aims to broaden our epistemological horizons by looking beyond Asad and Bhabha and instead locates itself on a solid methodological platform based on Ricoeur's hermeneutic philosophy. It is to an above all triangular task that this book is directed: to provide the first definition of cultural translation not limited to Asad and Bhabha but predicated on a clear, unambiguous and sustained engagement with the theoretical model on which it is built; rooted in the interlingual praxis of the translator; and applied to a wide range of examples drawn from across the social imaginary and beyond the world of letters.

What's 'wrong' with cultural translation?

Cultural translation's detractors have been vociferous in their criticism and any definition worth its salt must tackle these early on. An oft-cited niggle is use of the term 'translation' – which we might understand as the purposeful means by which a text written originally in one language is made meaningful in a new time and place to an audience that speaks another – in a metaphorical sense, to refer to things above and beyond the worlds of text and language. Principally, concern has focused on the use of translation's supposed transportational etymology that evokes the act of moving or carrying across from one place or position to another and changing from one condition or state to another. In the early Christian usage, for example, it suggested the 'bearing across' of the deceased from this world to the next or the physical transportation of a body from one grave to another. This is a trope which Rushdie exploits when he writes that in their journey across the globe, migrants become 'translated' people, 'borne across' from one cultural milieu to another. Where critics signal a problem is that it tends to be used to legitimize the application of an interlingual model of translation to all manner of topics of human migration. For Tymoczko, we should not place much stock in the idea that simply because translation's roots are suggestive of physical transportation we can then legitimately apply translation to all questions of the literal movement of peoples across the globe. While people may literally relocate themselves, she argues, one thing that all translators know is that words can never be relocated in such literal ways. Thus while the etymology of the word translation may indeed signal 'carrying across', in the interlingual practice of translation, translators emphatically do *not*. She writes: 'The word translation implies that the semantic meanings of a source text can be transferred intact to the target text, even when the words of the source text themselves are not carried across; the metaphor implies that there can be a translation practice that meets these criteria' (Tymoczko, 2010, pp. 107–8). A theory of cultural translation founded on the idea that meanings in translation are carried across unaltered semantically and semiotically, she says, is undermined by the very fact that this is precisely what does not happen when people migrate. In a similar vein, Chesterman writes that the major problem with establishing a theory of cultural translation on the transportation metaphor is that this historical sense of mobility is true only for the term in its English and Indo-European cognates. It does not hold for other languages such as Chinese, Finnish, Japanese, Tamil, Tibetan, Turkish or Vietnamese in which the corresponding term does not evoke carrying across but rather the mediation of difference (2010, p. 104). To build a paradigm of cultural translation-*qua*-human migrancy on the notion that translation means 'carrying across' is to proceed from an already Eurocentric hierarchy.

More broadly, however, what Chesterman terms the 'metaphorical extension of the concept of translation to cover non-textual modes of transfer' (p. 103) and which has elsewhere been described as the 'generalized' (Pym, 2009, p. 160), 'broadening' (Bachmann-Medick, 2009, p. 2) or 'inflationary' (Wagner, 2010, p. 98) use of translation to cover non-interlingual contexts, means the idea of translation itself 'risks being diluted into nothing' (Chesterman, 2010, p. 103). Indeed, according to the cultural translation entry in the *Routledge Encyclopedia*, 'Metaphorical usage could at worst hollow out the word "translation", not just into something that need not necessarily include more than one language but into something that primarily does not include more than one language – a factor, instead, of shifts and layering within globally dominant English without the need for bilingual translation to take place' (Sturge, 2009, p. 69). In other words, the development of translation thinking across a range of scholarly applications may uncover useful synchronicities and create opportunities for fruitful interdisciplinary debate; but in its infinite theoretical expansion it also runs the risk of becoming so broad it becomes meaningless (Pym, 2009, p. 159). Chesterman summarizes the consequence thus: 'If practically every kind of change or transfer or metamorphosis can be called translation, we shall soon need a different term to refer to what

Jakobson (1959), in his well-known semiotic classification – and extension – of the concept, called "translation proper" ' (2010, pp. 103–4).

If translation is now so vast in meaning, critics say, it no longer 'means' anything. Metaphors, by their very nature, beat about the bush and go around the trees; they never quite 'say' and always defer what they 'mean'. Too protean in our metaphorical extension of translation and we risk draining translation of its ability to refer to the practical realm of interlingual transfer on which it is based. It is this concern for the loss of the practical that goes to the heart of arguments against cultural translation, for there is a sense among its critics that those who theorize about cultural translation are not translators, are uninterested in grounding their theorization in the practice of interlingual translation and that on a fundamental level this is a Bad Thing. In this view, the very paradigm of translation, as something that is supposed to signify the production and exchange of ideas between different languages, is appropriated by cultural theorists with no real interest in or knowledge of the practice of professional translation. Thus for Trivedi, when the term translation is applied to life in postcolonial and diasporic contexts, as it is in Bhabha's conceptualization, it further extends the global reach of Anglo-American cultural studies, where the trope of translation has been appropriated without the need to actually learn languages other than English in order to do so. If such bilingual ground is worn away, he says, 'we shall sooner than later end up with a wholly translated, monolingual, monocultural, monolithic world' (2007, p. 286).

Trivedi's critique speaks to the fear that the uncontrolled enlargement of the idea of translation will threaten the hard-won attention to language issues and the rigorous analysis of texts that the field of translation studies has built for itself (Simon, 2009, p. 210). For Trivedi, cultural translation spells 'the very extinction and erasure of translation as we have always known and practised it' (2007, p. 282). Chesterman's suggestion is to take a step back from the use of metaphor and to keep discussions terminologically separate, using precise and distinct terms depending on whether we are talking about texts, ideas, cultural communities or individual people (2010, p. 106). Any extensions of terminology, he says, would have to be justified in terms of adding something to the study of immigration or other sociocultural phenomena, thus 'producing more benefits than costs in comparison to some other terminology' (p. 105). For Tymoczko, the problem is at base one of untrammelled interdisciplinarity: 'Many fields have been tempted to latch on to terms meaning "translation" as an ostensibly easy way out of their theoretical problems, not realizing how complex textual translation is and how many theoretical problems the subject brings with it' (2010, p. 110). The solution for Trivedi, meanwhile, is thus to cut off such interdisciplinary sharing entirely:

> One wonders why 'translation' should be the word of choice in a collocation such as 'cultural translation' in this new sense when perfectly good and theoretically sanctioned words for this new phenomenon, such as migrancy, exile or diaspora are already available and current. But given the usurpation that has taken place, it may be time for all good men and true, and of course women, who have ever practised literary translation, or ever read translation with any awareness of it being translation, to unite and take out a patent on the word 'translation', if it is not already too late to do so. (Trivedi, 2007, p. 285)

I wish to make four points at this stage. First, objections to a model of cultural translation based on a perceived sense of mobility associated with translation's etymology proceed from a particular *position* on what constitutes both the process of 'interlingual' translation and the role of the translator within it. Tymoczko criticizes cultural translation because interlingual translators supposedly do not 'carry across'. But surely something *is* carried across – not discrete words or meanings, replicated wholesale in some magic act of intercultural photocopying, but ideas, imputed by the translator into the text-for-translation, ideas that are inspired by what is offered in the same. By its very nature, moreover, translation involves using *different* words to stand in the place of the words of the source text. Is this not the very meaning of metaphor? Translation is not simply a metaphor *for* the carrying across of ideas from one page to another. Translation *is* metaphor. The point of looking to translation's etymological basis in transportational metaphors, surely, is that as with words, sentences, texts, ideas, bodies, bones and relics, with transportation comes *transformation*. Remember that the feast of the translation of Thomas à Becket celebrates not the movement of his remains, per se, but the fact that by relocating his earthly vestiges from one site to another, new life was breathed into his cult. Second, and following directly from the first, in response to critiques of cultural translation's English-language bias, D'hulst (2010) points out that in order to label such views on translation thinking as 'Eurocentric', we must assume the prior existence of some sort of 'neutral' view. There is in fact no such thing as neutral theorization, and while we should not ignore the presence of bias – epistemological or otherwise – we should not claim to advance value-free approaches outside of geopolitical context.

Third, the weight of the anti-metaphor argument – that cultural translation's application in fields outside translation studies circumvents the study of linguistic and textual aspects of translation (read: the authoritative knowledge produced by researchers in these areas) – should also not be exaggerated. The presence of the term translation in diverse intellectual domains beyond translation studies is hardly new, or, as Young puts it, 'translation theorists who now wish to shut the stable door are several centuries late' (2010, p. 358). Translation never really implied only the textual, interlingual brand, since both the textual usage and the metaphor of bodily transport go back to the same early medieval period. From this time, translation always implied change, in form or appearance:

> Those objecting to its extension to other activities will no doubt be distressed by the fact that the translations of Enoch (moving from earth to heaven without death) was first described in 1382, translation as transference from one medium or form to another (for example of a painting by an engraving) in 1588, of property 1590, as interpretation or explanation 1598, as enraptured 1643, as the transference of a disease from one body to another in 1665, in astronomy, in physics 1715. (Young, 2010, pp. 358–9)

As Pym wonders, is there really anything wrong with the use of metaphors in a mode in which metaphor already abounds? (2009, p. 159). Perhaps the problem, he says, is that the metaphors we associate with cultural translation have become 'dead' metaphors – 'images that we somehow accept as self-evident truths. The more conscious metaphors of "cultural translation" may thus help us think more critically about all kinds of translation' (ibid.).

Fourth, as a field of intellectual endeavour, translation studies must be confident in its development and allow its models – and the idea that translation is the preserve of the worlds of language and text is but one model among others – to be tried and tested, embraced, adopted and questioned:

> Translation proper gets a lot of mileage from the Forum respondents, but there is often what sounds like a rather disciplinarily proprietorial air to the many complaints about the metaphorical extension of the term translation from its 'proper' domain of transforming texts from one language to another. The problem with such complaints is that intellectual history is largely made up of the creative appropriation of metaphors from one discipline to another. (Young, 2010, p. 358)

Translation studies has spent many years arguing for the relevance of translation thinking across the social disciplines; we cannot simply put the genie back in the bottle the moment the take-up of translational models outside the field becomes uncomfortable. Rather than construe the presence of translation in domains beyond the worlds of language and text as 'losing ground' to cultural studies and others, we must consider how our models can be better exported across the humanities at large. The multiple points of departure the term translation offers with regard to the analysis of urgent issues of identity, ethnicity, integration, justice, tolerance and respect at a time of border crisis surely cannot help but strengthen translation studies at large, 'proving its appeal to contemporary thought and social action' (Simon, 2009, p. 210). Indeed, as a domain of intellectual enquiry, translation studies was itself built on the very practice of intellectual nomadism Trivedi decries. From the very translators we study to the discourses we employ when we do so, the scholarship has always followed an itinerant trajectory as we move from one subject area to another in a bid to better articulate how and why we translate. As Wolf (2009) recognizes, to ban the metaphorical extension of the idea of translation in formulations of cultural translation would ultimately mean rejecting any sort of interdisciplinary work whatsoever (pp. 77–8). Indeed, differences in scholarly perspective are essential if we are to raise our discursive game and usher in the age of rigorous, well-substantiated, evidence-based and transferable models of cultural translation its detractors call for.

I wish to now turn to two further critiques deserving of much more serious treatment and which, paradoxically, have received much less attention in the literature. The first, which attacks cultural translation from an ethical perspective, is the concern that imprecise theorization promises more than it can deliver and obscures both the global hierarchies of power and influence to which cultural translation claims to speak and the material effects on the daily lives of real people caught up in them. Here, the concern is not just with the definitional ambiguities cultural translation introduces, but the assumption that with it comes the relegation of real-world problems of cultural difference. Or, in Pym's words, 'the theories of cultural translation would thus be sweeping away the very otherness that they generally proclaim to espouse' (2009, p. 161). In our rush to prove the relevance of translation thinking to the world, we must not allow terminologically loose pronouncements and superficial statements to betray the very people we claim to serve with our work. As Pym puts it elsewhere, 'Who said that translation had to save the day? One senses that an immigrant would not ask how translation might be used in the interests of justice and democracy' (2010, p. 8). This is a view shared by Bery (2009), who signals a need to remember the 'who' of translation – the people who are actually affected – and not just the 'what' (p. 213). Introducing ideas from one field and applying them to another is all very well, but when it pits the ethical status of real people against inanimate objects, we impede rather than enrich communication between disciplines (Chesterman, 2010, p. 105).

There is an ethical price to pay, in other words, when we lose sight of the social and ideological powers in play and become distracted by what Ha calls 'chic intellectual language games' that satisfy the postmodern thirst for complexity but do not necessarily address the real-world problems that disproportionately affect people on the basis of their race, ethnicity or any other delineator of group identity (2010, p. 350). Theories, Pym writes, not based on empirical data and which display 'imprecise and contradictory thought, betray a short-term consumption of fashionable concepts, are ploys in search of academic power, and are deployed by fly-by-night intellectuals who will move on to something else next year anyway' (2009, pp. 160–1). As Pratt notes: 'People could indeed be forgiven for seeing this as another plumed display of intellectual authority by privileged metropolitans who don't know any languages and still want to uphold their monopoly on ideas. People could be forgiven for asking whether cultural translation serves to configure the traffic in meaning in the image of the free market' (Pratt, 2010, p. 94). It is tempting to dismiss these arguments as the spectre of disciplinary gatekeeping once again. But given the imprecise and obscure theorization that has dogged the cultural translation literature in recent decades, they underline the urgent need for precision: to elevate cultural translation above the level of fashionable *trope* to that of a measurable and transferable political *discourse* capable both of illuminating power relationships in the world *and* of criticizing them.

The second major challenge to cultural translation questions its methodological validity as a theory based on the practice of interlingual translation. Here, critique returns us to the perceived 'loss' that surrounds cultural translation's supposed repudiation of the so-called proper form of translation that deals with the problematics of transfer between multiple texts and multiple languages. In contrast to this latter form, Trivedi writes, with cultural translation we have a kind of translation, 'which does not involve two texts, or even one text, and certainly not more than one language. These are examples of what Bhabha, with his usual felicity, has in another context called "non-substantive translation" (in personal conversation). One could perhaps go a step further and, without any attempt at matching felicity, call it simply non-translation' (Trivedi, 2007, p. 286). Pratt takes this methodological concern a step further by claiming that at base, the interlingual model is ill-suited to the concerns of cultural translation because difference in life is in a constant state of organic change: 'The concept of cultural translation bears the unresolvable contradiction that in naming itself it preserves the distances/distinctions it works to overcome [...] Because it sustains difference, a translation paradigm is too blunt an instrument to grasp the heterodox subjectivities and interfaces that come out of entanglements sustained over time' (Pratt, 2010, pp. 95–6). In the attempt to overcome essentialism through the theoretical promise of a model predicated on the movement between languages, cultural translation in fact ossifies difference, by relying precisely on the very borders of language and culture it seeks to dissolve.

I will deal with each of these in turn. The weakness of arguments against cultural translation on the basis of supposedly incorrect understandings of the term translation begs the question: precisely who owns the rights to translation? It should come as no surprise that areas such as cultural studies and comparative literature are interested in translation, for the 'cultural' dimension of translation has always played a role in linguistic formulations; there cannot be a clear-cut distinction between translation 'proper' and its cultural sense precisely because in the creation of the linguistic categories upon which Trivedi bases his argument there is always something *more* than the merely linguistic at play. As Young notes, 'translation has always, in a Derridean sense, been an improper term, without a single, unitary meaning, always doubling back on itself to include a greater and sometimes even contradictory semantic range' (2010, p. 359). Moreover, what Trivedi describes as translation has never been a purely linguistic activity. The role of the translator – as an individual working within a specific set of audience requirements, constraints, needs and expectations to which her translation must be sensitive – requires intense ethical reflection on the relations between distant and often conflicting contingencies of text, society, people and culture. As an intellectual and creative process of reading and writing, translation's relationship to culture goes far beyond the narrow linguistic and textual theorization supported by Trivedi. To defend an a priori sense of translation as linguistic transfer would be both a limited and a limiting course of action indeed.

Implicit in Trivedi's words, furthermore, is the assumption that the 'otherness' with which translation engages is confined only to the interaction of translators with texts written in different languages. But what of the otherness we encounter all around us, or the fact that when we find ourselves encountered by other people we become 'others' to ourselves? Does not difference exist everywhere? Even when dealing with people or examples in one language does not automatically mean sameness. To say that cultural translation eschews linguistic paradigms of translation in favour of 'cultural processes' does not mean that we cannot detect movements we associate most closely with the linguistic work of translation, for, as I have already discussed, every understanding that takes place in the world is actively interpretive, in the sense that all things can and do mean more or less than they appear. We must never forget that the textual and linguistic problems with which interlingual translation deals start *before* we address the problem of transferring texts from one language to another, for the same modes of interpretation we associate with translation between languages also take place in the one language alone.

In this book, I argue that as with translation in the interlingual, intertextual, sense, cultural translation starts from a quest for understanding – of some form of source material and in the sense that some cultural, political or social stimulus in the world sets in motion the interpretive work of translation led by a human actor. If the practice of human communication involves the continual interpretation of stimuli in the social sphere, cultural translation in my conceptualization here delineates a model for *all* meaningful exchanges in the world and is therefore not a subsection of interlingual communication. The 'agents' of cultural translation, moreover, are not the privileged polyglot elite but every single one of us engaged in the practice of encountering and questioning difference in every aspect of everyday life. If 'language' is the communication of the contents of mind, words are but only one particular brand of human language; translation is therefore relevant to the study of all the ways in which we communicate the contents of the mind, whether we use words or not. If translation is both a priori to and at the very heart of human communication, then to restrict a dimension of human existence in which every human being on the planet shares is to immure within the privileged – and limited – walls of the academy what is ultimately a global social practice.

This brings me to my second point. Pratt rightly questions the inscription of cultural essentialism within the heterogeneous processes that cultural translation claims to cover. Given that we *do* use cultural translation to raise questions of migrancy, displacement and exile, there is surely value in imbricating the tools we have developed in translation studies for the analysis of interlingual transfer. Pratt worries that the application of translation implies the possibility of the reification of cultural difference, but we need to view this critique as just this: a possibility. To return again to Rorty, Pratt's construction of cultural translation as the sustenance of difference is a position no less contingent and no less valid than the construction of translation that orientates my own definition in this book. *Pace* Rorty, the two positions remain incommensurable, and, as such, are theories to be debated, extended and engaged with; but they are not facts and should not be treated as such. Translation as I conceive of it here is about infinite cultural production; it is about the processes of interpretation, distanciation, incorporation, transformation and emancipation most closely associated with the translation of texts that we witness in the construction and contestation of the cultural phenomena of everyday life. Translation in this view is interested neither in reifying *nor* surmounting difference but instead making use of it productively, and creatively, for emancipatory ends. Cultural translation as I conceive of it seeks not to overcome difference, but, as interlingual translation does, to create it.

That cultural translation has fostered such vociferous debate augurs well for the future. If there were not some kernel of social relevance which cultural translation taps into, one suspects we would not bother to comment on it at all and the term would simply slip away quietly from the academic scene. We might not yet be sure what it means, but its position in the critical imaginary gives it a certain substance. The need for precision, to make clear what we mean by the translational component in the collocation cultural translation and what role it plays in the model, means that the time has now come for cultural translation theorization to shape up or ship out. As Pym writes:

> For us, much as we might ignore the precise meaning of 'cultural translation', the questions raised here are among the most important and harrowing of our time. In Europe, the bodies of Africa are washed up on the beaches of Spain and Italy, second generations are burning *banlieues* of France, immigrants' houses are burnt in Germany, and the life-and-death dramas are acted out and on every day in the courts and tribunals. The problems of justice in such postmodern societies obviously require a lot more thought and work than is currently available in the talk about cultural translation. (Pym, 2010, p. 8)

Languages and cultural communities are not separate. People move and migrate and the way in which we respond to and interact with one another changes over time. As Pym is prepared to admit, cultural translation might just offer us a means of thinking critically about the many ways in which difference works in the world around us. Rather than ask why the term translation should be applied in other domains – as Young shows, this has been taking place since the fourteenth century and translation 'proper' seems to have thrived this long – we should instead ask why cultural translation exists as a distinct term in widespread usage. The question, in other words, is not how we should go about limiting cultural translation's use of the interlingual model but to ask why the interlingual model should be used as the foundation for cultural translation in the first instance.

Towards a definition of cultural translation

As I have argued, cultural translation theorization can be grounded most usefully in a solid foundation of the practice of the interlingual translator. By focusing on the specific actions of the translator vis-à-vis the texts they translate, we not only achieve a lens through which to identify translational movements across the social sphere, but, more important, we gain a way to *critique* them. It is with this task in mind that I return once again to Ricoeur, for by applying the practice of the interlingual translator to matters of human interaction and the attendant challenges of cultural difference, I argue that the social practice of everyday life in a globalized, multicultural, world means that on a daily basis every one of us is faced with interpreting that which we do not understand. For the same reason, it is not enough to remain at a distance, to retreat into the comfortable worlds we know. Difference is everywhere and we must reach outwards to engage with it, in an attempt to encapsulate that which we do not know within terms that we *do*. This outward-facing gesture of incorporation transforms the objects of translation irrevocably. But it also has the effect of causing us to question who we are and what it means to understand along the way – by exposing us to difference; by enriching the limited purview of our local language with this foreign importation *from the outside*.

It is precisely in the application of the interlingual model that we are able to broaden the horizons of cultural translation, to speak not just to questions of human migrancy, but across the spectrum of human endeavour, to discover how people and ideas are encountered, interpreted and transformed in ways that can be illuminated by what we know about translation – as a relationship with difference that leaves neither side unchanged. Fundamentally, cultural translation is considered here as the traceable presence of hermeneutic gestures of reading and writing in the construction and reception of a range of cultural phenomena present in the public sphere. As such, the book is imagined as a journey across the stages of thoughtful encounter in the everyday world we associate most closely with the interlingual translation of texts, from the translator's interpretation of a source to-be-understood, the same translator's distanciation from the objects of perception and the incorporation of otherness within regimes of the 'own', to the irrevocable transformation of difference and the eventual emancipation of the illusions of the translating subject along the way.

Chapter 1 considers the quest for understanding that lies at the heart of translation and is concerned with presenting the act of 'reading' as its primary gesture. Through a discussion of the subjectivity of the translator's 'gaze', this chapter challenges the assumption that a translation can stand unproblematically as a simple 'reflection' of the texts a translator translates. Chapter 2, meanwhile, considers the interpretive distance which separates the translator from the object of perception. Given the multiplicity of readings different translators' interpretations yield, any independent 'meaning' a text might be thought to contain is liberated from its author's original intentions. This places the translator at a distance: both physically 'away' and temporally 'after' the original time and place of a source text's production and reception. This chapter views translation as a doubly historicizing process in which both source text and translator are shown to be located in their historically contingent spaces, through an awareness of the judgement all acts of perception require. Translation can thus be construed as either a 'loss' to be mourned or an inaccessible 'past' that can be celebrated and memorialized. Chapter 3 considers the gesture of power on the part of a translator and how this process can be traced in the public sphere. Here, the focus for analysis is the map: as a written text that not only stands in place of but also distorts the realities it purports to represent. Translations can therefore be read as cartographic representations: as highly individualized accounts of a journey of interpretation that mediates – and contains – the different worlds it encounters.

Chapter 4 investigates the ways in which translation gives rise to new, resistant or renovatory interpretations of phenomena and considers the role of cultural translation in opposing the fixity of received knowledge. With reference to a range of art forms (poetry, pop art and online video music memes), it explores how an artist or creator's subjective appropriation of the objects of their gaze can lead to new, creative or resistant ideas, rejuvenating or subverting received notions and opening up different ways of thinking as a result. Chapter 5 considers the ways in which cultural translation can be operationalized in the critique of ideology and reflects upon a series of real-world cases where the 'meaning' of events remains strongly contested in the public sphere. Read through a translational lens, these cases are shown to be subject to a conflict of interpretations in which translation can be harnessed productively to suggest not only alternative ways of understanding these events but also as a first step towards critique. Across each of these five chapters, case studies of cultural translation demonstrate how these gestures of reading and writing can be witnessed and explored 'in action'. Throughout, I insist that as the presence of translational gestures in the cultural sphere, cultural translation is above all a hermeneutic enterprise. As such, it looks to its foundations in Ricoeur's hermeneutic philosophy and to Benjamin's complementary notions of survival, afterlife and 'fame', to raise translation both as a form of representation that appropriates rather than reflects the realities it represents and as a doubly historicizing process by which both the source text *and* the translator are shown to be located in their historically contingent spaces. It is this effect of hermeneutic humbling that creates the conditions for critique by challenging the interpreter's pretensions to *understand*. It is with this emancipatory objective that cultural translation seeks to make its strongest contribution.

1

Interpretation

Translation and the quest for understanding

The Plaça Reial is a handsome square in Barcelona's Gothic Quarter, just off La Rambla dels Caputxins. It is surrounded on four sides by porticoes concealing restaurants, cafes and nightclubs. Above the porticoes, ochre-coloured neo-Classical facades are adorned with elegant wooden shutters and Juliet balconies. The quadrangle itself is dotted with palm trees that gesture towards a large fountain that stands in the centre. The Plaça Reial was designed by Francesc Daniel Molina i Casamajó on the site of an old Capuchin monastery and was completed in the mid-nineteenth century. Today, it is a popular tourist destination and venue for local arts events. It was here that I found myself on a sunny afternoon in March 2014, having just finished a week-long interpreting assignment for the Departament de Justícia de la Generalitat de Catalunya Centre d'Estudis Jurídics i Formació Especialitzada. My task was to provide Spanish–English interpreting as part of a restorative justice training course for bilingual Catalan and Spanish-speaking social workers practising in the area. The training was to be facilitated by an international expert in restorative practices and would combine front-led slide show presentations with group-based interactive workshops and managed role-plays. The training would be delivered in English and it would be my job to interpret into Spanish every statement the facilitator made, and in turn, relay to him the participants' responses. In the run-up to the training, I organized a planning meeting with the facilitator. I asked for copies of the slides and any materials he was planning to distribute or make reference to as part of the training, as well as a list of bibliographic references. Armed with a foot of journal articles and textbooks I primed myself on key restorative approaches in operation across the world today and the major theoretical frameworks that drive them. Slowly, the information on the slides started to make sense. I could see where complex theoretical ideas on justice, society and community had been made relevant for practitioners working in concrete situations of community-based criminal justice delivery. One of our conversations ahead of the training went something like this:

'What about the lesson plan for the week?', I asked.

'Facilitation doesn't work that way', he said. 'Training workshops for diverse groups of adults are tailor-made to the specific group of participants undertaking any one training at any one time. We will cover specific restorative practices, and we can talk about these ahead of time, if you like. But the way in which we cover those elements has to remain organic. For it to mean anything to the participants, and for it to become in any way meaningful within the specific community contexts in which our participants are working, day in, day out, contexts in which only they are the experts, it has to be matched to them. It has to be a journey of discovery led by them, not us.'

For any interpreter attempting to prepare ahead for a project, nothing instils a greater sense of dread than the three words 'journey of discovery'. What if the participants wanted to know why one restorative approach was considered more appropriate than another, I wondered. What if they wanted more detail on a particular case study? Having designed high-level restorative justice systems across the world, the facilitator was equipped with the knowledge and expertise to handle such questions and give meaningful answers. But what if the answer he gave simply wasn't in my Spanish vocabulary? Everything would come down to deft lateral thinking, I reasoned. I might not know the specific Spanish or Catalan terminologies in common use within the Catalonian criminal justice sector. But if I understood something of the broader concepts themselves, what real-world settings they tend to relate to, what ideas drive their usage and what sort of future contexts they could be employed in, I could use *other* Spanish words – not to describe what the facilitator meant, but what *I* meant. Although I would not always be able to locate the precise concept within the audience's own realm of linguistic and professional experience, I could at least gesture towards a place of mutual understanding. But if the training was going to proceed organically, driven by the needs of the participants and rooted in their professional practice across a range of work settings, how could I prepare ahead every topic that could potentially be covered? How could I be sure that the quality of my interpreting would not slip when the direction of travel moved outside my own frame of knowledge? The problem I faced, in other words, was not one of vocabulary but one of *understanding*.

Sitting on the edge of the fountain, reflecting on this experience while I listened to a classical music recital, a lamppost caught my eye. It is one of two lampposts in the Plaça Reial that stand facing one another in empty space, equidistant from the fountain. Tall, dark grey iron columns bearing the crest of the city rise from polished marble pedestals with chamfered angles and fan out into crowns of red arms, ornately touched with gold, each supporting six lanterns. The lampposts were designed in 1879 by a young Antoni Gaudí, newly graduated as an architect. What caught my eye was not so much the ornateness of Gaudí's design – reason enough to stop and stare – but what sat atop the lampposts. It was a helmet of Hermes, a pair of wings spreading out from either side, its wrought iron painted gold. Monuments to Hermes and representations of his image can be found all over Barcelona, at the entrance to the Parc de la Ciutadella, on the Passeig Marítim de Mataró, the Banc d'Espanya on Plaça de Catalunya, the Museo de Cera, above the entrances to markets and stock exchanges along La Rambla de Catalunya and Passeig de Gràcia, to name but a few. I could find no more fitting a symbol for the central challenge of my interpreting assignment than the mythical co-founder of Barcelona, the messenger-god of Olympus.

In Greek mythology Hermes was the god of fertility, thieves, travellers and lies. As the son of Zeus, he was known for his athleticism and was often depicted as handsome, with feathered sandals, which he fashioned himself, a golden staff for herding cattle and a cap with the ability to render its wearer invisible. As the fastest of the gods, it was Hermes's job to ferry messages between the gods of Olympus and the people of earth by crossing the boundary separating the two worlds. His role was imperative – to translate divine mysteries beyond the capacity of human words into terms that mere mortals could understand. Without such a messenger the two realms would remain forever at a distance, mutually mysterious and mutually incomprehensible. The first task of hermeneutics, the philosophical method which takes its name from Hermes, is concerned with bridging gaps in understanding, and for many years was concerned with the interpretation of sacred texts, thought, too, to be the divine and mysterious 'word of God'. Starting life within the framework of biblical exegesis, it was viewed as a means for exploring how to understand and restore the divine intention of scripture following successive generations of Judeo-Christian reinscription.

And yet Hermes was also a deceiver-god and was known to play skilled tricks and to use his staff to make people hallucinate. As chief intermediary between humans and the gods he was tasked with something greater than simply transmitting messages; he had to use all the persuasive devices at his disposal to stand between these mutually mysterious and mutually incomprehensible worlds and convince his respective audiences of the value and significance of his words. He had to convince them to believe in what he was saying. He had to become an advocate for each side to the other. He had to involve himself in the messages he was charged with carrying. And as Homer recounts, when Hermes was born he jumped out of his cot and proceeded to hide all of Apollo's cattle. When Apollo discovered what he had done Hermes jumped back into his cot and protested his innocence. As divine messenger, Hermes *hides* as much as he reveals. In a contribution to a seminal edited collection on cultural translation in the anthropological context, Crapanzano perceived a similarity between Hermes and the work of the modern-day ethnographer: 'He presents languages, cultures, and societies in all their opacity, their foreignness, their meaninglessness; then like the magician, the hermeneut, Hermes himself, he clarifies the opaque, renders the foreign familiar, and gives meaning to the meaningless. He decodes the message. He interprets' (Crapanzano, 1986, p. 51). Both are charged with the safe passage of meaning between mutually exclusive parties and both become involved actively in the way in which such meaning is 'packaged'. As Crapanzano observes, the ethnographer tends to assume all interpretations are provisional, yet assumes a definitive reading nonetheless (ibid.). As the god of cunning, from the Old Norse *Kumandi*, meaning 'knowledge', Hermes was a *creator* of meaning as well as its messenger, and in this act of creation there is an aggressive as well as a life-giving dimension, for to show knowledge – to represent to another all that which is strange and unknown – we must also deceive. As Crapanzano points out, when Hermes took the job of messenger of the gods, he promised Zeus he would not lie. But this is not the same as promising to tell the whole truth (p. 53).

It is also useful to note the etymology of Hermes. His name, in the Greek form *herma*, is associated with the piles of stones that stood as boundary markers placed throughout Greece to protect travellers on their journey. The figure of Hermes thus stands for border-*limits* – for all that separates the upper and the lower worlds, for the co-existence of mutually mysterious and mutually incomprehensible realms of understanding that make mutual understanding impossible. As the emissary of the gods, he was both the god of boundaries, and, by extension, the god of border-*crossings*. Hermes is a reminder of both the limits and the very possibility of human understanding, for by being in the very business of crossing borders, he both confirms their existence and validates the desire to supersede them. The border-limits of human understanding thus contain their own invitation to be crossed, for their presence at once impedes and demands passage. In the mortal world we recognize these borders when communication fails, because we speak both to communicate and to conceal, always leaving certain things hanging in the air. As Steiner rightly observed, where human beings are concerned there are no spaces of absolute transparency because no two speakers mean exactly the same thing, even when they use the same terms, or if they do, we would have no way of demonstrating it independently. Understanding is so fraught with difficulty because between every message is what Steiner terms a 'middle' in which there is 'an operation of interpretive decipherment' (1998, p. 49). It is in this space, the space where Hermes operates, that 'translation' begins. Properly understood, Steiner writes, translation 'is a special case of the arc of communication which every successful speech-act closes within a given language' (ibid.). The very thing that makes translation impossible is also that which creates an imperative precisely for translation, for somehow we *do* manage to communicate with one another, to read one another's work, to hold international conferences, to trade commodities and to export goods. We can no more deny that translation happens than deny our breath, for it is quite simply what we do all the time. But in this hermeneutic view, translation is neither the absence of misunderstanding, nor the destruction of the border-limits that challenge our knowledge of one another. It is a cunning act of knowledge-creation across the border-limit, never complete, never neutral, always partial and always embodied. It is here that the journey of cultural translation begins.

The symbol gives rise to thought

The first principle behind Ricoeur's hermeneutic philosophy is that the problem of understanding is a feature of all language, not just sacred texts, and that 'language' is a primary feature of our being in the world. His initial project was to demonstrate the way in which the language we use, enshrined within the texts we create, is engaged in representing and better understanding human reality in some way: 'Because it is a world, the world of the text necessarily collides with the real world in order to "remake" it, either by confirming it or denying it. However, even the most ironic relation between art and reality would be incomprehensible if art did not both disturb and rearrange our relation to reality' (Ricoeur, 2008, p. 6). Texts are both inextricably linked to *and* riff off the world. It is the mimetic quality of human life that establishes Ricoeur's hermeneutics as a universal philosophy dedicated to the way in which we read not just texts but the narration of human lives. If in this worldly relevant sense hermeneutics is concerned with the decipherment of meaning wherever it is found then we must see the 'text' as only the beginning in our interrogation of meaning-making. This intellectual genealogy shares something with Benjamin, who was well known to Ricoeur:

> Every expression of human mental life can be understood as a kind of language, and this understanding, in the manner of a true method, everywhere raises new questions. It is possible to talk about a language

> of music and of sculpture, about a language of justice that has nothing directly to do with those in which German or English legal judgements are couched, about a language of technology that is not the specialized language of technicians. Language in such contexts means the tendency inherent in the subjects concerned – technology, art, justice, or religion – toward the communication of the contents of the mind. To sum up: all communication of the contents of the mind is language, communication in words being only a particular case of human language and of the justice, poetry, or whatever underlying it or founded on it. (Benjamin, 1996, p. 62)

Ricoeur maintained that even at the most banal level of conversation the polysemy of the words we employ requires a work of hermeneutics, because everything we say has more than one meaning when used outside of determinate contexts. Yet it is not simply the fact that words have multiple meanings that causes a problem for understanding. It is the fact that, from the very beginning, language is in the business of mystery, for it always points to something beyond itself. Ricoeur's point of entry into this line of thinking is the symbol, which he defines as: '*any structure of signification in which a direct, primary, literal meaning designates, in addition, another meaning which is indirect, secondary, and figurative and which can be apprehended only through the first*. This circumscription of expressions with a double meaning properly constitutes the hermeneutic field' (Ricoeur, 2004, p. 12, original emphasis). Like every sign, symbols stand for things they intend beyond themselves. But not every sign is a symbol, for unlike signs, symbols conceal a double intentionality. In addition to the primary intention a second intentionality is grafted upon it so that the obvious meaning also points to something else. Unlike technical signs these are not transparent. Symbols present such a challenge because their roots run deep. In this opacity is 'the symbol's very profundity, an inexhaustible depth' (p. 287).

Hermes fits this description, for while on one level he appears to be the fleet-of-foot intermediary between the upper and lower worlds of ancient Greece, a facilitator of communication, he is also the trickster-god of misunderstanding and personification of the ways in which the limits of opacity can only be superseded through active involvement. But this secondary reading of the legend of Hermes was teased out only through reflection on the paradox of the border, which Hermes simultaneously reinforces and supersedes. As with Hermes, symbols become a hermeneutic problem when meaning is 'concealed' rather than given; hidden in plain sight, they lend themselves to mystery and ambiguity:

> The symbol, I said, is constituted from a semantic perspective such that it provides a meaning by means of a meaning. In it a primary, literal, worldly,

often physical meaning refers back to a figurative, spiritual, often existential, ontological meaning which is in no way given outside this indirect designation. The symbol invites us to think, calls for an interpretation, precisely because it says more than it says and because it never ceases to speak to us. (p. 28)

Symbols have a double meaning where the literal signification points to a second meaning that can be understood only by considering the reference of the first to the second – in other words, by taking a contemplative 'detour'. It is the *plurivocity* of symbols, their inherent multiplicity of meaning, which gives rise to the possibility of opposed interpretations:

> By living in the first meaning I am drawn by it beyond itself: *the symbolic meaning is constituted in and through the literal meaning, which brings about the analogy by giving the analogue.* Unlike a comparison that we *look at* from the outside, symbol is the very movement of the primary meaning that makes us share in the latent meaning and thereby assimilates us to the symbolized, without our being able intellectually to dominate the similarity. This is the sense in which the symbol 'gives'; it gives because it is a primary intentionality that gives the second meaning. (p. 287, original emphasis)

This dimension is not to be confused with allegory, where we reach past the symbol to find the 'true' philosophical meaning it elides – the one that precedes the fable, which is only a poor disguise for a truth universally acknowledged. With symbols, by contrast, we are drawn into an enigmatic game, for they invite active involvement on the part of the interpreter: 'I am convinced that we must think, not *behind* the symbols, but starting from symbols, *according* to symbols, that their substance is indestructible, that they constitute the *revealing* substrate of speech which lives among men. In short, the symbol *gives rise to* thought' (p. 295, original emphasis). Wherever meaning is symbolic, where the surface meaning may elide another, less obvious meaning that depends upon the first, it is the work of hermeneutics to discover and reflect upon this. Ricoeur gives the example of the expulsion of Adam and Eve from the Garden of Eden. Myth, he says, is symbol developed through a narrative and this narrative expands over time. The Adamic myth is a symbol of exile, alienation; but as a second-order mythic narrative it also suggests certain universals of human existence in which we too can share. Beyond the story of Adam and Eve in the garden are themes of jealousy, desire and human arrogance that remain universal so long as these things remain part of the human condition.

According to Ricoeur, the practical work of thought involved in hermeneutics 'consists in deciphering the hidden meaning in the apparent meaning, in unfolding the levels of meaning implied in the literal meaning' (p. xiv). Inherent to this hermeneutics of decipherment is a desire for amplification – to interpret a symbol by being sensitive to the 'surplus of meaning' implicit in the symbolism that only a full reflection could bring out. This work of amplification aims to demystify, to unmask the unavowed, to 're-collect' meaning 'in its richest, its most elevated, most spiritual density' (Ricoeur, 2008, p. 16). Ricoeur's point is that the surplus of meaning is simultaneously that which requires us to interpret and that which makes all other interpretations possible. *Le symbole donne à penser* – 'What the symbol gives, gives rise to thought. This aphorism suggests that everything has already been said enigmatically, yet it is always necessary to start again when it comes to the dimension of concepts.' (p. 6) This is not about thinking without presupposition, but about starting to think *from* our presuppositions.

> The symbol is given to thought only by way of an interpretation which remains inherently problematical. There is no myth without exegesis, no exegesis without contestation. The deciphering of mysteries is not a science in either the Platonic or Hegelian sense or in the modern meaning of the word science. Opacity, cultural contingency, and dependency on a problematical interpretation-such as the three deficiencies of the symbol as measured by the ideal of clarity, necessity, and scientific order in reflection. (Ricoeur, 2004, p. 314)

We can draw three conclusions about symbolism: the first is its inherent plurivocity, which ensures that the symbol cannot survive outside of its unique situational context; the second is that the symbol's plurivocity simultaneously challenges understanding while issuing its own demand to be understood; and third, that this same symbol gives rise to the possibility of interpretations that are diametrically opposed.

Memes as cultural translations

What might the surplus of meaning – the work of reflection that arises from the co-presence of a literal signification suggestive of a secondary meaning that can only be understood by a detour through the meaning of the first – actually look like in context? In *The Selfish Gene* (2006) Dawkins wrote of the emergence of an all-new replicating entity, 'still in its infancy, still drifting about in its primeval soup' to challenge the prevalence of the gene as the primary means of securing evolution on our planet through reproduction:

The new soup is the soup of human culture. We need a name for the new replicator, a noun that conveys the idea of a unit of cultural transmission, or a unit of *imitation*. 'Mimeme' comes from a suitable Greek root, but I want a monosyllable that sounds a bit like 'gene'. I hope my Classicist friends will forgive me if I abbreviate mimeme to *meme*. If it is any consolation, it could alternatively be thought of as being related to 'memory', or to the French word *même*. It should be pronounced to rhyme with 'cream'. Examples of memes are tunes, ideas, catch-phrases, clothes fashions, ways of making pots or of building arches. Just as genes propagate themselves in the gene pool by leaping from body to body by sperm or eggs, so memes propagate themselves in the meme pool by leaping from brain to brain via a process which, in the broad sense, can be called imitation. If a scientist hears, or reads about, a good idea, he passes it on to his colleagues and students. He mentions it in his articles and his lectures. If the idea catches on, it can be said to propagate itself, spreading from brain to brain. [...] When you plant a fertile meme in my mind you literally parasitize my brain, turning it into a vehicle for the meme's propagation in just the way that a virus may parasitize the genetic mechanism of a host cell. (Dawkins, 2006, p. 192, original emphasis)

As a 'unit of cultural transmission' in the age of the Internet, the meme has now itself evolved, to secure its reproduction by means of what I insist here is best understood as *hermeneutic reflection*. By this I mean not only that memes are 'symbolic' par excellence in the sense that the modus operandi of the most viral of memes requires their audience to go beyond the surface-level meaning to appreciate hidden depths, but also that it is this very symbolic dimension that secures a meme's survival by increasing its chances of going viral. It is precisely in their inherent mysteriousness, the fact that memes engender a degree of detective work in order for their performative effect to be secured, that their contribution – to humour, wit, parody or politics – within the broader pool of cultural artefacts with which it competes is secured.

Consider the 'One does not simply walk into Mordor' meme. The phrase is a memorable quotation from *The Lord of the Rings: The Fellowship of the Ring* (2001). The quotation is taken from a meeting of the Council of Elrond at which it is revealed that the ring created by the Dark Lord Sauron can only be destroyed by throwing it into the fires of Mount Doom, a volcano deep in the fearsome territory of Mordor. Boromir, the character played by actor Sean Bean, warns of the difficulty of this task by observing that 'One does not simply walk into Mordor.' As is typical of memes, the 'One does not simply walk into Mordor' meme involves layering a variant of the phrase on which it is based – known in Internet terminology as a 'snowclone' – onto an image still taken from the film itself. In the 'One does not simply X into Mordor' snowclone, the word 'walk' is typically substituted to humorous effect. In the 'One does not simply *wok* into Mordor' meme, Sean Bean's face has been placed over the body of a chef; the 'One does not simply *Walken* to Mordor' meme layers a black and white headshot of actor Christopher Walken over a still from the film showing a dark plateau with Mount Doom in the background; and the 'One does not *silly walk* into Mordor' places Sean Bean's face over the body of John Cleese. In the first two examples we do not require too much hermeneutic decipherment to work out what is going on. They do require the reader to have seen the film, of course, and to understand that the fatuousness of Boromir's original phrase has sparked something of an Internet sensation; but, in the round, they do not have to point too far beyond themselves for the richness of their meaning to be revealed. However, for the 'One does not silly walk into Mordor' meme to function, for it to have any comedic effect at all, the reader must not only understand all of the foregoing; she must also understand the multiple – and multimodal – references that are being made simultaneously. First, the reader must understand that the background image of the besuited body of Cleese clutching a briefcase is taken from a sketch entitled 'The Ministry of Silly Walks', first screened as part of the *Monty Python's Flying Circus* (1970) television programme, in which the actor starred as a civil servant in a fictitious British government department responsible for administering grants for silly walks. Throughout the original sketch, Cleese walks in a variety of very silly ways. In the meme, Cleese's head has been replaced with that of Bean's and the phrase 'simply walk' has been replaced with 'silly walk'. Without a prior knowledge of the comedic genealogy on which this meme relies, the reader cannot decipher the hidden meaning behind the surface-level reference to *The Lord of the Rings*. To employ Austin's terminology, for memes to be truly *performative*, rather than just *constative*, that is, to do more than merely 'say' something of interest but to incite us towards some sort of action (such as clicking the 'share' or 'like' or 'retweet' icon and thus increasing the viral score a meme achieves), is to suggest to readers the existence of a shared secret to which, if they have the right background knowledge or experience (in this case, of 1970s British comedy), they too can be privy.

Translation, language and being

For Ricoeur, the very fact that language refers to the world – it does not simply 'say' things; it has something to say about them – meant that his reflections on the concealment of meaning through the symbol were only the beginning of a much bigger project. He observed that the objective of a sign, to stand 'for' something, is repudiated by its very nature as something designed to transcend itself. There is no closed system of intra-significant signs in language, only signs that express an extra-linguistic reality. Like pieces of Lego that make sense only when the mechanism by which they interlock with other pieces of Lego is made known, signs exist in the very condition of reaching outwards, beyond language, to the world. In the intention to signify, language becomes inextricably linked not just to the world but to the references it makes to a world outside itself. As Ricoeur observes, 'language speaks, that is, shows, makes present, brings into being. The absence of the sign from the thing is only the negative condition for the sign to reach the thing, touch it, and die in this contact' (2004, p. 258). When, for example, I once visited the toilets of a fashionable bar-restaurant in Belfast and was confronted with two separate doors offering me a choice between 'Olivia Newton-John', on the one hand, and 'Elton John', on the other, I did not actually expect to find a best-selling English-born singer-songwriter-performer lurking behind my chosen bathroom door. Instead I found the venue's humour charming and I made my choice. Discursive statements are statements of reality; not reality itself. Inherent within the symbolic materials we produce there is a simultaneous presence and an absence. Ricoeur gives the example of metaphor, which, like symbolic language, reaches outside itself to a world that it represents mimetically. But it does not reach outside of itself by itself; one employs the metaphor, as a living device. It is impossible to coin a new metaphor without being aware of what one is doing, and, in turn, the new metaphor creates a mystery for the reader unfamiliar with it. This requires the reader to think carefully about it and in so doing to become aware of the mystery involved in interpreting it. With metaphor, explains Simms, 'we say that something is something else, and in so doing assimilate the something else into the first something, despite the fact that on first appearance it does not belong there. This constitutes for Ricoeur a form of ordering the world by the imagination' (Simms 2003, p. 79). To declare that 'the law's an arse', 'yer head's a marley' and 'she's the quare girl', as we are wont to do in Northern Ireland, or that 'Achilles is a lion', to adopt Ricoeur's own example, is to say that something or someone both *is* and is *not* that to which they are being actively compared (2004, p. 249). Even the copula itself is othered by the fact that Achilles is both the same and not the same as a lion. By referencing a world it represents mimetically, yet simultaneously does not re-create, language contains its own othering. In this sense, a sign is a negative truth, since it can only stand 'for' something if it is *not* the thing itself. For this reason, metaphor 'forces conceptual thought to think more' (p. 303). It compels us to use the imagination interpretively, to roll up our sleeves and participate actively in the creation of meaning. As Simms notes, 'the work of interpretation involved in understanding a metaphor is itself a part of the knowledge arrived at. Metaphor is thus a point in language at which the objective facts of the world meet the subjective interpretation of the individual who interprets them – a point at which phenomenological truth is arrived' (2003, p. 74).

Ricoeur's point is that words have no 'proper' meaning on their own and meaning cannot be said to 'belong' to them. They are simply empty vessels and do not carry any meaning in themselves, for language always opens outwards and gestures towards something beyond itself and beyond the world of the speaker. 'Meaning' in language exists only inasmuch as we make language refer to the world:

> Only this dialectic says something about the relation between language and the ontological condition of being in the world. Language is not a world of its own. It is not even a world. But because we are in the world, because we are affected by situations, and because we orient ourselves comprehensively in those situations, we have something to say, we have experience to bring to language. (Ricoeur, 1976, p. 20–1)

This is significant, because it means that when it comes to the work of reflection that language stimulates, as is the project of Ricoeur's philosophical hermeneutics, the linguistic focus of our enquiry cannot be separated from the domain of lived experience. We speak because we have something to say. Language does not really exist until we employ it in a real-world situation of communication – until we imbue it with meaning by using it to say something about something *to someone else*. It is the instantiation of language through speech addressed to an interlocutor. As such, language is an open system. When we speak, we select certain meanings and exclude others; these choices produce new combinations, new sentences and new ideas. When this 'discourse' is understood by another, by the receiver to which it is directed, it becomes meaning: 'Just as language, by being actualised as discourse, surpasses itself as system and realises itself as event, so too discourse, by entering the process of understanding, surpasses itself as event and becomes meaning' (Ricoeur, 2008, p. 75). Speech is event: it is deliberateness of choice; it is reference; and, crucially, intersubjectivity, for language remains only potential until it is actualized by someone addressing their words to another. Because a speaker's signifying intentions are always relative to the situation and the audience to whom they are addressed, discourse never exists for its own sake. It is also always self-referential, precisely because signs in language remain empty until they are filled by a speaker who deploys them. At the same time as it makes reference to the world, then, discourse also refers back to the one doing the referencing. While the speaker can be identified through all manner of indicators such as personal pronouns, language, meanwhile, acquires no subject until someone actually speaks. It is only through this circular dialectic, by which a speaker engages with the world and puts into words that self-same engagement that meaning comes to mean anything. Ultimately, Ricoeur attests, '[l]anguage itself, as a signifying milieu, must be referred to existence' (2004, p. 15).

Benjamin offers a similar reflection in his essay, 'On Language as Such and on the Language of Man', in which he observed that by 'naming' the world around us, language becomes the communication of the 'mental being of man' (1996, p. 65). The language of a lamp, he says, communicates not the lamp itself, but the 'language-lamp, the lamp in communication, the lamp in expression' (p. 63). The lamp does not communicate by itself; we make it communicate. When we name it, it becomes a vehicle for communication, both with others and back to ourselves:

> What does language communicate? It communicates the mental being corresponding to it. It is fundamental that this mental being communicates itself *in* language and not *through* language. Languages, therefore, have no speaker, if this means someone who communicates *through* these languages. Mental being communicates itself in, not through, a language, which means that it is not outwardly identical with linguistic being. Mental being is identical with linguistic being insofar as it is capable of being communicated. (Benjamin, 1996, p. 63, original emphasis)

Language has no being. It is we who communicate things using language. Language does not communicate anything except the person behind it, who communicates *in* language – that is, using language, not 'through' it. This would be to imply that the 'thing' that is communicated is itself fixed and inalienable. What language communicates is not an essential quality but the 'mental being' of the one who communicates. In this infinite circle, the expressions of a mental entity, words, are but the communication of a self through language, not language itself (p. 63). When it comes to Ricoeur's hermeneutic project, which is neither interested in linguistic description nor semantic theory but in how the world relates to human beings through the mediation of texts, these insights are crucial, for they suggest that language is secondary: to the world and to ourselves. Yes, language is the medium through which meanings are conveyed; but as the communication of the contents of the mind it is a medium that 'belongs' properly to being:

> For us who speak, language is not an object but a mediation. Language is that through which, by means of which, we express ourselves and express things. Speaking is the act by which the speaker overcomes the closure of the universe of signs, in the intention of saying something about something to someone; speaking is the act by which language moves beyond itself as

sign toward its reference and toward what it encounters. Language seeks to disappear; it seeks to die as an object. (Ricoeur, 2004, p. 82)

In this way the referential function of language – the means by which it says something about something to someone else – is only the counterpart of another aspect which proceeds from our being in the world, for that which language 'says', ultimately, is something as pertinent about the one who is speaking as the one who is being spoken to. 'It is because there is first something to say', Ricoeur writes, 'because we have an experience to bring to language, that conversely, language is not only directed towards ideal meanings but also refers to what is' (1976, p. 21). Language, then, is the expression of our very ontological condition. As Benjamin attests:

> There is no event or thing in either animate or inanimate nature that does not in some way partake of language, for it is in the nature of each one to communicate its mental contents. This use of the word 'language' is in no way metaphorical. For to think that we cannot imagine anything that does not communicate its mental nature in its expression is entirely meaningful; consciousness is apparently (or really) bound to such communication to varying degrees, but this cannot alter the fact that we cannot imagine a total absence of language in anything. (Benjamin, 1996, p. 62)

Yet we speak both to communicate *and* to conceal, for as much as language-in-life is a performance by which human actors imbue words with intentionality, purpose and desire, we also leave certain things unspoken. Whether intended deliberately or not, there is always something hidden in our language. As Steiner reminds: 'The language of a community, however uniform its social contour, is an inexhaustibly multiple aggregate of speech-atoms, of finally irreducible personal meanings. The element of privacy in language makes possible a crucial, though little understood, linguistic function' (1998, p. 47). Because language belongs to being, in other words, it will always be aporetic. Consider these words of wisdom from the March Hare in *Alice's Adventures in Wonderland* (1869):

> 'Your hair wants cutting', said the Hatter. He had been looking at Alice for some time with great curiosity, and this was his first speech. 'You should learn not to make personal remarks', Alice said with some severity: 'it's very rude'. The Hatter opened his eyes very wide on hearing this; but all he *said* was, 'Why is a raven like a writing-desk?' 'Come we shall have some fun now!' thought Alice. 'I'm glad they've begun asking riddles – I believe I can guess that', she added aloud. 'Do you mean that you think you can find out the answer to it?' said the March Hare. 'Exactly so', said Alice.

'Then you should say what you mean', the March Hare went on. 'I do', Alice hastily replied; 'at least-at least I mean what I say-that's the same thing, you know'. 'Not the same thing a bit!' said the Hatter. 'Why you might as well say that "I see what I eat" is the same thing as "I eat what I see!"' (Carroll, 1869, pp. 96–8, original emphasis)

According to the March Hare's reproach, there is a distinct difference between meaning something, in the intentional sense, and for that which you say to be actually reflective of that which you mean by the time it reaches the person to whom you are speaking. The 'linguistic function' of which Steiner writes is the inescapable duplicity that surrounds our expressions of human life. As Steiner puts it, 'No two historical epochs, no two social classes, no two localities use words and syntax to signify exactly the same things, to send identical signals of valuation and inference. Neither do two human beings' (1998, p. 47). No two people will interpret the same statement in exactly the same way, because we imbue even apparently neutral terms with social, cultural, linguistic and political particularity and because 'understanding' does not depend upon universal criteria that are shared equally by all who understand. For Benjamin, this situation contrasts starkly with the time before the fall of the mythical city of Babel, a time when there was perfect understanding and total correspondence between signs and the things to which they pointed. In paradise, there was no need to name things, because things simply 'were':

> After the Fall, which, in making language mediate, laid the foundation for its multiplicity, linguistic confusion could only be a step away. Once men had injured the purity of name, the turning away from that contemplation of things in which their language passes into man needed only to be completed in order to deprive men of the common foundation of an already shaken spirit of language. *Signs* must become confused where things are entangled. The enslavement of language in prattle is joined by the enslavement of things in folly almost as its inevitable consequence. In this turning away from things, which was enslavement, the plan for the Tower of Babel came into being, and linguistic confusion with it. (Benjamin, 1996, p. 72, original emphasis)

What we face in our post-Babelian miasma goes deeper than just the polysemy of words or the ambiguity of sentences. It follows that if language is the expression of the contents of the mind, then the putative 'problem' of language is at base a problem of the incommensurability of *human experience*. When Benjamin writes that the paradisiacal language of humankind 'must have been one of perfect knowledge, whereas all later knowledge is again infinitely differentiated in the multiplicity of language' (p. 71), we can attribute this to the plurivocity of human experience as expressed in language and which makes the things we say mutually incomprehensible, since 'my' experience does not map directly onto yours. The mysteries of language thus consist partly in the fact that what is experienced by one person cannot be transferred wholesale to another.

The starting point for hermeneutics – as a method for deciphering meaning where there is mystery – is not simply that semantic meaning is distinct from symbolic meaning, or that the speeches we make or the texts we write are more than the sum of their parts. Hermeneutics insists that because the things we say and the things we write tell us something about the world, we cannot derive their meaning in isolation from the worlds to which they point:

> For the interpreter, it is the text which has a multiple meaning; the problem of multiple meaning is posed for him only if what is being considered is a whole in which events, persons, institutions, and natural or historical realities are articulated. It is an entire 'economy', an entire signifying whole, which lends itself to the transfer of meaning from the historical to the spiritual level. (Ricoeur, 2004, p. 63)

Because it is a philosophy of interpretation based on the lingual condition of *all* human experience, hermeneutics is committed to the idea that the significations that populate the world around us are neither totalities closed in on themselves, nor are they restricted to the world of text. Behind (and indeed, before!) texts there are real people with real motivations, intentions and desires. Each of these brings to bear an influence on the shape and nature of the texts that are created:

> To be sure, texts – mainly literary ones – are ensembles of signs that have more or less broken their ties to the things they are held to denote. But, amid the things that are said there are people, acting and suffering; what is more, discourses are themselves actions; this is why the mimetic bond – in the most active sense of the term *mimetic* – between the act of saying (and of reading) and effective action is never completely severed. It is only made more complex, more indirect by the break between *signum* and *res*. (Ricoeur, 2008, p. xi, original emphasis)

Although he takes lessons from semantic theory, Ricoeur embraces the textual model of interpretation wherever there is meaningful discourse and believed that it is in the nature of every being on Earth to communicate its mental contents. But he also believed that the communication of the contents of the mind was not limited to the making of speeches or the writing of text, traditionally conceived. Then, as now, our world is as much visual as it is verbal – if not more so today, with the rise of social media and the multimodal cultures of circulation that prevail in an Internet-connected age. Ideas predicated on received notions of 'text' no longer stand. One of Ricoeur's key contributions to hermeneutic philosophy was to extend the process of interpreting mystery within the words on a page to the process of 'reading' the world around us. If the basic premise of hermeneutics is that written works are possessing of meaning because they are reflective of life, then it follows that 'life' can be viewed as a narrative to be engaged with – 'read' and interpreted as we would a text and revealing of something about the human condition. In Ricoeur's fundamental revision, hermeneutics is concerned with interpreting any instance in which meaning is advanced and contested, for the textual model is only the means for discovering how the world relates to human beings and human beings to one another through language.

Thus while the prima facie concern of hermeneutics is the concealment of meaning in language – the 'circumscription of expressions with a double meaning' – Ricoeur's expanded definition of hermeneutics is not limited to symbols as expressions of multiple intention (Ricoeur, 2004, p. 12). His innovation is that we can apply the theory of the text to meaningfully oriented behaviour in the Weberian sense, to the production of any human act, inscribed as much in deed as in text, where meaning is contested. As with text, Ricoeur observes that in all manner of phenomena in the social sphere, we witness attempts to cope with problems of understanding, and, as with text, these human efforts to tackle conflict and complexity have a referential dimension in the sense that they project worlds that are more than their ostensive situation. Such social structures 'point toward the aporias of social existence, the same aporias around which mythical thought gravitates' (Ricoeur, 2008, p. 162). As with the textual model, we cannot understand meaningful patterns in the social sphere without the same kind of personal commitment that the reader deploys when grasping the complexity of the text. As readers as much of ourselves as one another, we embrace the rules of the text within a theory of action when we enter into thoughtful engagement with all manner of human expression, from the newspaper articles we produce and comment on, to the material we post and share on the Internet, the street graffiti we produce, the historical events we memorialize, the monuments we build and the politicians and celebrities we raise and destroy. To Ricoeur, these are all 'quasi-texts asking to be read' (2008, p. 33).

The common link between text and human action is its temporal character. As with storytelling, for example, which is marked, organized and clarified according to the moment in which it unfolds, so too action is historically contingent: 'Everything that is recounted occurs in time, takes time, unfolds temporally; and what unfolds in time can be recounted. Perhaps, indeed, every temporal process is recognized as such only to the extent that it can, in one way or another, be recounted' (Ricoeur, 2008, p. 2). We can speak of a 'discourse' of action in which something is transacted from one agent to another as a message might pass from one speaker to another through the process of interlocution. Certain actions also leave their 'mark' – and it is these marks that serve as the 'textual' inscriptions on which to base our hermeneutic enquiry. Just as we can interpret the internal and external relations of a text, we can examine the multiple connections of an action, for, as with text, actions contain an internal structure that has a reference to a world; and they project something outwards, connecting themselves to the wider world, analogous to the referential function of the text. Like metaphor, human action demonstrates mimetic qualities, for it is engaged in representing human reality in some way.

As a quasi-text, human action, 'like every other text, makes room for a kind of hermeneutic circle, inasmuch as one interprets it as a whole as a function of its parts and vice versa.' (Ricoeur, 2013, p. 34). The world is open-ended because the things we say, the texts we produce, the things we make and the things we do are also open to interpretation. In a bid to better understand the human condition and the ways in which it inscribes itself in mystery, Ricoeur looks to the signs produced in writing or by any other process of inscription equivalent to writing including 'all the sorts of documents and monuments that entail a fixation similar to writing' (2008, p. 140). These 'documents of life' encompass any 'expression of life' or 'cultural artefact' in the 'social imaginary', including events and public monuments, in addition to the actions of human beings themselves. It is Ricoeur's belief that the substitution and representing of things by means of signs is the very foundation of social life. It is the conflict of interpretations these processes of substitution and representation activate that enable the signs of human experience to mean all they can possibly mean. For Ricoeur, meaning in life is a text to be interpreted. He thus gives interpretation what he describes as a 'distinct' meaning:

> I propose to give it the same extension I gave to the symbol. *Interpretation, we will say, is the work of thought which consists in deciphering the hidden meaning in the apparent meaning, in unfolding the levels of meaning implied in the literal meaning.* In this way I retain the initial reference to exegesis, that is, to the interpretation of hidden meanings. Symbol and interpretation thus become correlative concepts; there is interpretation wherever there is multiple meaning, and it is in interpretation that the plurality of meanings is made manifest. (Ricoeur, 2004, p. 12, original emphasis)

Opening itself to multiple detours across the terrain of otherness – culture, society, politics, religion and the human sciences – Ricoeur's hermeneutics is committed to critical reflection on how explanation and understanding operate when we interpret the signs of humanity all around us. Viewing the world as textual, where human existence is expressed through discourse that invites interpretation, Ricoeur's hermeneutics remains essentially a theory of text, but which takes texts only as a starting point.

As with texts, actions have agents who own the actions that belong to them, and, as with texts, they also contain their own invitation to be interpreted, since both are diverse and multifaceted. The expressions of human life are constantly circumscribed with heterogeneous meaning: 'As a quasi-text, action derives its readability from the rules that connect it together, thanks to which we can say that in raising our hand, we vote; that in leaving a room we break off negotiations; in running down the street we take part in a riot; and so on' (Ricoeur, 2013, p. 34). Actions have meanings that are not immediately apparent but which give rise to reflection. Like language, human action is conflictual, for the plurivocity of an action allows it to be construed in a number of ways. We attempt to explain why a person did this or that, and when we provide motives and causes, we impute certain things to both the action and its agent, in an attempt to understand. But, as with text, one can always argue for or against a particular interpretation of an action:

> Could we not say that what can be (and must be) *construed* in human action is the motivational basis of this action, that is, the set of desirability characters that may explain it? And could we not say that the process of *arguing* linked to the explanation of action by its motives unfolds a kind of plurivocity that makes action similar to a text? (Ricoeur, 2008, p. 156, original emphasis)

When Ricoeur entitled his first collection of essays on hermeneutics the *conflit des interprétations* his contention was not only that all human experience is at base conflictual but also that the mediation of different positions in the world forms the basis of the hermeneutic project itself.

Understanding (as) the human condition

By saying that the actions of others can be construed in more than one way, that the expressions of life all around us give rise to a mystery that can be studied and interpreted, that life can be read and interrogated as we would a text, we show 'life' as a narrative to be read and engaged with. This is to presuppose not just that all human experience is, in principle, expressible, but that human experience *demands* to be said (Ricoeur, 2008, p. 36). This is the *Sprachlichkeit* that pervades all human experience – that the linguisticality of the world around us is more than the outward expression of an understanding and instead a never-ending search for meaning. So while Ricoeur's philosophical hermeneutics is interested above all in the mysteries of life in all its manifestations, it is the bigger picture, our very experience of life and the world around us, that is of ultimate concern. Thus the fundamental premise of hermeneutics is that because we gain meaning in life through our ability to represent the world around us through the things we say, the things we write and the things we do, human works are precisely possessing of meaning because they are reflective of life. By understanding these we understand something of the meaning of life. At base, then, Ricoeur's philosophy is one of life and one of reading:

> This is why philosophy remains a hermeneutics, that is, a reading of the hidden meaning inside the text of the apparent meaning. It is the task of hermeneutics to show that existence arrives at expression, at meaning, and at reflection only through the continual exegesis of all the significations that come to light in the world of culture. Existence becomes a self—human and adult—only by appropriating this meaning which first resides 'outside', in works, institutions and cultural monuments in which the life of the spirit is objectified. (Ricoeur, 2004, p. 21)

If we express our understanding of the world through signs, symbols, speech and writing, when we interpret such things, a certain questioning takes place. Since human life is a never-ending process of engagement, moreover, 'understanding' in the social sphere is dialectical in nature, since our activities in the social sphere are never fully introverted or introspective; we riff constantly off one another's interpretations. What Iser calls a process of 'mapping the open-ended world' is the intermediary step between understanding our representations of the world around us and *self-* understanding (2000, p. 9). Ricoeur's hermeneutics is therefore more than epistemological, in the sense of acquiring knowledge *of* the world; it is also ontological, for its primary interest is the study of how knowledge-production increases what we know of ourselves and enables us to question our being in the world. Being philosophical, Ricoeur's hermeneutics is concerned above all with the meaning and significance of life for us as human actors. If language is the vehicle through which meanings are conveyed and the meaning of life is given, to 'understand' language is to understand what it means to be human.

My definition of cultural translation

It is on this foundation of philosophical hermeneutics that I build my definition of cultural translation. *Pace* Ricoeur, my definition takes as first principles that it is through language that the imagination reaches expression and that words are only one particular brand of human language. It is through the full spectrum of human endeavour – whether word *or* deed – that we communicate our being in the world. To 'understand' human action, as our response to the world around us, is to discover human truths – as much about ourselves as others. I believe that 'understanding' is primarily a problem of understanding the expressions of mental life inscribed in the works of human endeavour all around us. 'Hermeneutics', then, is simply a description for what we do in life. Into this philosophical foundation I integrate insights gleaned from the concrete domain of interlingual translation. As is the project of hermeneutics, interlingual translation starts where there is mystery and proceeds to instigate an act of interpretation in a bid to understand. In the case of interlingual translation, this interpretive act is addressed towards the enigma of a foreign 'source' text – no less mysterious – written in another language, by another person, addressed originally to another audience, in another time and in another place. Hidden beneath the surface of the source is a surplus of meaning of great interest to a reader who cannot understand the language in which the text was written originally and who therefore remains stranded, left out in the linguistic cold. Like Ricoeur's interpreter of texts and human action, these hidden depths can only be plumbed through thoughtful reflection on the part of the translator, who labours to enable the source to mean all it can possibly mean when written again in the language of the translator's reader, in a different time, in a different place and for very different reasons than the original. By virtue of this shared interpretive project, both Ricoeur's hermeneutic theorization and the practice of interlingual translation are driven by a quest for *understanding*.

An interesting dimension distinguishes the interpretive practice of interlingual translation from the process of interpretation as it unfolds in Ricoeur's framework. In philosophical hermeneutics, the objects of interpretation are the mysteries of human discourse – whether inscribed in text or in human action – as the means by which human beings express themselves. 'Discourse' is precisely mysterious because it is always expressive, always referential, always reaching outwards to represent a world that it claims to describe. To 'understand' discourse is to step into a circular process of meaning-making by which the works of human endeavour interact with and diverge tangentially from the worlds they represent, long before the interpreter undertakes to understand. It is this quality that the process of interpretation at the heart of hermeneutics takes as its object of reflection. This is a project that interlingual translation shares: its target is the web of relations internal and external to the foreign source text that connects it to the worlds of meaning it represents. And yet as an audience-directed mode, translation also does something else, for its objective is more than to understand the production of meaning in another text. It is also to produce meaning in a text *of its own*.

As with discourse, translation involves an agent, the translator, and an addressee, the audience who will receive the translator's work. And, as with discourse, that which translation produces is also expressive, also referential, also making references outwards to the world. As with all human works, translation is mimetic in the sense that it reflects the world of another text, written by another, in another language, in another time and in another place. But it is also mimetic in the sense that translation both expresses what is in the world of the source text *and* it creates a world of its own, for it is only in the context of this translator-audience dialectic that a translation becomes meaningful. Translators must do more than read and interpret texts; they must also read and interpret the needs, knowledges and expectations of their target audiences and then they must create a text of their own to which their audiences can respond. Translation is therefore purposeful, intentional, and although it starts from an act of reading, it finishes with an act of writing which will then be read. Thus translations themselves can be viewed as texts-for-interpretation – as human endeavour, the outward expression of the contents of the translator's mind. *Translations themselves invite interpretation*, both because they have something to say about the world and because this view of the world can also be contested by those who read them. Translation may well start life as secondary to the endeavours of others, a methodology it shares with Ricoeur's hermeneutics. But translation's purposeful dimension – as an act of writing to be read by an identified audience – makes it also a primary mode of human expression, and, therefore, open to interpretation. Whereas philosophical hermeneutics addresses the dialectic between reader and text and between interpreter and social phenomena, translation deals in dialectics that are infinitely intersecting.

In this way, rather than relegating the practice of interlingual translation and its theorization to a subset of cultural studies, as some critics have worried, my definition of cultural translation places the interlingual dimension front and centre. This is an approach that fits with Benjamin's own view of translation:

> It is necessary to found the concept of translation at the deepest level of linguistic theory, for it is much too far-reaching and powerful to be treated in any way as an afterthought, as has happened occasionally. Translation attains its full meaning in the realization that every evolved language (with the exception of the word of God) can be considered a translation of all the others. (Benjamin, 1996, pp. 69–70)

By combining the interpretive methods Ricoeur identifies as part and parcel of the hermeneutic nature of our existence with a sensitivity to the decisive nature of interlingual translation, my definition of cultural translation shifts the locus of philosophical hermeneutics to address the deliberate, purposeful acts of interpretation that aim to impact specific audiences in specific ways. My approach to cultural translation is concerned with investigating how different people operationalize interpretation in different times and in different places in a bid to achieve different ends within different audiences. It locates in the social world of human expression political gestures of motivation, determination and desire we associate most commonly with the audience-directed nature of interlingual translation. In my definition, cultural translation applies the interpretive methods by which philosophical hermeneutics attempts to understand the unknown and deploys them deliberately in order to effect *change*. Cultural translation is thus a gesture of interpretation – of contested understandings of the objects of human expression that suffuse the practice of everyday life in the social sphere and the attendant gestures of thoughtful reflection and analysis this entails. But this gesture of interpretation is also accompanied by a simultaneous gesture of desire – to occasion different behaviours and different ways of thinking and acting within an identified audience. As such, not everything in the world is cultural translation. To qualify as cultural translation a phenomenon of human expression in the social sphere must be shown to engage in a contemplative work of understanding addressed towards a particular substance, but it must also have as its primary objective nothing short of the transformation of human hearts and minds.

2

Distanciation

Translation and the space-time continuum

'My name is Ozymandias, king of kings:/ Look on my works, ye Mighty, and despair!'. It is thought that it was the imminent arrival in England of a colossal granite bust of Ramesses II, the third pharaoh of the Nineteenth Dynasty of ancient Egypt, which inspired Shelley to publish these immortal words in 1818. 'Ozymandias', derived from a Greek transliteration of one of his throne names, is just one of the names by which we recognize Ramesses. In film he has been portrayed on numerous occasions as the pharaoh of the *Book of Exodus*, by Yul Brynner in *The Ten Commandments* (1956), Ralph Fiennes in the animated feature *The Prince of Egypt* (1998) and Joel Edgerton in *Exodus: Gods and Kings* (2014). In narrative fiction he is the subject of *The Mummy, or Ramses the Damned* (1989) by Anne Rice, the *Ramsès* series by Christian Jacq (1995–7) and features as a crime-fighting vigilante-turned-businessman in the critically acclaimed *Watchmen* comic series (1986–7) and graphic novel (2008) created by Alan Moore and Dave Gibbons with colourist John Higgins.

That he continues to inspire a cult of personality would leave the pharaoh well pleased. Throughout the sixty-plus years of his reign he dedicated himself to building public monuments to his greatness. He ascended the throne at the age of twenty-five and from about 1279 BC until his death in around 1213 BC, and on a scale beyond all others who preceded him, covered a territory stretching between the Nile Delta and modern-day northern Sudan with palaces, temples and statues, adding to or completing existing sites and sometimes inscribing his name over the names of his predecessors, securing his place in history by erasing the marks of his forebears and tagging their works as his own. His building work was prolific. He is responsible for establishing a new capital named *Pi-Ramesses* at the ancient site of Avaris – another boast to the greatness of both his name and his victory in battle – and for the twin temples at Abu Simbel in southern Egypt near the border with Sudan. At the entrance to the Great Temple in the same complex four giant statues of Ramesses rising twenty metres were carved out of the exterior rock, each depicting the pharaoh seated on his throne.

Over three thousand years before the completion of Mount Rushmore, Ramesses knew that the secret of everlasting life was to impress into the geology of the Earth a permanent record of his works at every opportunity. He built the temples in honour of his queen Nefertari and to commemorate his military prowess at the Battle of Kadesh against the forces of the Hittite Empire. The treaty he concluded with King Hattusili III around 1259 BC is today recognized as one of the earliest surviving peace accords, and a replica clay tablet displaying the text of the treaty hangs at the north entrance to the Security Council in the United Nations headquarters in New York. And yet the Battle of Kadesh was basically a draw. For over two centuries the Egyptian Kingdom had been locked in hostilities with the Hittite Empire for control of lands in modern-day Syria. By the time Ramesses ascended the throne there was no clear victor. In the pharaoh's revisionist account, however, which is narrated on wall after wall on many of his monuments, it was an all-out victory for the Egyptian Kingdom. Given the sheer magnitude of his works and the shrewdness of his marketing strategy, Ramesses well earns his epithet as 'the Great'. But as one of history's first spin doctors, his works also teach us something about the limits of human achievement and it is this dimension that plays an important role in the hermeneutic project on which I base my definition of cultural translation.

Ricoeur's philosophical hermeneutics starts where there is mystery – when the signs of human existence are separated from the things to which they refer. He believed that when the site of separation is spoken discourse, where 'interlocutors' are engaged in contemporaneous dialogue, the mystery can be solved because they share the same moment in time and space. This shared historical co-situation means that when one speaker addresses herself to another, she can compensate for the separation of signs from their things through the referential scope of the discourse she employs. That is, being part of a common situation, a speaker can attempt to 'show' the thing that is intended: 'This situation in a way surrounds the dialogue, and its landmarks can all be shown by a gesture, by pointing a finger, or designated in an ostensive manner by the discourse itself through the oblique reference of those other indicators that are the demonstratives, the adverbs of time and place, and the tense of the verb' (Ricoeur, 2008, p. 144). The dialogue is steeped in this situation; we pepper it with descriptives, demonstratives, proper names and oblique references, in a bid to point towards that which we mean. For this ostensive designation process to be successful, everything the speaker says and does depends upon how they are taken up in turn by the interlocutor:

> Facing the *speaker* in the first person is a *listener* in the second person to whom the former addresses him or herself – this fact belongs to the situation of interlocution. So, there is not illocution without allocution, and, by implication, without someone to whom the message is addressed. The utterance that is reflected in the sense of the statement is therefore straightaway a bipolar phenomenon: it implies simultaneously an 'I': that speaks and a 'you' to whom the former addresses itself. 'I affirm that' equals 'I declare to you that'; 'I promise that'. In short, utterance equals interlocution. (Ricoeur, 1995, p. 43–4, original emphasis)

Utterances carry within them the intention of being recognized for what they are by our receivers. When we make a promise we are also making a commitment; we are asserting to someone that we will undertake a certain action. If I make a promise to you I expect you to recognize my promise as such – both as words and as a commitment to act. Every utterance produces a certain psychological effect on the part of the receiver through which a speaker's intention can be recognized – what Ricoeur describes as the 'reciprocity of intentions' (1976, p. 19). The speaker thus leaves a trail of breadcrumbs for the interlocutor to follow. The beauty of the shared situation of spoken discourse is that the speaker can occasionally check if the interlocutor is following, and, if not, necessary corrections can be made. Questions such as 'do you know what I mean?', 'you know what I'm saying?', 'you dig?', 'you feel me?', 'capische?', and, my personal favourite, 'are you picking up what I'm laying down?' signal this referential co-dependency across a variety of registers.

I will make four points here about spoken discourse. First, statements do not refer, people do. Personal pronouns are just one of the indicators by which a speaker implicates herself in the act of referring to things in the world. In addition to being self-referential, discourse also designates the interlocutor, since the signs of language are empty until someone employs them in the work of referring to something real or imagined *in the course of saying them to someone else*. In this way, we can say that the structure of discourse is tripartite, referring simultaneously to its own speaker, to the person to whom one is speaking and to a reality beyond the words that are spoken. It is in the coming together of all three that meaning is created. Second, statements do not 'mean' on their own. It is their speakers who mean things and they do so with a particular listener in mind. Words have no 'proper' meaning in and of themselves and meaning cannot be said to 'belong' to them. It is only in the purposeful act of someone saying something to someone else that meaning is carried. Discourse never exists for its own sake. Third, because discourse refers back to its speaker at the same time as it refers to the world, the subjectivity of its own speaker is also identified because the speaker belongs to the situation of interlocution just as much as the interlocutor. The subjective side of meaning is the speaker's meaning, the self-reference of intentionality, while the objective side is the propositional content contained within the sentence. To 'mean' is not just what the speaker intends, but also what the sentence *does*. Because in spoken discourse there is an overlap between the subjective intentions of the speaker and the 'meaning' of the discourse, the identity of the utterance is simultaneously that which the speaker means and what their discourse says. But because in addition to a self-reference to the speaking subject, discourse also has an audience and a reference to the world, the signifying intentions of the speaker are always relative to the shared situation in time and space of each. Meaning is therefore only fulfilled when pointed towards someone else. As Plato noted, words on their own are neither true nor false and a combination of words may succeed in meaning something, but it can also point to nothing.

Fourth, and for these reasons, the character of dialogue is above all 'eventful', in the sense that it represents a fleeting moment of complicity between a speaker and an interlocutor, at a certain time and in a certain place. Every message also has a temporal existence, for messages only 'mean' something when someone, at a particular time and in a particular place, intended the discourse to be meaningful to someone perceiving it. As we go about the business of referring both to ourselves and to our respective others, we also go about the work of referring to the world around us, such that our speech also refers to the historical situation in space and time in which the speech takes place:

> There is no identification which does not relate that about which we speak to a unique position in the spatio-temporal network, and there is no network of places in time and space without a final reference to the situational here and now. In this ultimate sense, all references of oral language rely on monstrations, which depend on the situation perceived as common by the members of the dialogue. All references in the dialogical situation consequently are situational. (Ricoeur, 1976, p. 35)

Just as geotagging in the digital world records the latitude, longitude, altitude and bearing at the exact moment we take a digital photo or make a Facebook update, discourse contains its own geospatial metadata by which a 'here and now' of language-in-use is established. Despite the lingering possibility of mystery, it is by this spatiotemporal co-situation of interlocution that enables two interlocutors to work together in the shared space of meaning in a bid to solve it.

The resolution of mystery in the shared spatiotemporal situation of spoken language is best explained through a concrete example. Consider the famous 'Four Candles' sketch from the BBC television comedy series *The Two Ronnies* (1976) in which Ronnie Corbett played a shopkeeper who becomes increasingly frustrated with a customer, played by Ronnie Barker, whose demands appear to confound all reason. The setting appears to be a hardware shop and opens with the arrival of a customer clutching a shopping list. The customer reads out the first item on the list: 'four candles', he says. The shopkeeper disappears behind the counter and returns with four wax candles, which he sets down in front of the customer. Confusion ensues. 'No, fork 'andles', the customer explains, "andles for forks'. With the shopkeeper, the audience realizes that in the regional variation that marks the customer's Estuary accent, what sounded like 'candle' was in fact the confusing combination of the final phoneme /k/ in 'fork' and the beginning of the word 'handle', in which the /h/ is dropped. The customer proceeds to work his way through the list and with every item confusion reigns. Thanks once again to the dropped /h/, lettering for garden gates is mistaken both for pantyhose and a length of garden hose, while size nine shoes are taken for a foot-operated piston pump. The exasperated shopkeeper tries to clarify as much as possible about the remaining items before eventually giving up.

As the sketch suggests, dialogue can be fraught with problems. Both interlocutors want to achieve certain things from an exchange. In this case, the customer wants to fulfil his shopping list and the shopkeeper wants to sell him the items he seeks. But the shopkeeper repeatedly imputes unintended meanings and their dialogue is replete with misapprehension. And yet, because they are contemporaneous, they are somehow able to meet the customer's needs, in spite of the confusion. The shopkeeper listens to his requests and seeks clarification. The customer reiterates and paraphrases himself; he makes gestures, adds emphasis and uses different intonation. With every iteration of the shopping list the shopkeeper better grasps what the customer is intending. The dialogical nature of their conversation means that by the end of their question-and-answer exchange there is no longer any problem of understanding, because even when confusion does arise, both the speaker and the interlocutor work together to achieve consensus around what is 'meant'. Of course, it is more than dialogicality that secures mutual understanding in life, for everything that is said in dialogue takes place within a particular social context and historical tradition. The so-called short intersubjective relation shared by two interlocutors is always intertwined with 'long' intersubjective relations mediated by wider social institutions, roles, groups and classes. In the case of the shopkeeper and the customer, this includes the issues that arise from the use of Estuary English, or the terminology of hardware and household goods; the dialogue is only one element in a much wider ecology of historical situatedness. But when it comes to the specific problem of understanding, of agreeing and achieving meaning where there was contestation, it is the shared co-situationality of time and space that makes their communication 'successful'. It takes some time, involves no small amount of irritation, and more than a little explanation, but by the end of the dialogue, that which is 'said' – fork 'andles – in Ricoeur's terms 'turns toward the real', and the 'about which' – handles for forks – become one and the same thing.

The focus of Ricoeur's hermeneutics, by contrast, is what happens when discourse passes from speaking to writing, when, in other words, the object of interpretation is not the spoken word but the written text, a domain where, unlike speech, the agent of language and the audience to whom language is addressed no longer share the same moment in space and time. In a written text, that which is 'said', and the 'about which' that is the take-home message, no longer represent a shared goal that the speaker and the interlocutor work together to secure as a team. Because textual meaning and psychological meaning 'have different destinies', what the text signifies no longer coincides with what the author meant (Ricoeur, 2008, p. 80). A gap opens between monstration, on the part of the author, and identification, on the part of the reader. Here, Ricoeur maintains, is where the unknown adventure of the text begins.

Semantic autonomy

When text takes the place of speech a dialogical situation remains – not between a speaker and a hearer but between an author and a reader. Crucially, unlike the common situation of spoken dialogue, the two parties to the written situation no longer have anything in common. They do not share the same time and they are not in the same place. So as a phenomenon of its first reading, the reader is absent when the text was written and the writer is absent when the text is read:

> Dialogue is an exchange of questions and answers; there is no exchange of this sort between the writer and the reader. The writer does not respond to the reader. Rather, the book divides the act of writing and the act of reading into two sides, between which there is no communication. The reader is absent from the act of writing; the writer is absent from the act of reading. The text thus produces a double eclipse of the reader and the writer. It thereby replaces the relation of dialogue, which directly connects the voice of one to the hearing of the other. (Ricoeur, 2008, pp. 102–3)

As with speech, written text still makes 'reference' – poems, essays and works of fiction all tell of things, events, characters and states of affairs that are evoked but which are not there. But whereas in oral discourse interlocutors can mediate misunderstanding by pointing towards the objects their conversation is about, in the written situation, the act of pointing no longer exists. The 'double eclipse' of the writer from the reader and the reader from the writer means that the movement of ostensive reference is intercepted and can only be fulfilled by the task of reading. Without the author to act as guide, the reader is left in a state of suspense and must speculate as to what is meant.

Consider the iconic photograph of Princess Diana sitting on the bench in front of the Taj Mahal. During a tour of India with her husband the Prince of Wales in 1992, she visited the mausoleum on her own and sat for press photographs while Charles attended an event in Bangalore, over a thousand miles away. For the world's press, and endless numbers of spectators ever since, the photograph has served as a focal point for endless conjecture about the state of the Princess's marriage. Why was she sitting alone in front of the world's greatest monument to love? Had she been snubbed by her husband? Or was it she who had snubbed him? Were separate travel itineraries simply unavoidable when two of the most popular people on the planet go on tour? The day after it was taken, the photograph of the Princess sitting alone on the bench, now known affectionately as 'Lady Di's Chair', featured on the front page of newspapers across the world and her visit was widely interpreted as both a statement on her solitude and her husband's rejection of their marriage. In the public consciousness, the photograph became the moment that sympathy shifted from the stoic prince to the seemingly vulnerable princess. It became a cipher for their estrangement and Diana herself a blank canvas for endless contemplation. As with the story of the Princess of Wales at the Taj Mahal, where the world's press looked to other supposed examples of their marital discord and created a narrative of mutual bitterness, the exteriority of written discourse to itself invites *speculation*. To the text we bring all manner of prior knowledge and experience:

> The suspense that defers the reference merely leaves the text, as it were, 'in the air', outside or without a world. In virtue of this obliteration of the relation to the world, each text is free to enter into relation with all the other texts that come to take the place of the circumstantial reality referred to by living speech. (Ricoeur, 2008, p. 104)

When the reader and the writer no longer share the same space, in other words, written discourse must be made to speak for itself.

This situation is compounded by the fact that whereas speakers know exactly to whom they are speaking, so that all their messages are tailor-made to suit their identified audience, the reader of a text is undefined at the time of writing. Instead of being addressed to 'you', it is addressed to an audience that creates itself; in fact, the audience of writing is anyone who knows how to read. This universality of address means that writing escapes the 'momentary character' of the event of spoken discourse and explodes the limits of the face-to-face dialogical situation. Because neither the reader nor the author share the same space and time, the immediacy of the dialogical situation in which speakers and hearers participate in the live-event of human speech is replaced with a much more complex relationship in which the author is no longer the a priori site of meaning. From the get-go, there is thus a certain falsehood that we must rid ourselves of, for we tend to think we know 'who' the author of a text is – and, by extension, what they are 'saying' – because we derive the idea of the author from that of the speaker. But when text takes the place of speech there 'is' no speaker, in the sense of immediate self-designation. This is because:

> from the single fact that discourse is written down, it has a history that is no longer that of its author. This paradox is easy to understand. The meaning of what has been written down is henceforth separate from the possible intentions of its author and hence removed from any kind of psychologizing technique. What we can call the *semantic autonomy* of the text means that the text unfolds a history distinct from that of its author. The ambiguity of the notion of signification reflects this situation. To signify can mean what the text signifies or what the author meant to signify (in English: what does the text mean? What do you mean?). (Ricoeur, 2013, pp. 12–13, original emphasis)

Whereas in spoken discourse the subjective intention of the subject and the meaning of the discourse overlap, since to understand the speaker and to understand what the discourse 'means' is one and the same thing, in written discourse the author's intention and the meaning of the text cease to coincide because the verbal meaning is now dissociated from the mental intention (Ricoeur, 1976, p. 29). Moreover, every text has a historical context distinct from that in which its reading unfolds, since the act of reading occurs in a different time and place to the time and place in which it was written. Because of a text's 'double historical reference' – to the world of the writer, on the one hand, and the world of the reader, on the other – what is true for the psychological dimension therefore also holds for the sociological conditions under which the text was produced and received. This threefold semantic autonomy – in relation to the speaker's intention, to the economic, social and cultural circumstances of its production and to the economic and sociocultural milieu of reception – means that texts open themselves up to an unlimited series of readings:

> In short, that the work de-contextualizes itself, as much from the sociological as the psychological point of view, and allows itself to be recontextualized

in other ways is what happens through the act of reading. The result is that the mediation of the text cannot be treated as an extension of the dialogical situation. In dialogue, the vis-à-vis of discourse is given in advance through the colloquy itself. With writing, the original audience is transcended. (Ricoeur, 2013, p. 96)

A text can be viewed neither as a message addressed primarily to a specific range of readers, nor as part of a historical chain, but an atemporal object that has cut its ties with its own historical development.

Freedom from authorial intention

The practical consequence of the threefold semantic autonomy of the text is that the 'event' of saying by the author is now surpassed through the act of reading by the meaning of what is said, for its ostensive reference can now be completed by anyone who accesses the text:

> The dissociation of the meaning and the intention is still an adventure of the reference of discourse to the speaking subject. But the text's career escapes the finite horizon lived by its author. What the text says now matters more than what the author meant to say, and every exegesis unfolds its procedures within the circumference of a meaning that has broken its moorings to the psychology of its author. (Ricoeur, 2008, p. 144)

If the author's horizon is finite, the verbal meaning of the text breaks free from the moorings of psychological intention. Just as the text frees itself from the limits of ostensive reference, the text also frees its meaning from the confines of mental intention (Ricoeur, 2013, p. 59 and p. 144). What Ricoeur terms the 'matter' of the text now escapes the author's restricted mental horizon, so that what the text says now means more than what the author meant to say.

We witness this liberation from authorial intention at work in the phenomenon of the politician's words that come back to haunt them. UKIP – the UK Independence Party – is a right-wing political party in the United Kingdom. It has one member of parliament, three representatives in the House of Lords and nearly 500 local government councillors (about 2% of the total seats). In the 2014 European Parliament election UKIP topped the national poll in the United Kingdom, winning twenty-four seats. With a general election looming the next year, this swing towards the right shook the Westminster establishment to the core. As a result, in the months before the general election, party leader Nigel Farage became the subject of close media scrutiny. It was around this time that a woman named Louise Burns tweeted pictures of herself breastfeeding her baby under a large napkin while enjoying a Christmas afternoon tea treat with her mother and sister at the luxury London hotel Claridges. It turned out that a waiter and supervisor had told her that it was the hotel's policy for mothers to cover up while breastfeeding. Her tweet read: 'Asked to cover up with this ridiculous shroud while #breastfeeding so not to cause offence @ClaridgesHotel today' (Burns, 2014). A twitter storm ensued. The *Guardian* covered the story the next day and it was syndicated worldwide. On 5 December 2014, a few days later, Farage gave an interview on LBC radio in which he was asked about the Claridges controversy. He told the host that some people feel very embarrassed by breastfeeding, adding that 'it isn't too difficult to breastfeed a baby in a way that's not openly ostentatious' (LBC, 2014). When asked if Claridges was wrong to require Burns to put a napkin over the baby's head and whether a mother should go to the ladies' room instead, he replied: 'Or perhaps sit in the corner, or whatever it might be' (ibid.) That afternoon the *Guardian* headline ran: 'Nigel Farage says breastfeeding women should sit in a corner' (Wintour and Mason, 2014). A mass 'nurse-in' was planned to take place outside Claridges the next day. In the Twitterverse, meanwhile, Farage's words were picked over in great detail. Live and direct, a raft of tweets recorded the live liberation of the meaning of the UKIP leader's words from the limits of psychological intention:

> I'm going to have children so I can indulge in 'ostentatious breast feeding'. I'm imaging the be our guest scene from Beauty & the Beast (Reid, 2014);
> What exactly does 'Ostentatious Breastfeeding' involve exactly? Doing it as a landmark exhibition at the British Museum? (Tindale, 2014);
> Not a mother but what is 'ostentatious breastfeeding?' Does it involve a small brass band and a neon sign? (Hardman, 2014).

A Devon cake shop owner went one step further and tweeted a photograph of a 'Breastfeeding mums welcome' sign she had placed in the window: 'We're causing a bit of a stir. Love it. #Exeter #cakeadoodledo #getagrip' (Cakeadoodledo, 2014). The image attachment showed a white A4 notice affixed to the glass. Beneath the large 'mums welcome' headline was a statement in small type: 'If you are a Ukip supporter we politely ask, for the comfort of other customers, that you eat in the corner, or in the toilet, or under a large tablecloth that we can drape over you. We're sure you understand that, when people are eating, you don't want to have to look at a complete and utter tit' (Cakeadoodledo, 2014). Over the course of this debacle, Farage had insisted that his comments on breastfeeding mothers were 'wildly misrepresented' and that while he was not against breastfeeding he also respected the rights of private businesses with respect to their customers.

But as with 2012 US presidential candidate Mitt Romney's statement that as governor of Massachusetts he was given 'whole binders full of women' for jobs on his team, by the time Farage's interview was disseminated across the airwaves – that is, from the moment his audience exploded beyond the interviewer to whom he was speaking, so that anyone with a television, radio or Internet connection could access it – his comments on breastfeeding had become the subject of both intense scrutiny and intense parody. Whatever meaning he had intended for his words was by this stage beside the point, for this was something no longer in his gift.

Semantic autonomy creates a problem of interpretation not so much because the psychological experience of the author is incommunicable but because written discourse cannot be 'rescued' in the same way in which spoken discourse can make use of intonation, mimicry, intertextuality and referential gesture in order to facilitate understanding. In Ricoeur's terms, 'The surpassing of the intention by the meaning signifies precisely that understanding takes place in a nonpsychological and properly semantical space, which the text has carved out by severing itself from the mental intention of its author' (1976, p. 76). Without the presence of the author, in other words, only the meaning rescues the meaning. This goes against the Romantic view, summed up in the famous slogan, 'to understand the author better than he understood himself', by which the understanding of texts could be unlocked by exposing the other person thought to be contained therein. By understanding the dialogical situation through which an author's intentions were enacted upon his or her original audience, the exegete could follow this course backwards and finish with understanding the author. Ricoeur rejected this psychologizing impulse, by which we would extend to texts the same empathy with which we would put ourselves in the place of another person's consciousness: 'This undue extension maintains the romantic illusion of a direct link of congeniality between the two subjectivities implied by the work, that of the author and that of the reader' (2008, p. 18). For Ricoeur, what is to be understood in the text is not the one who is speaking behind the text, but what is being talked about, 'the *thing of the text,* namely, the kind of world the work unfolds, as it were, before the text' (p. 127, original emphasis). If the central task is not to rescue meaning from the author because the objective meaning is something *other* than subjective intention, then the task of 'understanding' must be directed somewhere else. Ricoeur's message is that to seek a return to the mental experience of the author is to miss the point: meaning starts with the author but this is only the beginning of the journey. By rejecting the notion of the text *qua* author we shift the interpretative emphasis away from uncovering hidden subjectivities and towards what is contained within the work itself – its sense and reference, the world it opens up – and in this way we enable it to recontextualize itself differently through the act of reading

(Ricoeur, 2008, p. 291). As Ricoeur observes, 'What the text means now matters more than what the author meant when he wrote it' (1976, p. 30).

Freedom from historical context

Benjamin captures these adventures of semantic autonomy with a tale from Book III of the *Histories* by Herodotus. The Egyptian king Psammenitus had been taken hostage by the Persian king Cambyses. Determined to break the spirit of his new prisoner, Cambyses gave the order for Psammenitus and many other chief nobles to be placed in the suburbs where the Persian victory procession would pass and contrived that Psammenitus would see his maiden daughter dressed as a slave, carrying a pitcher to draw water. When the daughters passed their fathers, shedding tears and uttering cries of woe, the fathers grieved for their children, weeping and wailing in return. But Psammenitus simply bent his head towards the ground. Then came Psammenitus's son, and with him two thousand other Egyptians, each with ropes around their necks and bridles in their mouths, on their way to be executed. Psammenitus watched the train pass by, and knew that his son was being led to death, but while the other Egyptians lamented the spectacle, Psammenitus stood alone, inscrutable, giving no more sign of mourning than when he saw his daughter. After they had passed, an old man approached the Egyptians, asking for alms from the soldiers. He was once a friend of Psammenitus and now had been stripped of all that he had. At this sight the king burst into tears, hitting himself on the head and calling out his friend by his name. Watchers had been sent to inform Cambyses of the king's behaviour as each train went by. Astonished at the news of what was done, Cambyses sent a messenger to Psammenitus, asking why he shed no tears when he saw his daughter humiliated and his son on his way to die, and yet when he saw a beggar, who was a foreigner in their land, he honoured him with pity. Psammenitus's reply was that his own misfortunes were too great for tears, but when a man falls into penury in old age, he well deserved them. When Cambyses heard his answer he himself was touched with pity and ordered that the life of the son be spared and Psammenitus brought from the suburbs into his presence.

Benjamin remarks that although Psammenitus explains his behaviour, the story itself remains infinitely provocative, as suggested by numerous attempts over the years to give account for the story. Montaigne, for example, believed that when the king saw the old man it was simply the straw that broke the camel's back. He was so full of grief already that it took only the smallest increase in emotional trauma for his resolve to crack and for the floodgates of his misery to be opened. Benjamin himself speculated that the fate of those with royal blood left Psammenitus so unmoved because he knew very well that this too would be his own fate. Grief in this case would have been pointless since nobles are always the first to be punished. The old man, by contrast, should never have been put in that position and therefore deserved every one of Psammenitus's tears. The point, Benjamin says, is that Herodotus's own report is the driest. We learn, for example, that Cambyses's messengers were too late to save the life of the son of Psammenitus and that 'he had been cut in pieces the first of all' (1996, p. 231). Herodotus does not tell us what effect this had, either on Psammenitus as the father, or on Cambyses, who had both ordered his execution and granted clemency. We learn only that Cambyses allowed Psammenitus to live with him from that point onwards: 'That is why this story from ancient Egypt is still capable after thousands of years of arousing astonishment and thoughtfulness. It resembles the seeds of grain which have lain for centuries in the chambers of the pyramids shut up air-tight and have retained their germinative power to this day' (Benjamin, 1999, p. 90). As Thompson notes in her own study of the story, there is thus no single interpretation that is decisive, precisely because Herodotus's stories are open-ended and disturbing. He is not in the business of uncovering singular truths but of arousing astonishment and stimulating thought:

> [I]f these stories have ranges of meaning beyond that of factual material, they still comprise just one facet of the historian's spectrum of evidence. They have their place as part of the whole composition, so that they illumine and are illumined by other forms of evidence. Thus Herodotus does not attempt to cut through the multiple stories to arrive at the real evidence, because to him the stories are not only real, but also the most rooted loci of meaning. (Thompson, 1996, 146)

The hermeneutic lesson here is twofold. On the one hand, it is with the passage of time that the mystery of stories deepens because, as the saying goes, inscription generates suspicion – the instant a text is dehistoricized from its original context of production and reception, its meaning in its own time is lost. And yet, on the other hand, the text endures. Readers still read. Despite the ravages of time the text continues to offer something; no longer what the author intended but something *else*. In Benjamin's terms, the information a text offers does not expend itself in the moment in which it was new: 'It preserves and concentrates its strength and is capable of releasing it even after a long time.' (1999, pp. 89–90). This lesson enables us to identify two distinct critical attitudes vis-à-vis the text. Either we can monumentalize the text by viewing it as a fixed and finite substance, rooted to the time and place of its production and reception and which can only be appreciated by grasping its wholeness intact, or we can historicize the text, by accepting that while the text is a product of its time, its reader is rooted in the present and engaged in a process of looking backwards. It is from the perspective of the reader that its meanings transcend the mental experience of its author and the conditions of its production and reception.

Our other case from ancient Egypt places in stark relief the futility of the former attitude. I emphasized that the reign of Ramesses the Great was characterized by an epic building programme dedicated to immortalizing his greatness for all eternity. One of his most magnificent constructions was the vast memorial temple known today as the Ramesseum, sited across the Nile from the modern city of Luxor, in the necropolis at Thebes, the city of a hundred gates. In 1820, Giovanni Belzoni, part antiquities dealer and part nineteenth-century Indiana Jones, published a first-hand account of his arrival in the great complex in which he evokes the properly awesome nature of the works of Ramesses:

> After having taken a cursory view of Luxor and Carnak, to which my curiosity led me on my landing, I crossed the Nile to the west, and proceeding straight to the Memnonium, I had to pass before the two colossal figures in the plain. I need not say, that I was struck with wonder. They are mutilated indeed, but their enormous size strikes the mind with admiration. The next object that met my view was the Memnonium. [...] The groups of columns of that temple, and the views of the numerous tombs excavated in the high rock behind it, present a strange appearance to the eye. On my approaching these ruins, I was surprised at the sight of the great colossus of Memnon, or Sesostris, or Osymandias, or Phamenoph, or perhaps some other king of Egypt; for such are the various opinions of its origin, and so many names have been given to it, that at last it has no name at all. I can but say, that it must have been one of the most venerated statues of the Egyptians; for it would have required more labour to convey such a mass of granite from Assouan to Thebes, than to transport the obelisk commonly known under the appellation of Pompey's Pillar, to Alexandria. (Belzoni, 1820, pp. 38–9)

One of the enduring symbols of the reign of Ramesses is the colossal statue we know today as the Younger Memnon, one of two vast granite effigies of the pharaoh that stood at either side of the entrance to the Ramesseum and whose landing in Deptford induced Shelley to give voice to the immortal god: 'My name is Ozymandias, king of kings:/ Look on my works, ye Mighty, and despair!' (1819, p. 72). It was Belzoni who removed the statue and transported it to England. While there appears to have been some disagreement over who had actually been behind Belzoni's commission to remove the bust, and whether or not it had been under the encouragement of the British Consul Henry Salt and geographer and orientalist Jean Louis Burckhardt, what is clear is that the trustees of the British Museum acquired the sculpture from Salt in 1822 and for several years it was displayed in the old Townley Galleries, which have since been demolished. By 1834 the Egyptian Sculpture Gallery in the British Museum was completed and because of the enormous weight of the statue and other pieces, the museum called on the British Army Royal Engineers to move them into the new gallery, under the command of Major Charles Cornwallis Dansey, who had had fought at the Battle of Waterloo nearly twenty years earlier. Indeed, as former director of the British Museum, Neil MacGregor, noted in the *A History of the World in 100 Objects* (2010) series, which was broadcast on BBC Radio 4 over the course of twenty weeks and subsequently published as a best-selling book, when the statue arrived in England it was quite simply the largest sculpture that the people of Great Britain had ever seen. 'And', MacGregor noted, 'it was the first object that gave them a sense of the colossal scale of the Egyptian achievement' (2010). Thought to date from about 1250 BC, the sculpture was a truly wondrous accomplishment for its time, as much for the beauty of its aesthetics as for the feats of engineering and logistics required to transport it to Thebes and construct it on site. Its eyes look downward, holding the spectator in its gaze, while the colour of the granite changes from the torso to the head, drawing the eye upwards towards a knowing smile. The upper body alone is some six or seven feet tall and weighs over seven tonnes. There is a hole at the torso's right breast, which is thought to have been made as part of an unsuccessful attempt to remove the statue by Napoleon's expedition party to Egypt at the end of the eighteenth century.

In the first book of the *Bibliotheca historica* by Diodorus Siculus we find a detailed description of the statue and its original surrounds. Paraphrasing Hecataeus of Abdera, he sketches the following picture:

> Ten stades from the first tombs, he says, in which, according to tradition, are buried the concubines of Zeus, stands a monument of the king known as Osymandyas. At its entrance there is a pylon, constructed of variegated stone, two plethra in breadth and forty-five cubits high; passing through this one enters a rectangular peristyle, built of stone, four plethra long on each side; it is supported, in place of pillars, by monolithic figures sixteen cubits high, wrought in the ancient manner as to shape; and the entire ceiling, which is two fathoms wide, consists of a single stone, which is highly decorated with stars on a blue field. Beyond this peristyle there is yet another entrance and pylon, in every respect like the one mentioned before, save that it is more richly wrought with every manner of relief; beside the entrance are three statues, each of a single block of black stone from Syene, of which one, that is seated, is the largest of any in Egypt,

the foot measuring over seven cubits, while the other two at the knees of this, the one on the right and the other on the left, daughter and mother respectively, are smaller than the one first mentioned. And it is not merely for its size that this work merits approbation, but it is also marvellous by reason of its artistic quality and excellent because of the nature of the stone, since in a block of so great a size there is not a single crack or blemish to be seen. The inscription upon it runs: 'King of Kings am I, Osymandyas. If anyone would know how great I am and where I lie, let him surpass one of my works.' (Diodorus, 1933, p. 169)

Many centuries later and there is still very little about this monumental figure that fails to inspire awe. Yet in addition to wonderment, Belzoni's account of his own first glimpse of the statue also suggests a very different dimension – decay:

> As I entered these ruins, my first thought was to examine the colossal bust I had to take away. I found it near the remains of its body and chair, with its face upwards, and apparently smiling on me, at the thought of being taken to England. I must say, that my expectations were exceeded by its beauty, but not by its size. I observed, that it must have been absolutely the same statue as is mentioned by Norden, lying in his time with its face downwards, which must have been the cause of its preservation. I will not venture to assert who separated the bust from the rest of the body by an explosion, or by whom the bust has been turned face upwards. The place where it lay was nearly in a line with the side of the main gateway into the temple; and, as there is another colossal head near it, there may have been one on each side of the doorway, as they are to be seen at Luxor and Carnak. (Belzoni, 1820, 39–40)

Compared to the blissfully 'blemish-free' sculpture that Diodorus Siculus described, the image of the broken body and its scattered remains is sorry indeed. It was the state of disrepair into which the statue had fallen by the time of its removal that captured Shelley's imagination, for his sonnet mocks the arrogance of the pharaoh's words inscribed on the statue's pedestal:

> I MET a traveller from an antique land
> Who said: Two vast and trunkless legs of stone
> Stand in the desert. Near them, on the sand,
> Half sunk, a shattered visage lies, whose frown,
> And wrinkled lip, and sneer of cold command,
> Tell that its sculptor well those passions read
> Which yet survive, stamped on these lifeless things,

> The hand that mocked them and the heart that fed:
> And on the pedestal these words appear:
> 'My name is Ozymandias, king of kings:
> Look on my works, ye Mighty, and despair!'
> Nothing beside remains. Round the decay
> Of that colossal wreck, boundless and bare
> The lone and level sands stretch far away. (Shelley, 1819, p. 72)

As if to say, 'King of kings, are you? See that your works have indeed been surpassed', Shelley's message is that the nature of power on Earth is transient and that no work, no matter how great, escapes the ravages of time. For his piece on the statue of Ramesses in the *History of the World in 100 Objects*, MacGregor interviewed Anthony Gormley, sculptor of the modern-day statue the *Angel of the North*, which stands on top of a hill near Gateshead in England. Its steel structure extends twenty metres in height, with wings measuring over fifty metres across and overlooks the southern fringe of Low Fell, once an eighteenth-century settlement established by miners. The sculpture itself is sited on a former colliery pithead baths, once an integral part of Gateshead's mining history and now reclaimed as a green space since the early 1990s. According to Gateshead Council's background document, Gormley cites three functions that the angel fulfils: 'firstly a historic one to remind us that below this site coal miners worked in the dark for two hundred years, secondly to grasp hold of the future, expressing our transition from the industrial to the information age, and lastly to be a focus for our hopes and fears – a sculpture is an evolving thing' (Gateshead Council, n.d.). In his contribution to MacGregor's piece on the bust of Ramesses, Gormley remarks that it is in the very material of the granite statue that the essential 'waiting quality of sculpture' is conveyed, that is, the relationship between the biological time of human life here on Earth and the eons of geological time onto which we inscribe our ideas (MacGregor, 2010). Sculptures persist while life dies, making sculpture a dialogue with death, a meditation on the ephemerality of human intention. Belzoni's journal offered a similar reflection: 'It appeared to me like entering a city of giants, who, after a long conflict, were all destroyed, leaving the ruins of their various temples as the only proofs of their former existence' (1820, pp. 37–8).

Despite the air of persistence that surrounds a sculpture, and the insistence of the human hand behind it, our monuments succumb to the ravages of time. Whether it is their physicality or their locality that changes, these changes transform irrevocably the intentionality that informed a monument's making. Today the statue of Ramesses stands in Room Four of the British Museum, where it dominates the space. But there is something about its present-day position as a museum piece that has the effect of normalizing what was once so properly awesome, for with increased ubiquity and access has come an increased feeling of the ordinary. The hundreds of thousands of visitors, each taking photographs with their smart phones and circulating them online; the coffee table books and tote bags with images of Ramesses printed on the front; every emanation creates an air of banality, of containment, of the appropriation of the pharaoh's legacy within the inseparable modern-day regimes of spectatorship and commercialization. Ramesses had indeed attempted to immortalize his image, but he could not control what happened to his likenesses after he was gone. For all his imperial grandeur and ostentatious boasts, something that seemed so unattainable has finally been captured and tamed. This meditation on the fleeting nature of empire has important lessons for the hermeneutic project of cultural translation. Like the granite legacy of Ramesses, to monumentalize the text as the essence of an author's vision is to presume a permanence, a persistence of vision and intentionality, that is refused by the passage of time. From the point of view of the reader in the here and now the author is already dead and buried and the text is but a relic of the past. The way in which a work unfolds over time is beyond the control of the author; it is only the footprint in the sand.

Action autonomy

As he grew increasingly concerned with matters of ethics and international relations, Ricoeur looked to the model of the text and to the refusal of fixity that accompanies semantic autonomy – whether in terms of how we construe the figure of the author or where we locate the site of meaning – as a basis for understanding human action in the world. He maintained that actions imprint their mark in space and time, leaving 'traces' that can be 'read' as we would the texts of authors. Every day, and throughout our lives, we create and engage with all manner of human works. Some of these are 'formal', such as the 'documents', 'deeds' and 'records' of human action. These include records of employment; test results; bank details; criminal records and, in the age of the Internet, memes; animated GIFs; photos on Facebook and Instagram; blogs; Tumblrs; tweets; YouTube videos; Vines, to name but a few. Others are 'informal', such as reputation, celebrity, blame and praise. All of these create 'persisting patterns' in our lives and have 'durable effects' (Ricoeur, 2008, p. 149). Even history itself is the ongoing and contested record of human action – it is the 'thing' on which we leave the traces of our human lives, in formal archives and in the narratives, myths and stories of public and private record. In this way, we can say that the process of recording human action is continual and, as with text, interpretive by necessity.

This complementarity with the world of text goes further. Before we can assign blame or give praise we must be able to speak of those actions as belonging to an agent who asserts and completes them. But a problem arises when the agent of an action is no longer present or available, when, in Ricoeur's terms, the action becomes 'detached' from its agent just as the text becomes autonomous with respect to the intentions of its author. It is then that the fate of the marks of public and private record escapes the control of their original agents and meaning becomes autonomous with respect to the intentions of their owners (2013, p. 28). Of course, some actions have a clear agent to which they can be attributed and their significance does not give rise to contested interpretations. But these are not the focus of Ricoeur's concern. He is interested specifically in the problem of understanding in those human situations where the meaning of events no longer coincides with the logical intentions of their agents, where, as happens with text, the meaning is 'depsychologized' to the point that the meaning *is in the action itself*. Consider the cyber attack on Sony Pictures Entertainment in 2014. On 24 November Sony announced that it had been hacked by a group calling itself Guardians of Peace, which had realized a massive data dump, including films not yet on general release, passports and visas of cast and crew members, film budgets and confidential contracts, employee workplace complaints, medical records, salaries of current and former employees, pre-bonus salaries of top executives and thousands of emails involving Sony staff, producers and stars. The putative rationale given for the leak was to force the cancellation of *The Interview* (2014), a political satire depicting the assassination of North Korean leader Kim Jong-un. The cyber terrorists issued a warning that they would attack all cinemas that screened the film. The film's two lead actors called off their promotional tour and numerous screenings in major cinema chains were cancelled. Eventually, Sony released the film online for rental and purchase on 24 December, with a limited cinema release on Christmas Day, but the episode raised important questions: living in an age of cyber warfare, how do we continue to assert and enjoy freedom of artistic expression? Should terrorists dictate creative content? Should business interests take precedence over the values of liberty?

But beyond questions surrounding the wisdom of pulling *The Interview* from general release, the hackers' actions also gave rise to a range of other wider-reaching and longer-term meanings. The leaked salary details of Sony employees suggested the possibility of a vast disparity in rates of pay between women and men (Roose, 2014). This disparity was not confined to Sony employees. Among the emails dumped by the hackers were details of differential remuneration rates between female and male film stars, exposing, for example, that Amy Adams and Jennifer Lawrence were paid significantly less than their male co-stars for their roles in *American Hustle* (2013). That there is lack of parity between rates of pay for male actors and female actors is not a new story in Hollywood. Nor is it possible to find easy correlations in the statistics that link gender with rate of pay. Many variables, such as age, decisions about parenting and caring, preferences for benefits, union membership and the role of agents have an impact. But when, two months later, Patricia Arquette used her Oscar acceptance speech to call for wage equality for women in the United States (Shoard, 2015); when, in May 2015, Charlize Theron confirmed that she would be paid the same as her male co-star for a forthcoming sequel and that she and her agents had used the hack to renegotiate her contract (*Elle*, 2015); or when, in June 2015, it was revealed that Jennifer Lawrence would be paid $8m more than her male co-star for a forthcoming role, the narrative that Hollywood's leading men are more bankable than its women is being challenged (Masters, 2015). These are just a few of the public statements issued in recent months by high-profile women working in the entertainment industry on gender differentials in pay and conditions and the culture of fear that prevents people from speaking out. By opening up the possibility of a counter-narrative, the 'story' of the Sony Pictures hack enjoys significance well beyond issues of freedom of expression surrounding a cancelled film release.

Just as texts are available to an undefined and theoretically infinite audience, human action is an open work. As with the Sony Pictures hack, every event has the potential to reach audiences beyond the immediate context of its original undertaking. Similar to the way in which a text breaks its ostensive ties with the sociocultural situation of its production and reception, 'meaningful action' – that is, action where there is richness of meaning, contestation and where, therefore, there is mystery – is emancipated from its original situational context and takes on relevance beyond the immediate circumstances under which it occurred. Remember that as a consequence of semantic autonomy in the written domain, a text's references are no longer ostensive to the world in which the work was written and received. In turn, this means that the act of reading enables a text to create all-new resonances in an all-new world of meaning particular to the reader. It is likewise that 'important' action can develop meanings that can be fulfilled in situations other than the one in which the action occurred originally: 'To say the same thing in different words, the meaning of an important event exceeds, overcomes, transcends, the social conditions of its production and may be re-enacted in new social contexts. Its importance is its durable relevance and, in some cases, its omnitemporal relevance' (Ricoeur, 2008, p. 50). In the same way that the fixation of speech gives rise to the surpassing of the event of saying by the meaning of what is said, the fixation of action in the doing is eclipsed by the significance of what is done, in the sense that an action is not only decoupled from the intentions of its agent but also gains consequences of its own, as it becomes inscribed in history. When it comes to the problem of human understanding, which is at the heart of Ricoeur's hermeneutic concerns, this latter point is important because it suggests the inherent danger when the meaning of an action not only spirals out of its agent's control, but also when it snowballs, changing shape organically, inexorably, as it takes on meanings beyond its agent's original intentions and affects audiences beyond those impacted by its original unfolding. In this way, Ricoeur maintains, human events contain the possibility of their own transcendence (2013, p. 29). The need for reflexion arises because our actions become embroiled in the wider course of human affairs:

> In the same way that a text is detached from its author, an action is detached from its agent and develops consequences of its own. This autonomization of human action constitutes the *social* dimension of action. An action is a social phenomenon not only because it is done by several agents in such a way that the role of each of them cannot be distinguished from the role of others, but also because our deeds escape us and have effects we did not intend. (Ricoeur, 2008, p. 148, original emphasis)

In a practical sense, when the doer of an action is present we need not ask who did this or that, since the meaning of the action and the intention behind it overlap. When baby Charlie is recorded biting his elder brother's finger in the viral video sensation, for example, very little mystery surrounds his actions (VO CS, 2012). The video clearly shows the elder brother placing his finger in Charlie's mouth; Charlie bites down and the elder brother cries out in pain while Charlie laughs. But with complex situations that are remote from their initial actions, we face a problem similar to that of textual interpretation. As with the reader of a text, the interpreting self stands in opposition to the other as 'author' of their actions, at a distance from their intentions as much in time as in space. In addition to placing the interpreter of the action at a distance from the psychological intentions that informed the unfolding of the event in the first instance, action autonomy also distances the agent and the interpreter from the significance of the action within the wider social ecology of human events. Whether reader of texts or interpreter of human events, it is this condition of distanciation that creates a mystery demanding to be understood, for as with textual interpretation, the interpretation of human deeds involves actions that are readable and meanings that go beyond the intention of their actors and which, as a result, give rise to conflicting understandings (Kaplan, 2012, p. 68).

From distanciation to appropriation

In the domain of ethnography, Geertz outlines a similar process at work in 'thick' description, a notion he attributes to Ryle's meditation on the subtle differences between a 'wink' and a 'twitch'. In Ryle's example, two boys swiftly contract the eyelids of their right eyes. In the first boy this is involuntary; the other, meanwhile, winks conspiratorially to an accomplice. At the thinnest level of description we construe the two sets of eyelid contractions as exactly alike. On the visual plain, for example, there may be no way to tell which was an involuntary twitch and which was a deliberate wink. And yet the difference between a twitch and a wink is vast: to wink is to attempt to send a message to an identified audience, perhaps furtively, according to an already understood code. For this secret message to be 'successful' the intended recipient must witness the wink and be aware of the code. A twitch, by contrast, can achieve neither failure nor success for it has no intended recipient, carries no message and is neither intended to be witnessed nor is hidden from others.

But, Ryle wonders, what if the second boy's wink were awkward and amateurish? What if, for example, a third boy were introduced, who mocks the second boy for his awkward attempts at winking? This third boy would imitate the second boy by also contracting his right eyelid in the ways in which the awkward winker had done. But the objective of the parodist would not be the same as that of the furtive winker. The third boy is not awkwardly attempting to send a covert signal to another; he is attempting to make apparent the awkwardness of the second boy for the amusement of his friends. The task of third boy fails if his friends are not amused or do not witness the parody. On a visual plain, the physical actions of the first, second and third boys may continue to be indistinguishable. But a 'thick' description of all three situations enables us to nuance our reading of the situation and to construe them as discrete attempts at meaning making. Different motivations, different success criteria, different causes and different effects are each in play and without careful reflexion the subtleties of their actions cannot be teased out. Thus when we attempt to 'understand' these actions through a thick rather than a 'thin' lens of interpretation, we open what Ryle describes as the beginning of a series of internal subordinate clauses to which we can easily add layer after layer of nuance. The second winker may reveal that he had not actually been trying to send a covert message but was instead feigning the action in order to fool the grown-ups into the false belief that he was trying to do so. When it comes to describing the work of the parodist we must then add yet a further level of meaning to his actions. The thinnest description of the parodist is broadly the same as for the involuntary eyelid twitcher; but, says Ryle, its thick description 'is a many-layered sandwich, of which only the bottom slice is catered for by that the thinnest description' (Ryle, 2009, p. 497).

For Geertz, the take-home message is that meaning is not an essential substance that is immediately available. It must be interrogated through thoughtful reflexion and with reference to the wider ecology of subordinate and interconnected layers through which the studied behaviours take place. He maintains that when we attempt to understand the 'imaginative acts' of human behaviour, as is the project of ethnography and on which I base my own interpretive investigations with regard to cultural translation, we do so precisely because they have taken on significance in their public unfolding. When it comes to identifying the object of 'understanding', then, it is not what is going on in a particular person's head, but the meanings that emerge from the realization of this person's being in public:

> Culture, this acted document, thus is public, like a burlesqued wink or a mock sheep raid. Though ideational it does not exist in someone's head; though unphysical is not an occult entity. The interminable, because unterminable, debate within anthropology as to whether culture is 'subjective' or 'objective', together with the mutual exchange of intellectual insults ('idealist!'—'materialist!'; 'mentalist!'—'behaviorist!'; 'impressionist!'—'positivist!') which accompanies it, is wholly misconceived. Once human behavior is seen as (most of the time; there *are* true twitches) symbolic action—action which, like phonation in speech, pigment in painting, line in writing, or sonance in music, signifies—the question as to whether culture is patterned conduct or a frame of mind, or even the two somehow mixed together, loses sense. The thing to ask about a burlesqued wink or a mock sheep raid is not what their ontological status is. It is the same as that of rocks on the one hand and dreams on the other—they are things of this world. The thing to ask is what their import is: what it is, ridicule or challenge, irony or anger, snobbery or pride, that in their occurrence and through their agency, is getting said. (Geertz, 1973, p. 10, original emphasis)

Whether text or the 'imaginative acts' that constitute human behaviour, the psychological dimension of meaning is now out of our hands. The author is as much distanced from the reader as they are from their work and the reader is as much distanced from the author as they are from the sociocultural context in which the work was realized. To 'read' is to be faced with a distance that stretches out before us: of time, space, culture, history, language, politics – everything that separates us in the here and now of understanding from the text in the 'there and then' of its original context of production and reception. *Distanciation*, in this sense, signals everything that makes 'understanding' impossible.

As with interlingual translation, total understanding would presume total synonymy, and, as in the case of interlingual translation, it would presume an interpretation 'so precisely exhaustive as to leave no single unit in the source-text – phonetic, grammatical, semantic, contextual – out of complete account, and yet so calibrated as to have added nothing in the way of paraphrase, explication or variant' (Steiner, 1998, p. 429). Translation, as with understanding, seems impossible. And yet, translators still translate, texts still get written and readers still read. We *do* somehow manage to speak to one another; our criminal justice systems sanction and rehabilitate those to whom responsibility for a particular action has been attributed; international conferences are held; commodities are traded; goods are exported; we travel internationally; we order food in foreign restaurants and use foreign public transportation systems; we interact with, make friends with, or fall in love with people from different religious, ethnic, linguistic, political, sexual and gender backgrounds. It is this very possibility within the realm of the impossible that requires us to revise how we define the task of translation, and, by extension, the very objective of 'understanding' itself. Ricoeur asks himself this very question:

> But what does it mean to be able to translate? This possibility, or rather this capacity, is not ascertained solely by the fact that we actually succeed in translating speech and texts from one language to another without totally prejudicial and, above all, entirely irreparable semantic loss. The possibility of translating is postulated more fundamentally as an a priori of communication. In this sense, I will speak of 'the principle of universal translatability'. Translation is de facto; translatability is de jure. (Ricoeur, 1996, p. 4)

We can argue about the extent to which translation happens 'successfully'. But the *translatability* of all things is the law, for all things can, in principle, be 'translated'. Distanciation problematizes translation, to be sure, and the criteria by which we measure the 'quality' of a translation enable us to deem some translations more appropriate to the circumstances of their commission than others. But all texts are at base translat*able*, since all texts continue to be 'about' something. They refer to a world; they address an audience. Simply because we are late to the party does not mean the party never took place. With Ricoeur we oppose what he calls the 'fallacy of the absolute text', a text that is hypostasized as an authorless entity:

> If the intentional fallacy overlooks the semantic autonomy of the text, the opposite fallacy forgets that a text remains a discourse told by somebody, said by someone to someone else about something. It is impossible to cancel out this main characteristic of discourse without reducing texts to natural objects, i.e., to things which are not man-made, but which, like pebbles, are found in the sand. (Ricoeur, 1976, p. 30)

Simply because interpretation is de-psychologized does not imply there is no such thing as authorial intention or that we dispense with the notion of authorial meaning. We *can* and *do* intend things when we speak, write and act and it is to this substance that we direct our efforts at understanding. In addition to shifting our focus away from the Romantic claim to the mental life of the author, we also renounce the Structuralist claim that the text is an end in itself. To say that reading breaks the web of references that bind a text inextricably to the situation commonly experienced by the author and the audience in the time and place of the text's production and reception is not the same as saying that there is no reference at all. The text is not absolute. It is free of its direct reference to its author and its circumstantial reality, but its references still allow the text to speak. The text is autonomous but continues to be 'about' something and in its autonomous trajectory away from the author and its situation of production and reception, symbolic expression opens up new modes of communication. In other words, signs still designate possible modes of existence. By recognizing that the text is more than a closed system we enable ourselves to look simultaneously inwards – to the internal world and structuring of the text – and outwards – to the something *else* the text advances.

This is about conceiving of the text dialectically: as an interpretive movement that moves constantly back and forth between the work's internal dynamics on the one hand, and, on the other, 'the power that the work possesses to project itself outside itself and to give birth to a world that would truly be the "thing" referred to by the text' (Ricoeur, 2008, p. 17). What is to be 'understood' is not the world of the author or the structures of the text but the opportunities it offers up for meanings that exist beyond it. This is a gesture that rejects the emptiness of relativism in favour of the possibilities for meaning that the text unfolds. By recognizing that the text is only the vestige of a fleeting moment of complicity between an author and their audience, and that this moment is now gone, we free ourselves from the 'narrowness' of the dialogical situation. There is no point hypostasizing the text as the symbol of authorial intention because the objective meaning of a text is something other than the subjective intention of the author. Thus we need not throw the baby out with the interpretive bathwater. Given that the meaning of a text is liberated from the subjective intention of its author, Ricoeur urges, 'the essential question is not to recover, behind the text, the lost intention but to unfold, in front of the text, the "world" it opens up and discloses' (2008, p. 33). The task of hermeneutics is not concerned with uncovering the psychology of the author but with the only element that a reader truly *is* empowered to act upon: the text itself. This injunction gives two distinct and unavoidable dimensions to the task of reading:

> As readers, either we may remain in a kind of state of suspense as regards any kind of referred-to world, or we may actualize the potential

nonostensive references of the text in a new situation, that of the reader. In the first case, we treat the text as a worldless entity; in the second, we create a new ostensive reference through the kind of 'execution' that the art of reading implies. These two possibilities are equally entailed by the act of reading, conceived as their dialectical interplay. (Ricoeur, 2008, p. 158)

Reading is precisely dialectical because the nature of understanding is precisely *lemniscatic* by necessity. If texts are abstracted from their authors and their surrounding world, and if we, as readers in the here and now, are prevented from reinstantiating their references by our condition of distanciation from the there and then of the text, then it follows that everything we do takes place *in medias res*. To read is to be faced primarily with a textual relationship that started long before we got there. In Ricoeur's terms, 'We suddenly arrive, as it were, in the middle of a conversation which has already begun and in which we try to orientate ourselves in order to be able to contribute to it.' (2008, p. 30). To fulfil the injunction to 'actualize' the references of the text in an all-new situation of meaning, we must reach backwards and across the medias res, to the 'past cultural epoch' of the text in a bid to access *hic et nunc* that which has already gone (Ricoeur, 2004, p. 16). By acting upon the text's potential to project new meanings into the world of reading in the present we open up new arcs of communication with the information the text offers. From the here and now of reading, references closed within the historicity of their original unfolding can therefore be made to speak in our own time and place. But because the interpreter remains fixed in the here and now and the object of interpretation in the there and then, interpretation is an infinitely extending work of distanciation and approximation in which the time and place of the interpreter remain the only constants. When it comes to articulating what goes on in the interpretation of a text, therefore, we can say that what we witness is a complex series of elliptical spatio-temporal relations – of reader to text, of text to the world of the author and of reader to the world of the text – such that only the reader stands in the space of meaning that writing advances.

These infinitely extending trajectories are illustrated in Zeno's paradox of Achilles and the Tortoise, which concerns a footrace between the two. Being slow, the tortoise is permitted a head start over Achilles. The premise is this: if each racer runs at a constant speed, the tortoise will progress very slowly and Achilles very quickly. Despite starting at a disadvantage, therefore, Achilles will very soon catch up with the tortoise, overtake it and win the race. But here is the paradox. During the time in which it takes for Achilles to cover the distance between his original starting point and the advanced starting point of the tortoise, the tortoise will have covered some distance of its own. To overtake the tortoise, Achilles would not only have to catch up with the tortoise but also to cover this extra distance the tortoise has by now covered. By this time, however, the tortoise will have advanced further, requiring yet more time for Achilles to cross this extra distance the tortoise has managed to cover. In other words, because the tortoise continues to move while Achilles is busy covering the tortoise's already covered ground, whenever Achilles reaches somewhere the tortoise has already been, he will always have a further distance still to travel. While the Greek hero always manages to make up the gap that separates him from the tortoise, the steady tortoise manages to create a new gap, which itself must be covered. Each new gap is progressively smaller, but because there are an infinite number of points where the tortoise has already been and which Achilles must traverse, the faster runner can never actually overtake the slower one. Or, as Aristotle recounts in Book VI of *Physics*, 'the slowest runner will never be caught by the fastest, because the one behind has first to reach the point from which the one in front started, and so the slower one is bound always to be in front' (1999, p. 161).

This paradox places in relief the twin arcs that extend backwards and forwards from the moment of reading in the present: that of the text, in its time and place, and that of the reader, in a time and place of her own. Like Achilles, the reader is at a disadvantage, since everything about the text – its internal structuring, its range of reference, its links to the world in which it was produced and received – remains out of the reader's reach. And yet, like Achilles, the reader extends herself towards the text, reduces the gap and draws herself closer. But the text remains ever-distant, forever progressing away from the reader's grasp. When it comes to Zeno's paradox, however, the philosopher elides one important dimension. If the tortoise were covering progressively larger distances between the two runners rather than smaller ones, Achilles would indeed be unable to catch up. But as long as the sheer speed of Achilles's pursuit enables him to make the gaps between them progressively smaller, he *will* eventually overtake the tortoise. We must not forget that somewhere within the infinite arcs of distanciation and approximation that accompany the act of interpretation, readers do read, translation does happen and at some point Achilles does overtake the tortoise. To read, to translate, to interpret – to understand – we participate in a dialectical game by which we draw ever closer and ever further from the objects of our hermeneutic desire. But as a process that is designed to culminate in an act of writing, translation itself is the means by which the distance is closed and the breach in the space-time continuum that separates the translator from the relics of the past is filled. It is this dimension that provides the platform on which I build my definition of cultural translation and to which the remainder of this meditation is addressed.

3

Incorporation

Objects in translation appear closer than they are! On the cartographies of interpretation

Right up until the early decades of the twentieth century, when British schoolchildren gazed at their classroom walls, the world was pink. At its height, the so-called empire on which the sun never set covered over fourteen million square miles and from its position of pink centrality, imperial Britain fanned outwards, surrounded by other pink land masses, from Australia and New Zealand, to the Indian subcontinent, much of Africa, Canada and a handful of Caribbean islands. As a form of global brand marketing, the pink map presented a powerful image of an island nation that was truly 'Great' Britain. Anderson writes that as a form of imperial logo, the map is 'an infinitely reproducible series, available for transfer to posters, official seals, letterheads, magazine and textbook covers, tablecloths, and hotel walls. Instantly recognizable, everywhere visible, the logo-map penetrated deep into the popular imagination, forming a powerful emblem (Anderson, 2006, p. 179). But as Colley observes in her study of the British Empire, the pink map in particular was also engaged in some cartographic sleight of hand (2010, pp. 4–5). The colouring gave the erroneous impression that the British Empire was the only imperial force in operation, when, in reality, the world was shared with other empires marketing themselves in a range of different colours – the colonies of France, for example, were usually depicted in purple-blue and Dutch colonies in yellow-brown (Anderson, 2006, p. 179). The singular use of colour made the territories of the empire appear more connected politically than they actually were. Its use of the Greenwich meridian also had the not entirely coincidental effect of placing Britain close to the heart of the represented world. Finally, because Britain itself was coloured in the same pink as the territories it controlled, any sense of smallness surrounding the British island was replaced with amazement at the vastness of its dominion. 'Like most cartographic exercises', Colley writes, 'it is not a simple depiction of the lie of the land, but in some respects a lie, or at least a calculated deceit' (2010, p. 5). To understand the translational gestures behind these cartographic manoeuvres, we must delve deeper into the hermeneutics of distanciation and interpretation by which we translate and pause to re-examine the conditions under which a translation is produced.

Between every writer and a reader is a reference to a world that has long since passed. In the double-blind situation of reading in the present, where the reader is absent when the text was written and the writer is absent when the text is read, the trajectory of the work departs from the author and the sociocultural situation of its writing and reception such that it no longer represents the voice of someone present. With the passage of time the work escapes the confines of authorial intention, transcending the psychological and sociocultural conditions of its production and reception and opening itself up to unlimited interpretations, themselves situated in sociocultural situations of their own (Ricoeur, 2013, p. 96). It is for this reason that a text is said to 'create its own public' because from the point of view of the reader 'understanding' is no longer synonymous with the subjective intention of the author. Rather than reifying the author as gatekeeper to the meaning of the text, it is the task of hermeneutics to embrace the possibility for meaning that the text offers beyond itself, in Ricoeur's terms, 'to restore to the work its ability to project itself outside itself in the representation of a world that I could inhabit' (2008, p. 18). 'Meaning', in this sense, is not an essence behind the text, a *telos* to be arrived at, but a *logos* in the Aristotelian sense. It is a process, an engagement, a reasoned interrogation with that which the text projects. Rather than an 'intuitive grasping of the intention underlying the text', it is an 'injunction' which comes from the text and which issues an invitation to think in a certain manner or to see things in a different way (Ricoeur, 1976, p. 88). Yet standing between the reader and the fulfilment of this injunction is a circumstantial reality that is both out of reach and which must be apprehended if understanding is to be achieved.

If every act of language is of its moment, with a temporal existence, fixed to the time and place of its uttering, then the act of reading, asynchronous with the past cultural epoch of the text, is above all one of confrontation – for the objects of understanding are self-contained reminders of not only everything that has gone but also everything that must be surmounted if meaning is to be made. It is this confrontational space that Steiner describes as the 'middle' between the text and the reader, the conversation that has already begun before the reader arrives, and in which there must be 'an operation of interpretive decipherment' (1998, p. 49). From the perspective of the reader, located after and away from the sociocultural moment in which the text was written and received, the 'past' of the text operates as a foreign country, for the condition of distanciation is above all one of estrangement. Consider what it means to be 'familiar' with something. From the Latin *familiaris*, it is suggestive of domesticity; of belonging to a family, household or community and with which something is shared; it implies being on intimate terms, enjoying a friendly or family relationship; things known from long association; the ordinary, the normal, the usual. Everything about the text, its symbols, allusions, references, its place in history, its political positioning, is both locked within the past cultural epoch of its original unfolding, and is, by definition, *un*familiar in the sense of being 'other' to that which we conceive of as our 'own'. To read is to be confronted not just with the inaccessibility of the author's intentions for the text and the circumstantial reality in which it was produced and received, but also with the presence of everything that does not 'belong' to us. *Appropriation* starts with a reader's desire to conquer this condition:

> The problem of writing becomes a hermeneutical problem when it is referred to its complementary pole, which is reading. A new dialectic then emerges, that of distanciation and appropriation. By appropriation I mean the counterpart of the semantic autonomy, which detached the text from its writer. To appropriate is to make 'one's own' what was 'alien'. Because there is a general need for making our own what is foreign to us, there is a general problem of distanciation. Distance, then, is not simply a fact, a given, just the actual spatial and temporal gap between us and the appearance of such and such work of art or discourse. It is a dialectical trait, the principle of a struggle between the otherness that transforms all spatial and temporal distance into cultural estrangement and the ownness by which all understanding aims at the extension of self-understanding. Distanciation is not a quantitative phenomenon; it is the dynamic counterpart of our need, our interest, and our effort to overcome cultural estrangement. Writing and reading take place in this cultural struggle. (Ricoeur, 1976, p. 43)

When it comes to the professional practice of interlingual translation upon which I base my definition of cultural translation, this dialectical 'struggle' manifests itself as a confrontation with the foreignness of the text-for-translation with respect to the language of the translation's end user. At its most basic, translation concerns rewriting a text written originally in one language for the purpose of being read in another. Faced with the foreign language, a language that the translator's audience does not understand, the translator must attempt to facilitate comprehension by locating appropriate alternatives to the language of the original text in the language of the translation's audience. As with appropriation, translation is animated by the presence of the 'alien' – in this case, the unfamiliar word of the foreign other. The translator's process is dialectical because it is characterized by a constant movement between the estranging word of the other and the familiar terrain of a language that a translator's audience knows and understands.

In the case of translating the 1978 film *Grease* for release in Spanish-speaking regions, for example, this dialectical struggle starts with the very title itself. Set in a 1950s high school in the United States, the title of the English-language theatrical release referred to the 'greaser' subculture associated with rock and roll, hot rod cars and motorcycles. The epithet referred to the slicked-back hairstyle modelled on the style of Marlon Brando and James Dean, which was greased with all manner of gels, creams and waxes. In English, the term 'grease' is polysemous. It is not just a hair product but also a lubricating oil that you add to the joints of machines; it is the fat you cook with in a pan or add to a cake mixture; and, in a figurative sense, it is the physical effort you put into fulfilling a particular task or objective. The term plays an important role from the beginning of the film. An animated sequence shows John Travolta's character Danny Zucco as he gets up from bed and makes his way through his messy bedroom to the bathroom, face obscured by his unruly mop. Comb in hand he stands in front of the mirror and proceeds to squeeze hair cream from a tube. A close-up of the tube shows drops of hair cream flying through the air, where they morph into the shape of the six letters of the film's title. Behind the letters the shape of an open-top motorcar fades into view – the car is 'Greased Lightning', subject of the famous musical number by the same name. For Spanish-speaking audiences, the title was translated variously as *Brillantina* and *Vaselina*, depending on the market region. Both *brillantina* and *vaselina* are generic terms (despite the latter's proximity to a well-known brand name) for semi-solid lubricating hair care products in common use in South America. But despite appearing 'generic' in the sense that the Spanish terms do not identify any hair care product in particular and refer simply to the function and purpose of the product itself, they are in fact totally particular, in the sense that they limit the term's linguistic possibilities to only one application: hair styling. Unlike the English term, *brillantina* and *vaselina* are not polysemous and do not open themselves up to the world of machines, hot rod cars, grease-monkey mechanics or the film's greaser gang, the T-birds. By opting for terms associated with the practice of styling one's hair, the Spanish translation localizes the reference to match the familiar context of its spectatorship.

But consider what it means to do this. If appropriation is the enactment of a desire to overcome 'estrangement', then to avoid the risk of confusion, alienation or even deception, the cause of such estrangement, the foreign word, is effectively replaced with the local. The sense of the foreign work must be absorbed by the translator and a second work produced, drawn from the translator's own tongue. If we think of the film's title as a mini 'text', the translator must not only absorb the presence of the English when producing a second text in Spanish; in this instance the presence of the foreign word must be totally obliterated. In broader terms, far in time and space from the original context in which the text was written, produced and received, translation is a function of multiple distances. A translated text does not seek to represent the intentions of the author of the original foreign text but the totality it projects before the translator and the translator's construction of such a world. Given that we have not yet found a way to travel through time and space, to overcome distanciation one's only option is to reach out across the distance to view it through a lens which is not strange but 'own'. In this sense, interpretation 'brings together', 'equalizes', renders 'contemporary and similar,' thus genuinely making one's *own* what was initially *alien* (Ricoeur, 2008, p. 114). It is for this reason that Ricoeur describes appropriation as the counterpart of distanciation: 'The purpose of all interpretation is to conquer a remoteness, a distance between the past cultural epoch to which the text belongs and the interpreter himself. By overcoming this distance, by making himself contemporary with the text, the exegete can appropriate its meaning to himself: foreign, he makes it familiar, that is, he makes it his own' (Ricoeur, 2004, p. 16).

If distanciation and appropriation exist in dialectical relation, as two sides of the same interpretive coin, what Steiner describes as the imposition of a 'native garb' of translation on the 'alien form' of the source language is in fact a gesture that attempts both to comprehend *and* to contain the text, for the journey outwards, towards the text of the other, is always a return journey (1998, p. 271). Out of the distance that was once closeness, in other words, appropriation effects an all-new proximity – not between translator and author, or author and audience but between translator and text, audience and translator. In the case of the translator, distanciation is more than the effect of being at a remove from the author of the text and the time and place in which the text was written. It is the ontological condition of being alienated in the present place of reading by the estranging quality distanciation creates. Appropriation, by extension, is a cognitive process of familiarization, a conscious embracing of the otherness of the other within the horizon of the own. 'Understanding', in this sense, always takes place within a historical horizon and 'meaning' is distanciated from subjective consciousness:

> For it is, paradoxically, in so far as we *belong* to an historical tradition that meaning is always at a *distance* from us in the immediate here and now. 'Distanciation' is the dialectical counterpart of 'belonging'. These two

> movements represent the twin arches of the hermeneutic bridge. The text thus becomes, for Ricoeur, the model for a belonging to communication in and through distance. In interpretation we endeavour to reappropriate those meanings that have been disappropriated from understanding. Hermeneutics, in short, is the attempt to render near that which is far – temporally, geographically, culturally, spiritually etc. It strives to recover that which has been removed. (Kearney, 1994, p. 110, original emphasis)

Semantic autonomy and appropriation thus go hand-in-hand, for with distanciation comes atemporalization, since the text has escaped both its author and its original addressee and it is now open to anyone who can read. This omnitemporality of meaning is the counterpart of historicity – the condition by which the reader, fixed in the reading present, must look backwards and across to the text, which is now a relic of the past. The problem that translation tackles, then, is not so much that the reader is separated spatially and temporally from the text-for-translation, the 'fact' of alienation, but the separation anxiety this state of alienated separation creates when it comes to attempting to understand. As Steiner notes:

> Resistant difference – the integral and historical impermeability, apartness of the two languages, civilizations, semantic composites–plays against elective affinity–the translator's pre- and recognition of the original, his intuition of legitimate entry, of an at-homeness momentarily dislocated, i.e. located across the frontier. At close quarters, say as between two European languages, the charge is maximal at both poles. The shock of difference is as strong as that of familiarity. The translator is held off as powerfully as he is drawn in. (Steiner, 1998, p. 399)

Distanciation is estranging because it is to be reminded that our access to the world is not immediate; that human understanding is fallible and cannot be assumed. The site of this struggle is therefore as much social as it is textual, for separation anxiety is not limited to the world of letters but permeates the myriad interactions and problematic understandings that characterize human existence in a globalized, interconnected world. The challenge distanciation creates is not so much the empirical state of separation between reader and text, self and other, but our desire, our continued *need*, to do something about it.

What is appropriation?

Two consequences attend the reader's distanciation from the text-for-interpretation. First, distanciation places the reader in a necessarily oppositional position vis-à-vis the text, since there is no mystery to be interpreted until the text is read. There exists no disagreement, no contestation, except in the condition of *being* interpreted. It is only when the text is actualized in the mind of the reader that the distance that separates the reader in the present from the time and place of the text's production and reception in the past is realized. Simply put, the text does not exist as an object of interpretation until the reader reads it. This leads to the second consequence: that the reader's opposition to the text is psychological in nature. That is, it is a state of separation that exists in the mind of the one who is in the position of reading a text. Indeed, it is the reader's opposition to the object of reading that creates the condition of 'reader' in the first instance. Without something 'to be understood' a 'reader' does not exist in order to read and understand.

Together, these insights shift the axis of meditation away from the subjective world of the author towards that of the reader. It is this reader-focused emphasis that forms appropriation's first principle:

> What is indeed to be understood – and consequently appropriated – in a text? Not the intention of the author, which is supposed to be hidden behind the text; not the historical situation common to the author and his original readers; not the expectations or feelings of these original readers; not even their understanding of themselves as historical and cultural phenomena. What has to be appropriated is the meaning of the text itself, conceived in a dynamic way as the direction of thought opened up by the text. In other words, what has to be appropriated is nothing other than the power of disclosing a world that constitutes the reference of the text. (Ricoeur, 1976, p. 92)

Given the text's autonomy with respect to the author and the sociocultural milieu in which it was produced and received, appropriation renounces any attempt to grasp the genius or the soul of the author as the one who talks 'behind' the text. For Ricoeur, that which must be appropriated is what he variously describes as the 'matter' of the text, the 'world of the text' and the 'thing of the text'. This projection of a world is, he admits,

> a possible world, to be sure, but a world nevertheless, a place I can think of myself inhabiting in order to carry out there my own-most possibilities. Without being a real world, this intentional object intended by the text as its outside-the-text constitutes a first mediation, inasmuch as what a reader can appropriate is not the lost intention of the author behind the text, but the world of the text in front of the text. (Ricoeur, 2013, p. 17)

Discerning this 'world of the text in front of the text' concerns making an important move away from the 'sense' of a text towards its 'reference', that is, 'from what it says to what it talks about' (Ricoeur, 1976, pp. 87–8). Whereas the sense is the ideal object that a proposition intends and this is immanent within the work, the reference is the value of the proposition, its claim to point towards reality. This latter quality is what Ricoeur elsewhere describes as 'what is being talked about, the *thing of the text,* namely, the kind of world the work unfolds, as it were, before the text' (Ricoeur, 2008, p. 127, original emphasis). We therefore have two distinct ways of approaching the text at our disposition:

> As readers, either we may remain in a kind of state of suspense as regards any kind of referred-to world, or we may actualize the potential nonostensive references of the text in a new situation, that of the reader. In the first case, in which we focus only on the sense, on its internal structure and relations, we hypostasize the text by treating it as self-enclosed, as a worldless entity; in the second, we create a new ostensive reference through the kind of 'execution' that the art of reading implies. These two possibilities are equally entailed by the act of reading, conceived as their dialectical interplay. (Ricoeur, 2008, p. 158)

In the first disposition, the reader seeks an essence located behind the text that governs how the work is structured. In the second, the reader looks beyond the text, away from its interior world towards the world it discloses before itself. By focusing on the reference in this latter way, we can engage with the text fully, to breathe new life into it in the here and now of reading.

To enter into understanding of a text is thus to follow its movement from sense to reference, away from its initial situation of discourse, away from the putative intention of the author and the structures of the text towards the possible world it establishes beyond itself through its power of reference (Ricoeur, 2013, p. 136). The nature of reference has an important consequence for interpretation:

> It implies that the meaning of a text lies not behind the text but in front of it. The meaning is not something hidden but something disclosed. What gives rise to understanding is that which points toward a possible world, by means of the non-ostensive references of the text. Texts speak of possible worlds and possible ways of orientating oneself in these worlds. In this way, disclosure plays the equivalent role for written texts as ostensive reference plays in spoken language. Interpretation thus becomes the apprehension of the proposed worlds that are opened up by the non-ostensive reference of the text. (Ricoeur, 2013, p. 60)

For Ricoeur, it is not about getting into the head of the author but interpreting the world that a work unfolds before us. Because it is written, there is no speaker present to explain things; instead, we must 'construct' its meaning for ourselves. Only one party, in this case, the reader, speaks for both. Along this road from configuration to refiguration, therefore, the text does not say; it offers. The text does not refer; the reader does. It projects a possible world but it is ultimately a world the reader builds for herself. It is the reader who is the 'real character who brings about the intersection of the (possible) world of the text with the (real) world of the reader' (Ricoeur, 2013, p. 18). For Ricoeur, the world of the text is not an empirical world, but 'my' world, the world as it unfolds itself to me and only to me. As such, it is unique to me and unique to my interpretation of the text:

> What we make our own, what we appropriate for ourselves, is not an alien experience or a distant intention, but the horizon of a world toward which a work directs itself. The appropriation of the reference is no longer modelled on the fusion of consciousnesses, on empathy or sympathy. The emergence of the sense and the reference of a text in language is the coming to language of a world and not the recognition of another person. (Ricoeur, 2013, p. 61)

As a result, the subjectivity of appropriation is not about projecting oneself onto the text, but allowing the text to disclose what it has to say to us. There is no intuitive grasping of authorial intention, only an impulsion leading us away from the text, an invitation to think in a certain manner, an incitement to see things in an all-new way. The text, Ricoeur asserts, seeks to place us in its meaning, such that 'intention' is not of the author but of the text, and it opens up a direction for thought. Interpretation is therefore not an act that proceeds *from* the text, but an act that is performed *upon* it. To comply with the 'injunction' of the text is to appropriate in the here and now the intention of the text, understood as whatever the text means for whoever complies with what it offers. In this sense, the text-for-interpretation is not a blueprint but a call to action: to look forwards, to focus not on what it says but what it offers. Reading is, above all, an act of belonging to the text.

Mapping the 'other'

To read, to interpret, is to place oneself in the meaning indicated by the relation of interpretation the text itself supports. But notice how the focus has shifted – towards readers and their world, their interpretation, their reading, their selfhood. Without the author to guide them, everything that unfolds in this relation between readers and text is led and developed by the readers alone. Benjamin gives the example of the difference between a reader and a man listening to a storyteller. Unlike the man listening to the story, who is in the company of the storyteller and enjoys his companionship, the reader of a novel is entirely alone:

> In this solitude of his, the reader of a novel seizes upon his material more jealously than anyone else. He is ready to make it completely his own, to devour it, as it were. Indeed, he destroys, he swallows up the material as the fire devours logs in the fireplace. The suspense which permeates the novel is very much like the draft which stimulates the flame in the fireplace and enlivens its play. It is a dry material on which the burning interest of the reader feeds. (Benjamin, 1999, p. 99)

We do not read from a space of empty time. Our readings, like history, are filled with the reader's presence in the here and now. In Ricoeur's words, 'every reading of a text always takes place within a community, a tradition, or a living current of thought, all of which display presuppositions and exigencies – regardless of how closely a reading may be tied to the *quid*, to "that in view of which" the text was written' (Ricoeur, 2004, pp. 3–4). Interpretation is therefore both embodied and historical. There is no understanding outside of history, for 'interpretation' gives life in the present, beyond the historical immediacy of the text in its original time and place. The impact of this on the nature of the reading we produce cannot be overstated, for it means that the very historical reality we claim to construct as an object of reading is also the very historical reality to which we belong and in which we participate (Ricoeur, 2008, p. 50).

Ricoeur's example is to describe reading as the performance of a musical piece, as delimited by the provisions of the written score but performed by an artist who actualizes the written annotations in the here and now:

> Bringing a text to language is always something other than hearing someone and listening to his speech. Reading resembles instead the performance of a musical piece regulated by the written notations of the score. For the text is an autonomous space of meaning that is no longer animated by the intention of its author; the autonomy of the text, deprived of this essential support, hands writing over to the sole interpretation of the reader. (Ricoeur, 2013, p. 56)

In Spanish, an actor is an *intérprete*; *una interpretación* is an artistic performance. By giving life to the thoughts and intentions of a particular person or group, a spokesperson in French is an *interprète*, speaking for and on behalf of another. From these we gain a sense of interpretation both as the embodied realization of a portrayal and as an act of agency, of one who represents the interests of others. Consider what happens when we make status updates, post content, comment on threads and share images, text and video on Facebook, Twitter and Instagram. In these, we commit to words our 'reading' of the world around us. But since every post and tweet is geotagged, we also imbricate something of the poster in the post itself. As Steiner observes, there is no 'unwobbling pivot in time from which understanding could be viewed as stable and definitive' (1998, p. 262). By creating its own pivot from which to understand, in this sense, the embodied nature of interpretation is best viewed as the hermeneutic version of photobombing, for to interpret is to place ourselves within the space of the text and to layer upon it our own particular representation of what we have read.

There is a note of caution here to which we must be sensitive. If the translator's task is primarily explicative – that is, to make graphic that which challenges understanding – explication is also always additive, since understanding is always situated and embodied. Interpretation therefore does not merely *re*state; it also *illustrates*. It does not show, in other words, it tells; and this is an important distinction. Benjamin's example in this regard is film – a means of reproduction he describes as anything but replicative:

> By close-ups of the things around us, by focusing on hidden details of familiar details of familiar objects, by exploring commonplace milieus under the ingenious guidance of the camera, the film, on the one hand, extends our comprehension of the necessities which rule our lives; on the other hand, it manages to assure us of an immense and unexpected field of action. (Benjamin, 1994, p. 536)

A person walking, a fish jumping, the camera can slow these down so that we see the tiniest detail of the clothes the walker is wearing, the droplets of water on the fish's scales. Like a translation, and as with all acts of explanation and understanding, the moving camera involves itself in the process: 'Here the camera intervenes with the resources of its lowerings and liftings, its interruptions and isolations, its extensions and accelerations, its enlargements and reductions. The camera introduces us to unconscious optics as does psychoanalysis to unconscious impulses' (ibid.)

In a 1965 newsreel produced by British *Pathé News* featuring a two-minute item on the production of maps for the Ordnance Survey, we can see these dimensions in action. The film opens with an exterior close up of the specialist equipment used by surveyors to 'plot' the land. A man appears, squinting one eye and peering into the viewfinder of an optical instrument with the other.

'An unobtrusive army of men on the alert spying out the land' says the narrator (1965). The film cuts to an interior shot of men at work at the headquarters of the Ordnance Survey Commission, poring over desks covered in maps and illuminated by spotlights. As the narrator speaks, we are shown close-up shots of precision mapmaking, as one man uses a ruler and a needle to trace the contours of a map on wax-coated graph paper. Another uses a scalpel to place miniscule street names on a red-coloured map. To make a printing plate of a map, we are told, a photograph must first be taken, a process that requires a vast camera system specially designed for the Ordnance Survey. We watch as men in white laboratory coats place a map in a vice-like frame and position it in front of the camera, which is held in a large scaffold. We learn from the narrator that it is the most advanced and accurate camera of its size in the world. A man in brown overalls prepares red and yellow paint for the printing press. A map showing roads, hills and place names will be photographed several times in different forms since only two colours can be printed at once from the 'meticulous blocks' they produce, says the narrator (ibid). Another man collects the coloured maps from the printing press and arranges them on a desk. We learn that the machine will print 5000 'spot-on' Ordnance Survey maps an hour (ibid.). The narrator leaves us with the following closing statement: 'If we hadn't been famous for anything else, mapmaking would have been enough to put Britain "on the map"' (ibid.). From the close-up shots of the precision equipment used for measuring the contours of the land and the delicacy with which we see the men construct the Ordnance Survey maps on paper and later produce printed reproductions, to the running commentary of the narrator and footage of bespectacled men holding scalpels and compasses, everything about this film tells us that mapmaking is a science; that it is a highly complex task, where accuracy and exactness are valued above all other qualities. The newsreel offers a portrayal in which the practice of cartography is venerated both as a source of national pride and, where precision is presented as a vector for verisimilitude, as a source of trust. But when construed as an act of understanding, this is less of a truth to be acknowledged than it is a position to be defended.

The model of text interpretation teaches that understanding has nothing to do with an immediate grasp of a foreign psychic life or with an emotional identification with a mental intention. What is appropriated is not something felt, but something released by the reference of the text, its 'power of disclosing a world'. If understanding is always mediated historically by the reader's location in the interpreting present, a paradigmatic act of embodied performance on the part of the reader, and if the text is no longer driven by authorial intention, what does it mean to appropriate its meaning to oneself? By turning to the world of cartography, we find a dialectic of distanciation and appropriation in which similar acts of reading, interpretation and understanding are present. Maps, as with translations, are interpretations that aim to conquer a remoteness: they appear as representations on our computer screens, satnav apps, atlases or desktop globes, and act as guides to that which is normally physically inaccessible. When faced with uncertainties in our immediate geography, we turn to maps as a source of guidance. In an unfamiliar city, we consult a street map and suddenly the metropolis opens up before us. By seeking their counsel, an unspoken agreement passes between the reader and the cartographer; we accept the authority and authenticity of the knowledges they reflect. They are explications that quite literally make graphic the worlds from which we are prevented from accessing directly because of the distance that separates us. And yet, by definition, maps are representations: they are hermeneutic interpretations of the territories on which we live and as such are also always additive.

Many modern maps are based on a projection created by sixteenth-century cartographer Gerardus Mercator for use in navigation. Despite the status of the Mercator projection as the go-to model for hundreds of years, the Mercator exaggerates its scale towards the poles, giving an erroneous picture of the relative size of different territories. Countries such as Greenland come out roughly the same size as the African continent, when, in reality, the latter is some fourteen times larger. By making many countries appear smaller than they really are, this is a projection that gives the impression that certain territories are more important than others. It is for this reason that Huggan describes maps as paradigmatic structures, for they 'conceptualise, codify and regulate' the vision we hold of a particular landscape (1994, p. xv). In 1974 Dr Arno Peters launched a controversial counter-projection to challenge the primacy of the Mercator. Peters was not a cartographer but a historian and his project was political: to oppose the charge of Eurocentrism and Western privilege that enhanced the global North to the detriment of the South in received projections of the Earth. The Peters map preserves equal area and retains a rectangular grid of latitude and longitude, making all countries a more accurate size in terms of their relation to one another. However, the shape of countries in the Peters projection continues to be distorted, and compared to the Mercator map it appears to stretch land masses vertically. According to the *New Internationalist* obituary for Peters, who died on 2 December 2002, aged 86, Peters did not engage with his most vitriolic detractors; many contended that he had plagiarized an earlier map published in 1855 by the Reverend James Gall; others resented his intrusion into a field in which he was not expert (*New Internationalist*, 2003). Despite this opposition the Peters Map was adopted by the UN, aid agencies, schools and even became the subject of an episode of the television series *The West Wing* (1999–2006).

The obituary notes that what fewer people realize is that the map was itself a sequel to his earlier *Synchronoptische Weltgeschichte – Sychronoptic World*

History, published in 1952 and arranged in tabular form with time running along the top and regions running down the side, so that the reader could see at a glance what was happening around the globe at any one time: 'Noticing that in most histories of the world Europe got more attention than Africa, Asia and Latin America combined, Peters decided to create a history which gave equal weight to each century in human history and to each region' (*New Internationalist*, 2003). Although it engages in distortion of its own, what the Peters projection demonstrates is what Huggan calls the 'potential for discrepancy that exists between the model (or modelling system) and the "reality" represented by the model' it purports to represent (1994, p. 6). No map is without some degree of distortion, given that all maps utilize some form of scientific projection to calculate land mass and to determine the shape and size of territories. When depicted on paper their representation of the world they represent is never 'distance-factual'. As a giant semiotic system, the map is the product of 'conventions that prescribe relations of content and expression in a given semiotic circumstance' (Fels and Wood, 1986, p. 54). The Peters projection, like the Mercator, is a rectangular-based system and thus gives rise to continued misrepresentation. But when judged alongside the political project of his previous work, perhaps achieving the best representation was not the point: the constructedness of the cartographic exercise in the Peters map is explicit for all to see. It is a translation that makes no claim to an absence of hermeneutics.

A similar moral is brought into play in a parable by Jorge Luis Borges, translated in *Dreamtigers* (1964) as 'On Rigor in Science'. The short story, which is presented fictionally as an excerpt from 'Suarez Miranda: *Viajes de Varones Prudentes*, Book Four, Chapter XLV, Lérida, 1658', is worth reproducing here in its entirety:

> ... In that Empire, the Art of Cartography reached such Perfection that the map of one Province alone took up the whole of a City, and the map of the empire, the whole of a Province. In time, those Unconscionable Maps did not satisfy and the Colleges of Cartographers set up a Map of the Empire which had the size of the Empire itself and coincided with it point by point. Less Addicted to the Study of Cartography, Succeeding Generations understood that this Widespread Map was Useless and not without Impiety they abandoned it to the Inclemencies of the Sun and of the Winters. In the deserts of the West some mangled Ruins of that Map lasted on, inhabited by Animals and Beggars; in the whole Country there are no other relics of the Disciplines of Geography. (Borges, 1964, p. 325)

As the story highlights, all attempts at representing the Earth on a flat piece of paper are doomed to failure, since either the true shape of the world around us or the true distance between its topographies will inevitably be lost. The map of the Empire in the story promises complete coverage of the lands it controls, yet the image of it rotting in the deserts of its own territory exposes the absurdity, naïveté or egoism behind the desire for a metonymic 'point by point' reflection of the topographic realities the map purports to reflect. 'The provisionality of cartographic representation', explains Huggan, 'renders maps, and the areas or territories they claim to represent, incomplete, indeterminate, and insecure' (1994, p. xvi). In a mimetic sense, he says, 'the function of the map topos has never been purely "representative"'; simply put, therefore, 'maps lie; they inevitably differ from the reality they purport to represent' (p. xv and p. 3). Huggan is not so much exercised by the deceits of cartographic appropriation as by the injurious gestures of selection and discrimination that accompany it:

> The map's efficacy as a claim, like its impact as a political weapon, rests on the combined effect of its diverse strategies: the *delineation and demarcation* of territory; the location and nomination of place; the *inclusion and exclusion* of detail within a preset framework; and the choice of scale, format, and design. Many of these strategies are obvious, but some are subliminal, reflecting the subtlety with which maps operate as forms of social knowledge or as agents of political expediency. (Huggan, 1994, p. 9, emphases added)

Maps, as with translations, are social constructions that serve as technologies of control in which power is exercised precisely through the judicious 'delineation and demarcation' not just of territories but of the lived experience they represent. By 'othering' the lands it represents, the map not only reduces the other to a second-order discourse – an object of representation – but, crucially, places the one who produces the map in the ultimate position of power, as the one who also does the selecting and discriminating. Through this kind of cartographic 'orientalism', maps can be divorced from the social consequences and responsibilities of their exercise, transformed into not only graphical representations but also discourses that seek to carve up and contain the world. As Winichakul notes, 'a map anticipated spatial reality, not vice versa. In other words, a map was a model for, rather than a model of, what it purported to represent' (1997, p. 110). In this way, maps imply the existence of 'empty' spaces, waiting to be 'named' into existence by the act of mapping which traces topographical identities onto them. Somewhere between the cartographer's observation of the world and its subsequent representation, the two become asynchronous and discourses of power and authority are extended along the way. Maps are not carbon copies but simulacra of a vision of reality mediated through the cartographer's gaze. We can read a map as we would any text or translation: as influenced by the hermeneutics of the one who produced it.

Appropriation as containment

Three interrelated aspects of appropriation stand out so far. First, appropriation starts where there is an ontological state of separation from the objects of our interpretation. Second, this state of separation displaces the figure of the author as the historical agent of meaning because 'meaning' is both sited in the here and now and is constructed by the reader in the interpreting present. In Steiner's words, the translator 'must actualize the implicit "sense", the denotative, connotative, illative, intentional, associative range of significations which are implicit in the original, but which it leaves undeclared or only partly declared simply because the native auditor or reader has an immediate understanding of them' (Steiner, 1998, p. 291). De-psychologized thus, interpretation is not concerned with what is going on in the author's head but with the fruit of the dialectical relation between a reader and the text. 'Appropriation' is not so much targeted at discerning what the text 'means' but what the text can possibly mean to *us*. Third, and because this imaginative encounter is concerned first and foremost with bringing into the present space of the reader everything about the text that challenges the immediacy of understanding, interpretation is distinguished by the immediacy of its character. But remember that translators, readers and interpreters the world over are living, thinking, beings, immersed in social, cultural, political, historical and geographical contexts of their own. That which we interpret, therefore, we also transform. It is an interpreter's performance of the object of perception and as such a difference is created between that which is interpreted and that which interpretation yields. In the context of interlingual translation, Benjamin offers a well-known image of this predicament, in which the text is a language forest and the translation is left outside: 'it calls into it without entering, aiming at that single spot where the echo is able to give, in its own language, the reverberation of the work in the alien one' (1999, p. 77). The translational 'echo' that returns from the language forest is often confused for the intentional voice of the author, but to Benjamin it is the echo of an enquiry the translator herself initiates.

The significance of these insights goes well beyond the world of text. They suggest that if the purposeful interpretation of the world around us is animated by a desire to conquer the distance that separates us from our respective others, then 'understanding' is at base a self-directed mode of ontological struggle with the otherness all around us. It is for this reason that Ricoeur describes understanding as the dialectical counterpart of being in a given situation of interpretation, because understanding is 'the projection of our ownmost possibilities at the very heart of the situations in which we find ourselves' (2008, p. 61). As we shift our emphasis away from understanding the other towards understanding the world of the work, we also shift how we view the very task of understanding. It is not an objective procedure but the expression of an ongoing process of a reader understanding herself in front of the work. Understanding the text thus produces a certain circularity that reaches outwards and arches back to the reader's own self-understanding. Within this hermeneutic circle:

> An interpretation is not genuine unless it culminates in some form of appropriation (*Aneignung*), if by that term we understand the process by which one makes one's own (*eigen*) what was initially other or alien (*fremd*). But I believe that the hermeneutical circle is not correctly understood when it is presented, first, as a circle between two subjectivities, that of the reader and that of the author; and second, as the projection of the subjectivity of the reader into the reading self. (Ricoeur, 2013, p. 61, original emphasis)

That which we contain through interpretation we make our own. Despite the notion that interpretation is about the opening up of possibilities, therefore, these possibilities must be realized in the here and now of the reader. All the reader can do is to make the text their own, to incorporate and to contain, bringing it into the body of the local and closing down the interpretive possibilities the foreign text presents within the framework of the familiar:

> The translator labours to secure a natural habitat for the alien presence he has imported into his own tongue and cultural setting. [...] The foreign text is felt to be not so much an import from abroad (suspect by definition) as it is an element out of one's native past. It had been there 'all along' awaiting reprise. It is really a part of one's own tradition temporarily mislaid. Master translations domesticate the foreign original by exchanging an obtrusive geographical-linguistic distance for a much subtler, internalized distance in time. (Steiner, 1998, p. 365)

As a process of incorporation, appropriation is 'a proximity which suppresses and preserves the cultural distance and includes the otherness within the ownness' (Ricoeur, 1976, p. 43). In the context of translation, we appropriate the foreign under the category of the same. Translation in this sense both preserves and overcomes distance, for it both acknowledges that which is different and inscribes it within its own creations. To translate, therefore, we must impose boundaries and limitations upon what a text possibly *can* mean. As a homeward movement, moreover, translation is ultimately a gesture of containment – what Steiner describes as the 'portage home of the foreign "sense" and its domestication in the new linguistic-cultural matrix' (1998, p. 351). There is thus a territorial dimension to our acts of understanding, for the text is a foreign land over which the translator seeks to establish dominion: 'We encircle and invade cognitively. We come home laden, thus again off-balance, having caused disequilibrium throughout the system by taking away from "the other" and by adding, though possibly with ambiguous consequence, to our own. The system is now off-tilt' (Steiner, 1998, p. 316). As Steiner observes, there has been an outflow of 'energy' from the text-for-translation to the world of the translator; but somewhere between seizure and surrogacy, the task of taking 'home' becomes synonymous with taking 'away' (p. 398). With the desire to overcome the strangeness of the foreign there is also a desire to possess – to reduce, compress and contain.

Translation as the exercise of sovereign authority

Consider the case of an island archipelago known to some as the Spratly Islands, located off the coasts of Malaysia, the Philippines and southern Vietnam in the South China Sea. It spans almost 800 islands, islets, reefs and atolls, covers a land mass of approximately one-and-a-half square miles in size and is spread across an area of over 150,000 square miles. It is largely uninhabited, has no indigenous population and is subject to multiple overlapping claims, two of which – Brunei and Malaysia – appeal to the United Nations Convention on the Law of the Sea, which recognizes an 'exclusive economic zone' stretching 200 nautical miles from the coastline of a state. The Convention draws a distinction between the 200-mile exclusive economic zone, which confers a 'sovereign right' on the area below the sea, and what is known as the 'territorial sea', which extends outwards for twelve nautical miles from the baseline of a coastal state and which confers full sovereignty over both airspace and seabed. In the same archipelago, within the 200-mile exclusive economic zone that extends from the Philippines, in an area that is also claimed by the People's Republic of China, lies a submerged reef known to Philippine claimants as *Ayungin*, *Ren'ai Jiao* in Chinese transliteration and by others as the 'Second Thomas Shoal'. In 1999 the Philippine Navy grounded the vessel BRP *Sierra Madre* at the reef and has maintained a small military presence on board ever since. The ship was constructed originally for the US Navy during the Second World War and ownership later transferred to the

Philippine Navy; in July 2015 it was reported that the navy had been quietly reinforcing the rusting hull and deck to prevent it from disintegrating (*Reuters*, 2015). As a commissioned navy ship considered on 'active' duty, under the 'Mutual Defense Treaty Between the Republic of the Philippines and the United States of America' signed on 30 August 1951, the Philippines could request US military assistance if the BRP *Sierra Madre* were attacked.

Fifteen miles from Second Thomas Shoal, meanwhile, is a once-tiny coral islet known by some as 'Mischief Reef' and which is at the centre of a vast Chinese land-reclamation project. Over the course of a few years, China has reclaimed thousands of acres from the South China Sea, turning reefs, which it refers to as the *Nansha* islands, which are under water at high tide and therefore not considered land under international law, into permanent artificial islands. The area is thought to be rich in mineral and oil deposits, but claims that its reserves could be as strong as the Kuwait region have not yet been proved through exploration. Ownership of land in the area could also offer a strategic advantage in terms of establishing a presence in a major sea route worth trillions in trade and blocking sea-borne threats to South China (Etzler, 2014). According to a position paper of the Government of the People's Republic of China 'on the Matter of Jurisdiction in the South China Sea Arbitration Initiated by the Republic of the Philippines',

> China has indisputable sovereignty over the South China Sea Islands (the Dongsha Islands, the Xisha Islands, the Zhongsha Islands and the Nansha Islands) and the adjacent waters. Chinese activities in the South China Sea date back to over 2,000 years ago. China was the first country to discover, name, explore and exploit the resources of the South China Sea Islands and the first to continuously exercise sovereign powers over them. (Ministry of Foreign Affairs of the People's Republic of China, 2014)

The Spratlys have become a cipher for competing claims to sovereignty where even the maritime territories they represent appear to be in a state of constant evolution. In the statement, China locates its claim to territorial dominion over the islands in the power to *name*. By placing a mark upon the metaphorical space of the land, through the word, China succeeds in containing the islands, if not in international law, then at least in the moral imaginary. It is through this hermeneutic gesture that competing claims to the contested space of the Spratlys are read and expressed.

For Tuan the physical world exists without values. The subjective experience of space manifests itself in what he calls the 'landmarks' of a place, which operate as markers, visible features of the way in which we perform our identity on the spaces around us. It is we who familiarize this alien space-without-values, imbuing it with ritual, attaching sights, sounds and smells, ascribing feelings, meanings and ideologies to it. When we impose signs and landmarks on places that relate to particular identities, loyalties and agendas – naming strategies – we familiarize empty human space and make it 'place'. These traces operate as clues to the multiple readings and meanings we attach to the lived human experience of the physical world around us. These markers simultaneously signal belonging but they can also divide, displace and exclude. Places in this sense are 'duplicitous' because their meanings are not only multitudinous but also change over time, depending on who uses them, why, where and when. As it passes through these continua of ascription, the identity of a place multiplies exponentially, expanding and contracting over time according to the way in which it is lived and experienced. New interpretations of space graft yet more identities, creating an aporia between the object as a discrete geographical reality and the object as we experience it (Tuan, 1977, p. 146).

Places, as with 'translations' bear an 'embodied' relationship to the world. They are constructed by living people, touched by the traces of multiple reconstructions and as such are never 'complete' but performed (Cresswell, 2004, p. 37). This is the 'place-ballet' through which space becomes more of a social construct than a series of discrete places in their own right (Buttimer and Seamon, 2015, p. 163). Each person will view space differently and, as such, space is constantly evolving over time. The 'spirit' of a place, in other words, exists in the eye of the beholder, for 'seeing' creates a distance between self and other, interpreter and object. For Tuan, because what we see is 'out there', all seeing creates a difference. We view the landscape not as it actually is but as we frame it to be, for places exist not as independent realities waiting to be rendered successfully, but as place-objects constructed from the interpreter's own perspectives, knowledges and expectations. When time elapses between the lived experience of a place and its subsequent interpretation, a variation occurs. The 'truth' of a place disappears and it is overshadowed by the subjective experience and outlook of the one doing the interpreting. Tuan puts this succinctly: 'If time is conceived as flow or movement, then place is a pause' (1977, p. 198).

In the context of the Spratlys, competing claims to territorial sovereignty function as translations: embodied, partial realizations of a particular worldview. Just as no 'true' knowledge of a place exists except as framed by its beholder, no text exists to its interpreter outside of its original geopolitical landscape. Just as the enactment of place is both a way of viewing the world around us and a way of understanding our subject-position within it, the translator's gaze on the space of the text is ultimately a mode of *looking*. As a practice equally engaged in the creation of difference, translation ascribes meanings onto the space of the text, whose values are no longer synonymous with those of the author but which must be constructed by the translator on her own. Because we are distanced from the author's role in determining the meaning of the text, the text is an autonomous space of meaning in which we dispense with authorial control. Despite this imaginative leap into the hermeneutic unknown, a journey outwards into the terra incognita of the foreign text, translation is ultimately a journey homeward-bound, decontextualizing the text, opening up its potential to project possible worlds, expanding the infinite possibilities for understanding located within it, but, importantly, fixing what is seen and read within the terrain of writing. In the final analysis, the translator must settle on only one of the infinite possibilities it raises, 'pausing', to use Tuan's term, the text's infinite trajectory in the present space of interpretation. Steiner describes this as the translator's 'interpretive attack and appropriation' and maintains that as comprehension's etymology shows, one 'comprehends' not only cognitively but also by encirclement and ingestion (1998, p. 415 and p. 314). The translator's response is just one of numerous continua of interpretation through which the space of a text passes as it migrates through appropriation from its 'past' reality in time and space to its new home in the present place of translation. It is the translator's positionality within the interpreting 'present' that informs how the translation takes shape. To the present-day translator, the space of the text is not just an object, in the sense that the translator can look upon it, but also a way of looking, as the product and object of a hermeneutic enterprise. When viewed as 'texts', the changing geopolitical status of the Spratly Islands suggests they are not only places in a constant state of translation, constructed and reconstructed in different times and places, but are also the space of competing interpretations and conflicting approaches to how the space should be owned and conceptualized. The lesson for our study of hermeneutics is that while appropriation enables us to open up the infinite possibilities for understanding that emerge from differential interpretations of the phenomena of our world, appropriation also requires us to fix upon only one.

4

Transformation

Translation as revolution

Lichtenstein: A Retrospective was shown at the Tate Modern between 21 February and 27 May 2013 and was the first full-scale exhibition of the artist's work in over twenty years. Co-organized by the Art Institute of Chicago, it brought together over one hundred of Lichtenstein's most celebrated paintings and sculptures and fostered renewed debate about the significance of his work. One of the key pieces in the touring retrospective, and perhaps his most famous painting of all, was *Whaam!*, a diptych from 1963 that Lichtenstein had based on a comic strip pane published the previous year in the *All American Men of War* series by illustrator Irv Novick and published by DC Comics in 1962. In Lichtenstein's enormous painted version, one of several in which he depicted scenes of aerial combat, a fighter pilot sends a rocket hurtling through the sky. It speeds across from left to right, exploding an enemy jet in a spectacular flash of red, yellow and white. According to the Tate's exhibition guide webpage, 'Lichtenstein carefully reworked his source image by cropping, eliminating detail, deleting or editing speech bubbles and making the rocket trail horizontal rather than diagonal, thereby sharpening the drama and giving more weight to a single enemy. The result is not just the story of a dogfight, but a compositional tightrope act' (Tate London, n.d.).

Lichtenstein's paintings of war and romantic melodrama became an overnight success but they also provoked harsh criticism. For some, he was the architect of pop art, venerated for his distinctive cartoon style, but for others he was a copycat; a plagiarist, not an artist. As the Tate material notes: 'In 1964 *Life* magazine facetiously queried "Is he the worst artist in the US?" – a question that riffed on a headline 15 years earlier in a 1949 *Life* magazine feature on Jackson Pollock which asked laconically: "Is he the greatest living painter in the United States?"' (ibid.) Lichtenstein was well known to have been inspired by popular culture and constructed his work as an ongoing dialogue with received approaches to art and art criticism. What accounts for a critical reception of his work that equates methods of imitation, simulacrum, parody and play with plagiarism and plunder? To answer this, we must delve further into the causes and effects of appropriation.

As an attempt to overcome the distanciating estrangement that separates the translator from the object of understanding, translation is an encounter with otherness that *contains*. To make the foreign familiar, translation must incorporate. It must draw near to the foreign text and possess it, bringing it into the body of the local. In the autonomous space of meaning from which appropriation begins, a text becomes decontextualized. The relationship it bears to the time and place of its production and reception – to its sociocultural moment in history – is out of the translator's reach. In translation, references become decoupled and all-new values are ascribed, expanding exponentially its potential to project new possibilities for understanding. And yet, at the same time, the translator distils this infinite horizon of possibility into a singular reading in the here and now of writing. By making it their own, translators, as readers in the first instance, mould the text according to their own reading. As an 'interpretation' of the text that also breathes life into the words of the other text and makes them anew, translation is above all a version-creating exercise. It is neither an innocent nor an automatic activity. It is a dynamic mediation born of opposition between a reader and a text, between what is 'ours' and what is 'theirs', between the security of the familiar and the alienation of the unknown, and, as such, starts with an imaginative encounter with 'otherness' and ends when the self-same otherness is immured within the translator's own interpretive frame.

According to Steiner, the 'ideal' scenario within this context would be a translation that operates as a 'total counterpart', a 'perfect "double" ', of the original, a 're-petition – an asking again' (1998, p. 318). In the face of translation's containing gestures, this is an ideal that sets out a demand for equity:

> Translation fails where it does not compensate, where there is no restoration of radical equity. The translator has grasped and/or appropriated less than is there. He traduces through diminution. Or he has chosen to embody and restate fully only one or another aspect of the original, fragmenting, distorting its vital coherence according to his needs or myopia. Or he has 'betrayed upward', transfiguring the source into something greater than itself. The paradigm of translation stays incomplete until reciprocity has been achieved, until the original has regained as much as it had lost. (Steiner, 1998, p. 415)

In Steiner's 'hermeneutic motion' this compensatory stage of translation is directed towards the restoration of balance. It is an act of 'reciprocity' between the translation and the source, between the two languages that have been interrupted by the translator's 'interpretive attack and appropriation' (p. 415). In this way, Steiner maintains, it forms part of the very moral fibre of translation (p. 316). Through 'tact' and 'intensified moral vision', the translator creates 'a condition of significant exchange' by which there would be translation without loss and the 'order' between the source and receiver would be preserved (pp. 318–19). This idealized conceptualization is consistent with representations of the translator as a 'conduit' or intercultural 'ambassador' charged with ensuring the safe passage of otherness from the time and place in which the text was produced to the time and place of its translation and reception. And yet, as with most touristic travel, a translation's itinerary tends to be homeward-bound, for while the process may begin as a journey to the land of the other, a return ticket is usually implied.

When it comes to the concrete practice of interlingual translation the driving force behind this homeward journey is the receiver of a translation – the audience towards which the translator directs her words. When I translate a Golden Age play from Spanish into English so that it can be adapted for the British stage (as I did with Lope de Vega's *El castigo sin venganza* for the Theatre Royal Bath in 2013), there is no sense of 'exchange' – understood as something transactional or reciprocal, a mutual giving and a receiving – with Lope de Vega as the author of the play. He is long since dead and cannot participate in any dialogical interaction with me. Nor do I enter into a 'dialogue' with the text itself. The play neither speaks back to me when I question it nor does it respond to me when I translate it. My strategic choices, my approach to translation, have no effect on the seventeenth-century Spanish-language text. It does not transact with me. It does not reciprocate. Confronted with my translation both text and author are silent. It does not 'give'; I 'take'. As the translator, my understanding of Lope's play is properly that of a 'source' text: it is my point of departure, the raw materials, the inspiration from which I will construct my English translation. In a hermeneutic sense it is the 'world' of dramatic possibilities I will read into the text and appropriate. In the double-blind situation of reading and translating Lope's play today, any sense of 'exchange' that has any bearing on the shape of the translation is not with the historical author but with the artistic director of the theatre company who commissioned me to produce it.

Distanciation separates the interpreter from the object of interpretation – from the foreign author and the historical context in which the text was produced and received. Translation starts with a desire to understand the text's relationship to this foreign world across this distance and it ends with an interpretation intended to be understood by audiences in the here and now. Translation's priority, indeed its very raison d'être, is to facilitate understanding among an identified audience, and, as such, it is purposeful, targeted and deliberate. It is an intention, a desire enacted on the part of the translator and performed, one hopes, in both the translation she produces and on the part of the audience that receives it. When it comes to conceptualizing the task of translation, therefore, we would do better to orient ourselves away from a notion of 'exchange', that is, away from what is or is not lost when we appropriate our objects of interpretation and instead towards everything we stand to gain when we do so. The Hollywood phenomenon of the 'reboot' shares many features with this approach to interlingual translation. In the reboot, the continuity of an existing series of fictional works is disrupted to introduce new characters and plot lines. When studio executives hired J. J. Abrams, best known for his behind-the-scenes roles in blockbusters *Armageddon* (1998) and *Cloverfield* (2008) to direct the first in a new Star Trek film franchise, it was precisely the potential for freshness and creativity in 'translation' that critics celebrated:

> Mr. Abrams doesn't treat 'Star Trek' as a sacred text, which would be deadly for everyone save the fanatics. But neither does he skewer a pop cultural classic that, more than 40 years after its first run, has been so lampooned (it feels like there are more 'South Park' parodies than original episodes) it was difficult to see how he was going to give it new life. By design or accident, he has, simply because in its hopefulness 'Star Trek' reminds you that there's more to science fiction (and Hollywood blockbusters) than nihilism. (Dargis, 2009)

While certain elements in the reboot remain recognizable to audiences familiar with the original works, such as the continued presence of the original Kirk, Spock, Uhura, Bones, Chekov, Sulu and Scotty characters, new elements or twists on familiar themes are introduced. In Abrams's reboots, which include *Star Trek* (2009) and *Star Trek into Darkness* (2013), Spock and Uhura are involved in a romantic relationship and Spock's home world, Vulcan, has been destroyed. Reboots depend upon the existence of already well-known source material and, as with translations, they appropriate their source material for the sole purpose of moving their intended audience in some way. In the reboot, there is also a commercial imperative at work. Studios expand their revenue potential by piggybacking on the success of proven models, securing a new generation of fans and reinvigorating the franchise for existing ones. In this context, the 'voice' of the original Star Trek 'author', Jean Roddenberry, is lost and the shape of the original Star Trek universe has been transformed radically. In this sense, only Abrams and the creative team behind the reboots have the agency to 'speak'; it is their story, their visuals, their ideas, their cast and their script behind the latest emanation of the Star Trek model. But this need not be characterized as a 'loss', for there can also be tremendous gain, as another newspaper story on the reboot suggested:

> Sure enough, Abrams's Star Trek zips along, fuelled by state-of-the-art special effects, agreeable young actors and a generous measure of comedy. By focusing on Spock and Kirk as novices finding their footing, and putting their gut-vs-logic dynamic at the heart of the film, Abrams gives non-followers plenty to hang on to, but also pays homage to familiar Trek tropes: Bones says: 'I'm a doctor, not a physicist!'; Scotty says: 'I'm giving her all she's got!'; and Leonard Nimoy, the original Spock, makes a cameo to symbolically pass on the torch. For advanced-level Trekkers, there are in-jokes and seismic events hardly anyone else will notice. This is the first time, for example, we see how Kirk cheats Starfleet's notorious Kobayashi Maru test, as mentioned in Star Trek II: The Wrath of Khan – an event, indeed a sentence, that will mean absolutely nothing to the rest of us. (Rose, 2009)

In the context of interlingual translation, when a translator's interpretative judgement is committed to writing it is the translator who speaks – with the sole intention of influencing an audience in some way. Steiner's vision of an 'ideal' translation that makes up for the loss of 'order' through 'exchange' and 'compensation' would in reality entail a uniquely *self*-centred gesture, for translation cannot help but direct itself towards its own context of production and reception. That is, towards the translator's audience. As with the *Star Trek* reboots, translation can engage in thoughtful 'nods' to its antecedent text, a text to which it owes its very existence, as the pre-existing model from which a translation is shaped. But if, as Steiner maintains, the 'perfect' translation should act as a 'double' that repeats a message without distortion, then this is a brand of translation that will always let us down. If, however, translation's very distorting processes can be viewed as part and parcel of a process of creative renewal, we go some way towards a view of translation not as containment, but as revolution.

Remember that the task of translation starts with a demand: to understand a mystery. To do so we must reach out across a distance of time and space and make the objects of interpretation our own. But we need not accompany this act of interpretation with mourning for the loss of the source. To read involves inhabiting a textual world that is not our own. We must participate in its performance and let it affect how we respond as readers. Even though, for example, we know that the characters of a novel are not 'real' in the material sense, by being drawn into their lives, their worlds and their concerns we 'believe' in them nonetheless. When we read we make an investment in the inherent value of the text. Before appropriation, then, is a profound *belief:* in the presence of something worthy of appropriation. In Steiner's model this is the first stage of the hermeneutic motion in which we find the translator's 'initiative trust, an investment of belief' in the meaningfulness of the text-for-translation, for if translation is above all the outward demonstration of an act of understanding, then translation must, by extension, start with an act of trust (1998, p. 312). Indeed, the very fact that translation has been called for is testament to the prior assertion that there is something 'there' – the foreign language, the foreign object, the mysterious act, the difference of the 'other' – to be understood. Like the hermeneuts of old, who began their reading of the Bible with prayer and devotion, seeing language not as literal but as figurative, mysterious and with many levels of meaning, the brand of modern hermeneutics both Steiner and Ricoeur espouse is one of rigour and introspection. It aims not to restore that which has been appropriated but to enter into thoughtful engagement with the text: 'Being methodical, penetrative, analytic, enumerative, the process of translation, like all modes of focused understanding, will detail, illumine, and generally body forth its subject' (Steiner, 1998, p. 316). Simply because lossless translation is impossible does not mean that there is nothing to be gained from the process. Texts speak about a world. As long as the things which texts address remain in human experience, they will continue to tell us something about human existence when we share in them. Simultaneously, we also acknowledge the presence of something we do not understand. This in turn implies a recognition of our lack of comprehension in the face of the misunderstood, of the fallibility of our own understanding and, at the same time, a commitment to do something about it. Hermeneutic trust, in this sense, is humbling. It is an initial emptying of our interpretive cache. It is an acknowledgement that there is something in the world of the other text that we need to fulfil a lack in our own. It asks not what the 'other' means, but what the other's text can possibly mean *to us*:

> The over-determination of the interpretive act is inherently inflationary: it proclaims that 'there is more here than meets the eye', that 'the accord between content and executive form is closer, more delicate than had been observed hitherto'. To class a source-text as worth translating is to dignify it immediately and to involve it in a dynamic of magnification (subject, naturally, to later review and even, perhaps, dismissal). (Steiner, 1998, p. 317)

As a result, something is added to the status of the original, because of the investment the translator makes in it. As Arendt wrote in her introduction to Benjamin's *Illuminations*, there is tremendous value in looking to the works of our world in this way:

Like a pearl diver who descends to the bottom of the sea, not to excavate the bottom and bring it to light but to pry loose the rich and the strange, the pearls and the coral in the depths, and to carry them to the surface, this thinking delves into the depths of the past – but not in order to resuscitate it the way it was and to contribute to the renewal of extinct ages. (Arendt, 1999, p. 54)

The 'sea-change' that translation ushers in is that of the new delights that can emerge when an original text in translation is extended and renewed. In the case of Stieg Larsson's *Millennium* series (2005–7), for example, with the posthumous translation of his novels into English came massive international appeal and feature film trilogies in Swedish and English. To conceptualize translation as posterior to the original is to focus only on the sense of derivation – of following after – and misses out on the sense of preservation – of keeping it in the public mind – that also accompanies it. It is, in Benjamin's terms, the 'ever-renewed latest and most abundant flowering' of an original life a text has already led (1999, p. 72). Indeed all of a work's retellings, remakes and revisions are part of this lineage, which is tantamount to the achievement of posthumous 'fame' for the author:

The history of the great works of art tells us about their descent from prior models, their realization in the age of the artist, and what in principle should be their eternal afterlife in succeeding generations. Where this last manifests itself, it is called fame. Translations that are more than transmissions of subject matter come into being when a work, in the course of its survival, has reached the age of its fame. Contrary, therefore, to the claims of bad translators, such translations do not so much serve the works as owe their existence to it. (Benjamin, 1996, p. 255)

The act of translation brings a focus, and an audience, to the source text in ways in which would not have been possible otherwise. Beyond opening up greater access to a work for monolingual readers, the success of a translation can also give rise to commissions for myriad other translations in a multitude of languages, bringing to light writers known only in their own regions, or revealing the significance of a body of work hitherto undervalued or known only to a precious few.

Translation as transformation

As Benjamin reminds us, because translation comes later in history than the source texts on which it is based, it thus 'marks their stage of continued life' (1996, p. 254), for the translator's distanciation from the text is not the first distanciation. As works in their own right, texts are distanced first and foremost from themselves over time. Transformation is part and parcel of translation precisely because, as Benjamin points out, the text is already something living and this living thing is already a product of its own time. No text, whether a source or a translation, can stand out of time. Even before the translator comes along to transform it, the source text is always in the process of transformation, taking on new forms and new significance in new times and places:

> For just as the tenor and the significance of the great works of literature undergo a complete transformation over the centuries, the mother tongue of the translator is transformed as well. While a poet's words endure in his own language, even the greatest translation is destined to become part of the growth of its own language and eventually to be absorbed by its renewal. Translation is so far removed from being the sterile equation of two dead languages that of all literary forms it is the one charged with the special mission of watching over the maturing process of the original language and the birth pangs of its own. (Benjamin, 1996, p. 256)

To cast appropriation in a purely negative light simply because the source text is changed is to forget that when it comes to translation's source material 'change' is already a natural part of the lifespan of such material. The key to reorienting our conceptualization of the task of translation, therefore, is the fact that when it comes to the evolution of texts, ideas and cultural practices, both the 'source' and 'translation' are bound together in mutual interdependence.

Consider the *Mona Lisa* (c. 1503–9), the most famous painting in the world. Even the name by which we know it is a translation, for the early sixteenth-century painting by Leonardo di ser Piero da Vinci, and which hangs in its own room in the Denon wing of the Louvre in Paris, in the museum's English-language catalogue is listed as 'Portrait of Lisa Gherardini, wife of Francesco del Giocondo, known as the *Mona Lisa* (the Joconde in French)' (Louvre, n.d). It was acquired by King François I of France in 1518 and has been housed in the Louvre since the late eighteenth century. Since 2005 the portrait, on a poplar wood panel, of a little-known Florentine woman has hung in a specially refurbished gallery designed to cope with the millions of tourists who flock to see that mysterious smile. As I describe it to you I know that you already know the smile to which I refer. Already you visualize that face. That knowing look. The way her hands sit atop one another. You have seen all this before and were drawn in, even before I reminded you of it here. In what Benjamin describes as the 'age of mechanical reproduction', this is because most of us already 'know' the Mona Lisa. As one of the most written about, most talked about, most mysterious figures in the art world, we are already well familiar with her. We have seen her before, perhaps not in the Louvre itself, but in one of the many likenesses that have circulated globally since its first acquisition – in books, such as Dan Brown's bestseller *The Da Vinci Code* (2003) and films such as *Mona Lisa Smile* (2003) and *The Da Vinci Code* (2006) adapted from Brown's novel. We also see her image printed on any number of gallery gift shop products, on posters, postcards, scarves and tote bags. Who was the real identity of da Vinci's sitter? What were his reasons for painting her? Was the background imagined or based on a real landscape? What is she thinking behind that enigmatic smile? In global circulation, the image of da Vinci's muse has proliferated to such an extent that anyone can become an art critic. She is, as Sassoon writes, 'an open text into which one could read what one wanted' (2001, p. 10).

As a text open to infinite interpretation, the Mona Lisa has inspired numerous readings, from Marcel Duchamp's *L.H.O.O.Q* (1919) in which the subject is depicted sporting a goatee beard and moustache, to Salvador Dalí's *Self Portrait as Mona Lisa* (1954), in which the familiar visage and twisted moustache of the artist himself can clearly be seen within his reproduction of Mona Lisa's face. Duchamp's piece, meanwhile, is regarded as one of his 'readymades' – manufactured, often mundane *objets trouvés*, usually bearing no pre-existing artistic function, adapted in some way and submitted as art in a challenge to received notions of aesthetic value in the art world. In the case of *L.H.O.O.Q*, a pun on the French pronunciation of the letters and their suggestion of the phrase *Elle a chaud au cul*, which Duchamp was thought to translate as 'she has a fire down below'. The *objet trouvé* in the case of *L.H.O.O.Q* was a cheap postcard reproduction of the Mona Lisa onto which Duchamp drew a moustache and beard and added the title. In the age of the Internet, of course, where pastiche of this nature has become commonplace, da Vinci's work has become quite simply 'the most visited, most written about, most sung about, most parodied work of art in the world' (Battersby, 2013).

This is a form of translational pastiche that is not possessive but symbiotic, for with every parody, every hodgepodge, potpourri reproduction, the Mona Lisa's fame grows. Although its homeward-directed, *familiarizing* tendencies may well result in the diminution of the painting's unfamiliar 'otherness', from the perspective that an image downloaded to one's computer from the Internet is a poor substitute for experiencing the painting oneself, the fact is that none of these parodic translations would exist without it. In this sense, translation is a mode that depends upon the presence of otherness – on the previous life of a work – for its very existence. It is appropriative, to be sure, but in its dependence upon this previous life it also makes its source material shine, for it is the work that gives life to the translation.

As Benjamin writes, what draws the reader to the novel 'is the hope of warming his shivering life with a death he reads about' (1999, p. 100). The reader receives life from the text, and the text, to echo Benjamin's words, achieves its afterlife. If the life lines of reader and work are interlinked, in this sense, then the existence of one is linked inextricably to the other. As Steiner writes, 'Where the most thorough possible interpretation occurs, where our sensibility appropriates its object while, in this appropriation, guarding, quickening that object's autonomous life, the process is one of "original repetition". We re-enact, in the bounds of our own secondary but momentarily heightened, educated consciousness, the creation by the artist' (Steiner, 1998, p. 27). To adopt this 'heightened' consciousness is to translate in the knowledge that the source text retains an autonomous life and that while translation is a revivification of such, it is a revivification within the confines of an autonomous life *of our own*. The consequence of this life-giving re-enactment is that while the source and translation are mutually interdependent, the translation has no power to obliterate the source, for it remains free to enjoy a future of its own. The lines of the two are intertwined and interdependent; yet each takes its own direction and each enjoys its own source of sustaining power. In this sense, what Steiner worries is the 'empty scar in the landscape' after the open-cast mine of appropriation closes (p. 314), for Benjamin is renewal, an opportunity to actually honour the original instead of destroying it. Translation thus has the power to illuminate, as well as to contain.

At the heart of this proposition is a paradox: that translation can 'repeat' the work of another while creating simultaneously an original work of its own. Steiner's term, 're-enactments', is apt to describe the process of cultural translation at work in the phenomenon of live-action remakes of famous works of art. In the 'art remake', people pose as well-known works of two-dimensional art, remade in three-dimensions and photographed, using costume, makeup and lighting and without any digital post-editing. In 2011 a competition for the best art remake was hosted by the Booooooom blog, one of the largest art blogs on the Internet, run by Vancouver-based artist Jeff Hamada. According to the competition rules, photographers were required to 'reference classic works of art' and 'put all your creative energy into re-creating and re-staging the image' (2011). The submissions are displayed on the Booooooom blog alongside copies of the original works on which they are based. Live-action Frida Kahlo's are shown, complete with stick-on eyebrows, a mocked-up Van Gogh's bedroom in Arles and even a vintage suitcase with clothes arranged in block colours and separated by a black belt to imitate one of Mondrian's famous blue, white, yellow and red compositions. Hamada cites as inspiration a photo spread by artist Miranda July for *Vice* magazine in

2009 in which she poses as extras from classic films (July, 2009). She starts the piece with the following note:

> Dear Julie,
> Do you ever feel like an extra in your own life? It seems like I'm forever stuck in the background, watching other people say and do all the things I feel inside. One day I'm gonna surprise everyone with my talents. They will be laughing and crying and texting me so often that I will be annoyed.
> Until then,
Sandy (July, 2009).

Below the note are a series of stills taken from classic films such as *The Godfather* (1972) and *Kramer vs. Kramer* (1979), each followed by a stylized photograph of July dressed as one of the extras in the background of the original stills. In a still from *Grease* (1978), for example, the original still shows Frenchie and the other pink ladies sitting on a cafeteria table, crowded around Sandra Dee as she sings one of the main numbers. The still captures the moment one of the background singers, her hair up and scarf tied around her neck, sings her heart out, the emotion of the moment captured on her face. In July's meticulous re-enactment every detail is recreated, from the hairstyle and scarf, to the angle at which the original singer is sitting. In a review for *Bitch* magazine, Briar Levit wrote the following:

> I find myself checking out all the details. I compare the original still to her image – scrolling back and forth repeatedly to verify the facsimile she's created. But in the end, I still ended up asking the question 'why'? once I was done looking. What's the point? Is this just a chance for her to play dress up? To flex some ironic costume muscles? What is she saying here? (Levit, 2009)

We might ask a similar question in the context of cultural translation: what is to be gained by construing these re-enactments as a translational dialectic between a reader and a text? In both these cases, what we witness are photographic snapshots of real human beings coming together in ways imagined by a photographer, *qua* reader, engaged in recreating a real-life piece of source material already in existence. Each re-enactment features alongside an example of its artistic stimulus and in both, the costume, makeup, lighting, composition and positioning suggest the artists have been scrupulous in their attempts at similitude. And yet even as these images assiduously recreate the source inspiration, there are subtle and not-so-subtle departures from the originals and it is precisely this transformative dimension that make these re-enactments so arresting. In July's magazine spread, her re-enactments are shot against a pale grey background, which has the effect of making her extras springboard off the background towards the spectator. Whereas in the films themselves, the extras exist at the literal and metaphorical margins of the screen – almost out of shot, in the background, in the corner, some with their backs turned, others with only their faces visible – in July's re-enactments they become the focus of our attentions, lead characters in the film of their lives. While in Hamada's art re-enactment competition, it is the three-dimensional, living, breathing, nature of the photographs that transforms original elements in the artwork into real objects in everyday life. Again, Benjamin's approach to translation offers insights into this process:

> It is clear that a translation, no matter how good, cannot have any significance for the original. Nevertheless, it stands in the closest connection with the original by virtue of the latter's translatability. Indeed, this connection is all the more intimate because it no longer has any significance for the original itself. It can be called a natural connection, and more precisely a vital connection. Just as expressions of life are connected in the most intimate manner with the living being without having any significance for the latter, a translation proceeds from the original. Not indeed so much from its life as from its 'afterlife' or 'survival' [überleben]. Nonetheless the translation is later than the original, and in the case of the most significant works, which never find their chosen translators in the era in which they are produced, indicates that they have reached the stage of their continuing life [Fortleben]. (Benjamin, 1997, p. 153)

By construing translation as a posteriori to the text-as-historical object – an integral part of its translational afterlife – we alleviate ourselves of the burden of looking backwards, to the perceived loss of substance the source text suffers when it is translated. If we construe translation as a forward-looking writing practice, which proceeds *from* the text but does not overwrite it, then we need not view translation as the obliteration of the source, since its lifeline continues *in spite of* the translation. Paradoxically, then, while the translation's very life-force depends upon the existence of the source, the source is free to enjoy a life of its own.

Benjamin illustrates this idea with the example of the translational 'tangent' and its relationship to the source text 'circle' from which it proceeds. Touching the circle at only the brief and single point of encounter in time and space between a text and a translator, the tangent of translation moves on to take its own course, creating a life and a future of its own (1996, p. 261). For translation to create something 'new' from an existing idea, there must first be an acknowledgement both of the value of the original idea from which such newness is inspired and the point at which such newness will depart from the original. Translation is a simultaneous embracing of the possibilities of departure and an acknowledgement of the place from which its journey begins. In the curation of both Hamada and July's series, for example, it is interesting to note that the 'source' material on which these translations are based is always actively referenced, whether through the provision of a still from the classic film, in the case of July's study of movie extras, or whether in the provision of a descriptive text and image to accompany the provision of the original artwork in the remake project. In effect, the source continues to live on within and inside the translation, because without it the artist's performative effect could not be achieved. The creative work of restaging and re-enacting depends on the audience's prior knowledge of the source and the translation acquires its status precisely because of the visible presence of the source within it. Rather than loss, containment and annihilation, translation of this sort is celebratory, for its very value lies in the audience's knowledge and awareness of the source on which it is based. Translation thus honours the original precisely because its very success depends on its relation with, and not replacement of, the source on which it is based. In both cases, the source is far from diminished but is in fact augmented – whether in Hamada's case adding to the prestige of the original masterpieces through creative imitation, adding to their Benjaminian 'fame', or in July's case shining a spotlight on hitherto overlooked human presences in the original films. In each of these cases, translation includes even as it excludes. It incorporates and contains, but it also builds upon and celebrates. In the Spanish sense of the word *presenciar*, both to be present *and* to bear witness to, appropriation thus functions to *presence* the source rather than to absent it.

Translation as renovation

In hermeneutic terms, what first appears to be a gesture of possessive approximation, overcoming the distance by containing the foreign, is in fact a more nuanced process of refutation *and* recognition, of repudiation and embracement across a distance. For Ricoeur, it is 'a proximity which suppresses and preserves the cultural distance and includes the otherness within the ownness' (1976, p. 43) To read, to translate, is to both preserve and to overcome distance. It is an act of intercultural outreach that simultaneously confirms the presence of difference, acknowledges the challenges to understanding it poses and welcomes the creative possibilities it offers. It is for this reason that translation is not totally totalizing. Although a profound intention lurks behind interpretation, 'that of overcoming distance and cultural differences and of matching the reader to a text which has become foreign, thereby incorporating its meaning into the present comprehension a man is able to have of himself' (Ricoeur, 2004, p. 4), by incorporating such differences within the domain of the local, translation is something other than 'overcoming' otherness, since the otherness continues to intend on the translation in ways that mean it is never truly obliterated. As Benjamin remarks, 'A real translation is transparent; it does not cover the original, does not block its light, but allows the pure language, as though reinforced by its own medium, to shine upon the original all the more fully' (1999, p. 79). When we focus only on what has been lost to the distance we miss out on what can also be gained. Because it is through interpretation that we understand the text, and that which we 'understand' is our own construction of that which the text presents to us, interpretation involves breathing new life into the text. It means riches are released. It is, to recall a previous metaphor, a moon that both illuminates, as well as obscures the source. In this, appropriation's positive, 'compensatory', side emerges, for translation can offer the text a range of survival it would otherwise lack:

> The relations of a text to its translations, imitations, thematic variants, even parodies, are too diverse to allow of any single theoretic, definitional scheme. They categorize the entire question of the meaning of meaning in time, of the existence and effects of the linguistic fact outside its specific, initial form. But there can be no doubt that echo enriches, that it is more than shadow and inert simulacrum. We are back at the problem of the mirror which not only reflects but also generates light. The original text gains from the orders of diverse relationship and distance established between itself and the translations. The reciprocity is dialectic: new 'formats' of significance are initiated by distance and by contiguity. Some translations edge us away from the canvas, others bring us up close. (Steiner, 1998, p. 317)

The transformative nature of translation can thus be seen as an end in itself. In the case of the art-selfie, where gallery spectators photograph themselves in front of a famous work of art, it is tempting to view this as a form of mechanical reproduction that does 'harm' to the original. It is common for galleries to have a formal policy on visitor photography, for example, with some enforcing a total ban through their network of exhibit attendants. Intellectual property, loss of income through approved merchandise, a risk to the safety of patrons or damage to property are chief concerns. Flash photography in galleries and museums is disruptive and emits light at potentially damaging ultraviolet wavelengths, while lingering crowds waving tablets and selfie sticks in the air risk obscuring works and obstructing emergency exits. From one perspective, given the cult of celebrity that surrounds paintings like Vermeer's *Girl With a Pearl Earring* (c. 1665) and Van

Gogh's *Sunflowers* (1888), without an overt camera policy, the risk of selfie-stick-related health and safety incidents increases exponentially. In the age of the digital camera, moreover, visitors no longer need to exit through the gift shop to purchase a lasting visual record of their favourite works. In the United Kingdom, where national museums established by act of parliament permit entry free of charge, the financial implications of threats both to the health and safety of their visitors and workers and to the overall bottom line are not insignificant. In a climate of diminished state-funding for the arts, however, the problem of camera-wielding visitor numbers is not helped by the commercialization of public art in recent decades – from the rise of crowd-pleasing retrospectives of established artists to museum-sponsored 'must see' lists of works. In many galleries the long-held common practice is to permit non-flash photography for 'personal, non-commercial' purposes in the main display halls where access is often free of charge, but to prohibit photography in pay-per-view commercial exhibitions. Yet some, such as the Prado, continue to uphold a total ban on photography of artworks. Indeed one of the bastions of photography-free museum spectatorship in Europe was the National Gallery in London, which changed its policy in August 2014 following the introduction of free Wi-Fi. A statement released by the National Gallery press office said:

> As the use of Wi-Fi will significantly increase the use of tablets and mobile devices within the Gallery, it will become increasingly difficult for our Gallery Assistants to be able to distinguish between devices being used for engagement with the Collection, or those being used for photography.
>
> It is for that reason we have decided to change our policy on photography within the main collection galleries and allow it by members of the public for personal, non-commercial purposes – provided that they respect the wishes of visitors and do not hinder the pleasure of others by obstructing their views of the paintings. (Furness, 2014)

Note the air of futile inevitability. There is no suggestion of any improvement in visitor experience that arises from an open policy on personal photography, only the sense that the sheer ubiquity of mobile devices makes enforcing a ban no longer sustainable. The reversal was reported as an admission of defeat in the face of camera phone technology and the death nail for quiet contemplation and deep engagement with museum exhibits. Recounting her last visit to MOMA, *Daily Telegraph* Arts Editor-in-Chief Sarah Compton wrote that the space 'was full not just of viewers but of photographers; it was impossible to stop, think and look at a painting amid the jostling crowd' (2014). It is an odd thing, she muses, the desire constantly to capture what you see, even before you have allowed yourself the chance to see it:

Presumably this is the fate that awaits the National. All those Impressionist landscapes, the Renaissance crucifixions, and Leonardo's sublime Virgin of the Rocks – just so much background for another selfie, or a group shot of your mates.

Actually, I just about understand the desire to mark one's presence in a particular spot by recording yourself there. What I absolutely fail to comprehend is the impulse to point and shoot the image in front of you. There are postcards in the shop, reproductions online. Why on earth do people want to fill their camera rolls with photographs of paintings? (Compton, 2014).

What seems to truly rankle about the use of camera phone technology in the gallery hall is the fear that our obsession with technology distracts us from the 'real' purpose of public art: to enter into thoughtful engagement with the works we see. We are generation 'clickbait', incapable of concentration in the age of short-form Internet lists. More interested in telling people what we are doing than actually doing it ourselves, we visit galleries not to look at works of art but to say we have 'seen' them. To capture works of art through the lens of a camera without appearing to look at them ourselves first is to prioritize consumption over contemplation, to record, repost and retweet, rather than reflect upon what we see. 'Today, the real permanent collection is the one we all store on the cloud', Archie Bland wrote of the National Gallery's reversal in the *Independent* (2014).

In one sense, this is only the latest stage in a much older debate. In his essay 'The Work of Art in the Age of Mechanical Reproduction', Benjamin writes of how works of art were always reproducible by hand; it was with the advent of photography in the early twentieth century that every work of art could be reproduced on a massive scale. 'Even the most perfect reproduction of a work of art is lacking in one element: its presence in time and space, its unique existence at the place where it happens to be', he writes (2005, p. 98). Reproductions have no historicity, no moment in time and space; they are timeless. The concept of 'authenticity', he observes, tends to be tied to the physical presence of the original work of art – chemical analysis of ancient manuscripts, for example, enables their provenance and age to be established. A manual reproduction of a work which dispenses with the presence of the original, tended to be branded as a forgery and the original preserved all its authority. This is not the case, however, with 'technical' reproduction:

> The reason is twofold. First, process reproduction is more independent of the original than manual reproduction. For example, in photography, process reproduction can bring out those aspects of the original that are unattainable to the naked eye yet accessible to the lens, which is

adjustable and chooses its angle at will. And photographic reproduction, with the aid of certain processes, such as enlargement or slow motion, can capture images which escape natural vision. Secondly, technical reproduction can put the copy of the original into situations which would be out of reach for the original itself. Above all, it enables the original to meet the beholder halfway, be it in the form of a photograph or a phonograph record. The cathedral leaves its locale to be received in the studio of a lover of art; the choral production, performed in an auditorium or in the open air, resounds in the drawing room. (Benjamin, 2005, pp. 98–9)

In the age of the art-selfie, gallery visitors post their photographs on Facebook and Instagram. The images can be shared, reposted, retweeted, captured by search engines and downloaded to computers all over the world. Thanks to the cultures of circulation that propagate and promulgate the spread of cultural material around the world in the blink of an eye, a grand master can hang in a gallery in New York and can feature as someone's office screensaver. With every click of the camera, swoosh of a selfie-stick and social media share, something of the majesty of the source work is diminished; its prestige, its grandeur, becomes less. And yet 'majesty' and 'prestige' are experiential qualities. The original's depreciation is not real, it is imagined. When a photo is taken of a grand master and shared on social media, copies circulate around the world, but the work itself hangs unchanged in its gallery space. Its substance, the glory of its material achievement, is undiminished.

What Benjamin describes as 'the desire of contemporary masses to bring things "closer" spatially and humanly' (2005, p. 100) is the technique of reproduction that detaches the reproduced object from the domain of 'tradition', in the sense that it facilitates the creation of many reproductions and in so doing substitutes a plurality of copies for a unique existence: 'Every day the urge grows stronger to get hold of an object at very close range by way of its likeness, its reproduction. Unmistakably, reproduction as offered by picture magazines and newsreels differs from the image seen by the unarmed eye. Uniqueness and permanence are as closely linked in the latter as are transitoriness and reproducibility in the former' (ibid.). But by allowing the reproduction to meet the receiver half way, by bringing works 'closer' in his or her own particular situation, the object that is reproduced is also reactivated. It is precisely the destructive dimension that gives rise to catharsis, the renewal of the traditional value of cultural heritage through reproduction and renovation. The same mechanics of technical reproduction that enable a work to be possessed, contained and appropriated are also the very processes that release positive change. As Nina Simon, executive director of the Santa

Cruz Museum of Art and History at the McPherson Center and author of *The Participatory Museum* (2010) writes:

> When visitors take photos in museums, few try to capture the essential essence of an object or create its most stunning likeness. Most visitors take photos to memorialize their experiences, add a personal imprint onto external artifacts, and share their memories with friends and families. When people share photos with each other, either directly via email or in a more distributed fashion via social networks, it's a way to express themselves, their affinity for certain institutions or objects, and simply to say, 'I was here'. (Simon, 2010, 176)

For Simon, an open photography policy goes hand in hand with a visitor-centred approach that is focused on participation and engagement. Restrictive policies militate against visitor inclusion and a sense of private ownership over works of art that belong to the nation. Visitors use photography and selfie-taking as a way to make meaning of their gallery, museum or exhibition experience and they do so in a way that is entirely different from their interaction with official merchandise. Photographs and selfies are records of their personal and social experiences, not deliberate or professional likenesses, of master works. This is something that cannot be bought in the museum gift shop: the experiential moment of spectatorship. A form of appropriation is at work here, but it is not one that brings damage to the source. As long as security, health and safety and flash photography restrictions are not infringed upon, it is a form of appropriation that in fact brings honour to the source material.

When people share their photos online they succeed in promoting museum content. It is free marketing for the institutions that house great works of art and which could result in increased ticket sales through increased exposure and awareness. Simon notes how digital texts have the greatest impact when consumers are able to circulate, reuse, adapt and remix them. With every Facebook share, for example, the reach of Vincent Van Gogh's *Sunflowers*, on display in the National Gallery, is extended exponentially. But more than this, it is in the creative interaction with cultural objects that photographs of museum works shared on social media enable Internet users to make meaning of the exhibits; to inhabit them in ways that make them meaningful *to them*. In the National Gallery's own explanation for relaxing the photography policy there is a recognition of both of these things: that memorialization is important to a visitor's experience and that this also brings prestige to the works that are captured. Rather than diminishing them, the works achieve an increased spotlight. According to the National's Director of Public Engagement: 'We know that when people feel inspired they often like to share the moment, so along with the free Wi-Fi service we are now welcoming visitor photography: from now on people will be able to share their experience of the Gallery and its paintings with friends and family through social media' (National Gallery, 2014).

This is about cultural translation that does not seek to reproduce but to transform. It is about adapting how we conceptualize the relationship between the text and its translation, the work and the art-selfie. When we bemoan the infinite possibilities for technical reproduction that more relaxed photography policies open up, we perceive the link as pernicious. But to view gallery photography in translational terms, proceeding from a hermeneutics of appropriation by which a spectator draws near to, contains, transforms and celebrates a work through interpretation, is to suggest that the best way to keep translation's sources alive is in fact to translate them:

> To grasp the true relationship between original and translation, we must undertake a line of thought completely analogous, in its goal, to those taken by critical epistemology in demonstrating the impossibility of a reflection theory. Just as in critical epistemology it is shown that there can be no objective knowledge, or even the claim to such knowledge, if the latter consists in reflections of the real, so here it can be shown that no translation would be possible if, in accord with its ultimate essence, it were to strive for similarity to the original. For in its continuing life, which could not be so called if it were not the transformation and renewal of a living thing, the original is changed. (Benjamin, 1997, p. 155)

As an interpretive process, 'objective' knowledge of the source is impossible; if it is likeness that we strive for then translation will always mean failure. The 'true' relationship between source and translation is altogether more messy, for while they stand in relation to one another it is not in terms of likeness. Translation's bridging of the gap between a translator and a text that is distanced both from its author and the time and space of its production and reception is makeshift at best – it is a muddling-through, a feeling of the ways, rather than a confident lead. Benjamin's famous example is the problem of 'bread' – the German *Brot* and French *pain* both intend the same object but their modes of intention are entirely different. The place they hold in society, the cultural practices they signal, are completely distinct. The two words are not interchangeable. For this reason, he writes that translation 'is only a somewhat provisional way of coming to terms with the foreignness of languages' (1999, p. 75).

If similitude is not the goal, what, then is the true task of the translator? If, as hermeneutics teaches, the making of meaning between a speaker and an interlocutor is an 'event', the act of reading creates an all-new meaning event. Thanks to writing, the world of the text breaks free from the limited world of its author and creates a similar emancipation with its reader, transported beyond the finite horizon of the original audience. The task of translation is not concerned, as previously believed, with finding, locating and uncovering – the so-called maxim 'understanding the author better than he understands himself' – but with creating, constructing and innovating. Because translation is an above all interpretive process, we need not see its 'afterlife' as a totalizing by-product of a failed imitation game but the production of something *else*. When judged from a translational perspective, then, the degree to which Lichtenstein's *Whaam!* coincides with the image from the *All American Men of War* comic book series is really not the point. As with Benjamin's translational tangent and the circle of the source text, the moment of contact between the two pieces is brief. As with the tangent, Lichtenstein's piece takes its inspiration from the comic before launching off to make its own way in the world. As the Tate exhibition guide itself states, Lichtenstein deliberately reworked his source image by changing details thoughtfully: '"I was interested in using highly charged material [in] a very removed, technical, almost engineering drawing style", Lichtenstein said' (Tate London, n.d.). Thus he retains the basic formal structure of his stimulus, but also adds to it, augments it, adapts it. By removing a chunk of mountainside from the background of the left hand panel and two fighter jets from the right, he simplified his version of Novick's original, removing some of the distractions and training the eye. Visually, the clarity of Lichtenstein's image invites the eye to follow the rocket's trajectory from the jet on the left towards its explosive impact with the jet on the right. The ball of fire the explosion releases is more vivid, more intense in shape and colour than Novick's, and by changing the colour of the letters of 'WHAAM!' from red to yellow, the eye charts a course from left to right, in parallel with the rocket's trajectory, from the yellow of the speech bubble to the explosion on the right, the colour of the letters connecting with the nucleus of the explosion at the centre of the destroyed plane. Perhaps the most arresting dimension of Lichtenstein's transformation was that he took something so small that it could be held in the hand, crumpled up and thrown away, destroyed by rains or carried away on the winds and raised it to the size of metres, not millimetres – from comic strip to canvas, a painting that could hang and draw spectators, not readers. He took something almost ordinary and in so doing his stylized transformations served to produce something political. To judge on the basis of how successfully it reproduces the original DC Comic pane, or to dismiss it as unoriginal in itself, is to miss the point. By Benjamin's measure, Lichtenstein's work is simply doing what a translation does: 'Translation is removal from one language into another through a continuum of transformations. Translation passes through continua of transformation, not abstract areas of identity and similarity' (1999, p. 70).

By embracing the continua of transformation through which the source passes we learn to better manage our translational expectations. To punish a translation for discontinuity with the source on which it is based is not only to misplace the transformative hermeneutic on which translation is predicated but also to elide the great rewards such a process affords.

Translation as revolution

Beyond the transformation of source material, what is it exactly that makes translation precisely so rewarding? When it comes to a viral video parody such as 'Bruce Springsteen & Jimmy Fallon: "Gov. Christie Traffic Jam" ("Born To Run" Parody)', which was aired on 14 January 2014 as part of the *Late Night* programme, what is it that can be gained by translation's transformational agenda? In the video, Jimmy Fallon appears as 1980s-era Bruce Springsteen, complete with sleeveless denim shirt, aviator sunglasses and a mop of curly black hair held behind a tight red bandana. Clutching a guitar he starts playing the opening chords to Springsteen's unofficial New Jersey anthem *Born to Run* (1975). The 'source' material for this translation is clear, and at the beginning the translation strategy seems to be one of maximum proximity to the source. But although Fallon's impersonation of Springsteen's voice and singing style is almost pitch perfect, we realize that the lyrics of the Springsteen original have been changed. According to the *Huffington Post*, which covered the story and transcribed the lyrics on their website, the opening lines of Fallon's parody, are:

> In the day we sweat it out on the streets stuck in traffic on the GWB
> They shut down the tollbooths of glory because we didn't endorse Christie
> Sprung from cages on Highway 9
> We got three lanes closed, so Jersey get your ass in line
> Ooohhh, baby this Bridgegate was just pay back
> It's a bitch slap to the state Democrats
> We gotta get out but we can't
> We're stuck in Governor Chris Christie's Fort Lee New Jersey traffic jam
> (Luippold, 2014).

At this point the real Springsteen joins him on stage, dressed identically to Fallon and clutching a guitar of his own. Standing together they take turns to sing the revised lyrics together. As with the phenomenon of the art re-enactment, this is a translation that vacillates between proximity and distance, at times echoing the source material closely and at others departing from it radically. As with art re-enactments, the performative effect of the translation actively depends upon the audience's prior knowledge of the source material. In such translations, the source is not elided but actively required for the translation to function. The effect in the art re-enactments is to valorize the original masterpieces, to venerate them as worthy of reproduction by attempting to reproduce them as accurately as possible in three dimensions. In the Fallon parody, the source is both seen – through the presence of Springsteen himself and the way in which Fallon is dressed – and heard – in the melody of the song and in the way in which he mimics Springsteen's voice and singing style. But the effect is different. When Fallon sings about Governor Chris Christie and bad traffic on the 'GWB', we witness a translation that not only pays tribute to Springsteen as a subject worthy of imitation but which also has a point to make. It is this that both gestures towards the true 'source' of this translation and which must be understood by its audience if it is to achieve its performative effect. The true subject of parody in this instance is not Springsteen, but Christie. The GWB is the George Washington Bridge, which connects northern Manhattan across the Hudson River with Fort Lee, New Jersey. It is one of the busiest bridges in the world and is used by millions of vehicles a year. The bridge is owned and operated by the Port Authority of New York and New Jersey, which builds and oversees much of the infrastructure critical to trade and transportation across the New York/New Jersey region. At rush-hour on 9 September 2013, and without prior warning to the public, the Port Authority closed two of the three lanes carrying traffic from New Jersey to New York. In Fort Lee the closure caused traffic chaos. Emergency medical services could not respond to emergencies, children could not get to school. For four days the world's busiest motor vehicle bridge became a car park before Patrick Foye, then executive director of the Port Authority, and who had not been informed about the closings, ordered the lanes to be reopened. On 14 September a Port Authority spokesperson emailed a statement to a local newspaper columnist claiming the lane closure was due to a traffic study. On 1 October 2013 the *Wall Street Journal* published an email sent by Foye on 13 September in which he described the closure as 'abusive', 'hasty and ill-advised' and potentially a violation of federal and state law. Soon after, the New Jersey State Assembly Transportation Committee opened an investigation (*New York Times*, 2015). On 8 January 2014 emails and text messages subpoenaed by the committee connecting appointees and associates of Christie to the closures were leaked. The cache of documents suggested that a top aide had ordered the lane closure to punish Fort Lee for not endorsing the governor for re-election. Among the documents was an email dated 13 August 2013 from Bridget Anne Kelly, a deputy chief of staff to Christie, to David Wildstein, a school colleague of Christie and director of interstate capital projects at the Port Authority. Kelly wrote: 'Time for some traffic problems in Fort Lee'. 'Got it', Wildstein replied (ibid.). Later text messages made light of buses filled with school students stuck in traffic: 'They are the children of Buono voters,' Wildstein wrote, referring to Christie's opponent Barbara Buono (Zernike, 2014). Following a 16-month investigation, US attorney for New Jersey, Paul J. Fishman, announced on 1 May 2015 indictments against Bridget Anne Kelly and Bill Baroni, former deputy executive director of the Port Authority, who were charged with nine counts, including conspiracy to commit fraud by 'knowingly converting and intentionally misapplying property of an organization receiving federal benefits' (Zernike and Santora, 2015). Wildstein pleaded guilty at the United States District Court in Newark to conspiracy to commit fraud and conspiracy against civil rights (ibid.).

Fallon's parody is a translation of its time – it fuses two distinct sources, Springsteen's *Born to Run*, with its notes of breaking free, its anthemic associations with working communities in New Jersey and the GWB scandal, adapting the former and transforming the latter irrevocably. The subsequent fusion is as reverential of Springsteen as it is scathing of the politics surrounding the traffic lane closure. It is about deliberately harnessing translation's transformative potential for very specific reasons, riffing off its source material to satirize revelations that lane closures on the world's most heavily used bridge had not been undertaken for traffic research purposes but for political payback. To read Fallon's parody in this way is to work *with*, rather than *against*, the hermeneutic flow. If, as Benjamin warns, 'the fundamental error of the translator is that he holds fast to the state in which his own language happens to be rather than allowing it to be put powerfully in movement by the foreign language' (1997, p. 163), the true task of translation is to not only give rise to the possibility of newness, but also to ensure *we are not left unchanged* in the process. We gain from Benjamin the notion that the translational encounter with otherness is not just one of interpretation, but also one in which the foreign source has the power to affect the local receiver, to emancipate it through the challenge of the foreign.

Consider a second viral video, this one produced by environmental campaign group Greenpeace in July 2014 entitled 'LEGO: Everything is NOT Awesome' (GreenpeaceVideo, 2014). The video was released as part of Greenpeace's global 'Save the Arctic' campaign to prevent Royal Dutch Shell from drilling in the Arctic waters off Alaska. Greenpeace claimed that the oil company risks destroying the region's unique marine environment and aggravating global warming. Against this backdrop, the Greenpeace video focused on a partnership between the oil company and Lego, which dated back to the 1960s. Greenpeace accused the oil giant of trying to hijack the magic of Lego and its positive associations across the world in order to distract attention from its environmental impact. Greenpeace's Arctic campaign leader said at the time: 'It is using Lego to clean up its image and divert attention from its dangerous plans to raid the pristine Arctic for oil. And it's exploiting kids' love of their toys to build lifelong loyalty it doesn't deserve. It's time for Lego to finally pull the plug on this deal' (Greenpeace, 2014). The video itself, a film short produced by London-based creative agency Don't Panic, begins innocently enough. The camera pans across a winter scene made of pieces from the Lego City Arctic range and shows floating ice, sea birds, polar bears, huskies, indigenous people fishing and ice hockey and football being played. Heavy machinery, a Shell tanker truck and Shell employees with beaming faces appear. In the background a female voice sings to a slow piano accompaniment: 'Everything is awesome/ Everything is cool when you're part of a team/ Everything is awesome/ when you're living on a dream/'. As the lyrics sound, the camera shows a Shell flag atop a flagpole, zooming out to reveal that it stands on a vast oil platform. A close up of a man in a pinstripe suit standing on the deck of the rig, smoking a cigar.

We watch as oil starts to seep from the spot where the drill dips into the ocean. It creeps across the water towards the winter wonderland in the background. Dead Lego fish float on the sea of black. A tide of thick liquid starts to engulf the peaceful scene. The fisherman, polar bear and huskies are now surrounded by the oil. Their bodies are no longer fully visible. A helpless Lego Arctic fox cub is overcome by the dark tide. As the short ends we see a polar bear scrambling to climb the last remaining iceberg in a sea of oil. On top of the iceberg is another Shell flag. The camera cuts away from the polar bear and zooms in on the encroaching oil as it covers the very last white Lego stud; the Lego logo that is printed on the circular stud is eventually covered in black. The camera zooms out and the iceberg is gone, submerged in oil. Only the Shell flag remains, rising from the black. Text flashes on screen: 'Shell is polluting our kids' imaginations. Tell Lego to end its partnership with Shell' (GreenpeaceVideo, 2014). A link to an online petition is given at the very end.

Here, as in Fallon's parodic video critique of the GWB traffic lane scandal, the Greenpeace short depends upon the prior knowledge of its audience, without which, the sheer drama of the appeal would be lost. Without this knowledge, however, the message remains clear enough: Greenpeace believes Shell is endangering the environment in the Arctic and that Lego should end its partnership with them as a result. But a familiarity with the *Lego Movie* (2014), a computer-animated action adventure set in a Lego world and which itself harks back to the stop-motion brickfilms of the 1980s and 1990s, enables Greenpeace to add irony and pathos to the appeal. The two lead characters in the *Lego Movie*, Emmet and Lucy, fight and defeat the evil Lord Business, saving the universe from his empire the Octan Corporation. When the oil engulfs the Arctic scene in the Greenpeace short, Emmet and Lucy can be seen holding hands as oil surrounds them from all sides, covering their feet and legs and rising up their bodies. Meanwhile the lead song from the *Lego Movie*, ' "Everything is Awesome!!!" Tegan and Sara featuring "The Lonely Island" ', a fast-paced and upbeat number, is covered in the Greenpeace short by a melancholy female voice. The fun of the original song is instead replaced with a slow lament. Greenpeace's message is that unlike the film, where the Lego world which Emmet and Lucy battle to protect is a happy and harmonious one, everything in the Arctic is most emphatically *not* awesome.

This is a translation that makes a virtue of the appropriative hermeneutic at the heart of every translation process: of the proliferation and extension of meanings and possibilities beyond the finite horizons of the original, fusing the cute with the diabolic and taking its audience beyond the world of a beloved children's brand and the frivolity of the *Lego Movie* and harnessing their transformation for resistant aim:

> A big motif for our campaign is the casting of the familiar with the unexpected. With the film, we decided to remix the hit theme tune of the Lego Movie 'Everything is Awesome' because we knew Lego fans would get the reference and respond to it. The track is slowed down and becomes a haunting accompaniment to the catastrophe unveiling on screen as oil floods over an impressive and intricate build. Using a cover of the Lego Movie theme tune was a risky move, but we knew we had a right under freedom of speech to parody it for our protest. And we chose to take the risk of copyright conflict because we were sure the irony wouldn't be lost on Lego fans. The song got our message across better than anything else could. (Polisano, 2014)

Greenpeace organized other campaign activities, including delivering the petition to the company door in Denmark, setting up tiny banners on the models of Big Ben and the Eiffel Tower in Legoland in Windsor and distributing 5,000 mini figures to dozens of local groups to take to Lego stores and engage directly with the public. According to the video's makers, it has received over seven million views, over 57,000 YouTube 'likes', over 150,000 Facebook and Twitter shares and driven over 680,000 petition signatures (Don't Panic, n.d). On 9 October 2014 it was announced that Lego would not renew its marketing contract with Shell. Steiner writes that no language, no cultural ensemble or symbolic set imports from the outside without risk of being transformed (1998, p. 315). Translation should be an encounter with the foreign that does not leave us unchanged. If the translator's distanciation from the text means appropriation will always transform the text in irrevocable ways, an opportunity exists to turn this transformative hermeneutic into creative, resistant, potential to deliberately disrupt the status quo and perhaps even to change hearts and minds along the way.

5

Emancipation

Translation as a critique of ideology

On 19 May 2015 Belfast County Court ruled that a Christian-run bakery in Northern Ireland had discriminated against a customer by refusing to fulfil an order for a cake carrying the words 'Support Gay Marriage' which was intended for a private function marking the International Day against Homophobia. Gareth Lee had placed the order on 9 May 2014 at a Belfast branch of Ashers Baking Company and paid in full for a cake bearing the image of Sesame Street puppets Bert and Ernie and with a logo of campaign group QueerSpace. Two days later the company contacted him to say the order could not be processed. In October 2014 the Equality Commission for Northern Ireland, which has a statutory duty to enforce anti-discrimination legislation, brought a case against Ashers on behalf of Lee and following a three-day hearing in May 2015, a judge ruled that the firm had discriminated against Lee on the grounds of sexual orientation. In her courtroom remarks, District Judge Isobel Brownlie stated:

> My finding is that the Defendants cancelled this order as they oppose same sex marriage for the reason that they regard it as sinful and contrary to their genuinely held religious beliefs. Same sex marriage is inextricably linked to sexual relations between same sex couples which is a union of persons having a particular sexual orientation. The Plaintiff did not share the particular religious and political opinion which confines marriage to heterosexual orientation. The Defendants are not a religious organization; they are conducting a business for profit and, notwithstanding their genuine religious beliefs, there are no exceptions available under the 2006

Regulations which apply to this case and the Legislature, after appropriate consultation and consideration, has determined what the law should be (*Gareth Lee v Ashers Baking Co Ltd et al* [2015], at 43).

Outside the courtroom, Paul Givan, of the Democratic Unionist Party (DUP) and member of the Legislative Assembly for the Lagan Valley constituency, spoke to assembled media about the ruling and was recorded by the *Belfast Telegraph* giving the following statement:

> There will be deep consternation right across the community in Northern Ireland at this finding that a Christian family that have conducted themselves with the utmost graciousness and dignity throughout this case have been found guilty of discrimination. The challenge to the politicians in Northern Ireland is to what type of society we are going to live in. Is it a society where Christians are to be subject to this type of attack on their faith, because that's what it is regarded amongst the religious belief; that this is an attack and an assault on people's deeply held sincere convictions. (Williamson, McAleese and McKeown, 2015)

The 'challenge to the politicians in Northern Ireland' is a reference to the DUP's plans for a so-called conscience clause that would enable Christian businesses to lawfully restrict the provision of goods and services to individuals where the provision of such would conflict with the religious beliefs of the business owners. On 8 December 2014, several months prior to the ruling and following the Equality Commission's initial decision to bring legal proceedings against Ashers in October 2014, the DUP released a consultation document entitled 'Consultation on the Northern Ireland Freedom of Conscience Amendment Bill'. The document was circulated in support of a planned Private Members Bill to the Northern Ireland Assembly in which Givan would propose to amend the Equality Act (Sexual Orientation) Regulations (Northern Ireland) 2006. According to the DUP website, 'The document provides the background to this Bill being brought forward, including recent legal action taken by the Equality Commission. It also outlines a range of questions for those responding to the consultation as well as a copy of proposed draft legislation which would be introduced' (DUP, 2014). In the language of the draft legislation, businesses would be granted an 'exception based on religious belief' to the provisions of the equality act such that:

> Nothing in these Regulations shall make it unlawful (a) to restrict the provision of goods, facilities and services; or (b) to restrict the use or disposal of premises, so as to avoid endorsing, promoting or facilitating behaviour or beliefs which conflict with the strongly held religious

convictions of A or, as the case may be, those holding the controlling interest in A. (Givan, 2014)

In February 2015, Sinn Fein announced that it would make use of the 'petition of concern' facility, put into place to safeguard the protection of minorities from the imposition of political decisions that do not achieve cross-community support, to effectively veto the bill if it came before the Assembly. In what ways do we witness a translational agenda at work in this case and what lessons might be learned for similar examples?

Whether we conceive of appropriation as possessive or transformational, this is not the final stage in translation's hermeneutic journey. Once 'meaning' no longer coincides with what the author intended, no privileged authority exists beyond the world of the text to mediate diverging interpretations. To 'understand' the text is above all to impute significance, to different areas and different aspects, at different times and in different places. In Ricoeur's words, it is about 'producing the best overall intelligibility from an apparently discordant diversity' (2013, p. 57). Without the author to guide us, the only choice we have is to roll up our sleeves and take the plunge ourselves. Every act of reading, in this sense, is predicated ultimately upon an act of *judgement*:

> The text as a whole and as a singular whole may be compared to an object, which may be viewed from several sides, but never from all sides at once. Therefore the reconstruction of the whole has a perspectival aspect similar to that of a perceived object. It is always possible to relate the same sentence in different ways to this or that other sentence considered as the cornerstone of the text. A specific kind of onesidedness is implied in the act of reading. This onesidedness grounds the guess character of interpretation. (Ricoeur, 1976, p. 78)

Just because there is always more than one way to construe a text, however, does not mean that all interpretations are equal. While there are no rules for making 'good' guesses, there are methods for validating the guesses that we do make (p. 76). It is the reader's job to show that their interpretation of a text is more probable than any other. This is something other than showing that one reader's conclusion is 'true' while another's is 'false'. Validation is not the same as 'verification': 'it is an argumentative discipline comparable to the juridical procedures used in legal interpretation, a logic of uncertainty and of qualitative probability' (p. 78). Judges, for example, have discretionary powers with regard to the law precisely because we say there is 'room for interpretation'. In order to ensure that a judge's ruling is not arbitrary, their interpretation is subjected to validation – precedents are consulted, evidence is presented, arguments are made, interpretations are defended or prosecuted, and, on the balance of probability and in the light of the available evidence, conclusions are weighed. Like the parties to a legal case, readers must build their case for support, attempting to prove beyond all reasonable doubt that their interpretation is the most probable in the light of all that is known about a text. We submit our understanding to the scrutiny of the court of public opinion, we advance an argument and we await a ruling.

How do we build this case for support? What does it mean to defend an interpretation against everything that is known about a text? How do we balance the 'onesidedness' of our interpretation with the needs of maximum probability? Because guesses are always putative and open to further interpretation, we must set them against a panorama of potential meanings:

> Congruence and plenitude, these are the principles an explanation should satisfy. Plenitude has to do with probability and offers a qualitatively 'better' account. Plenitude is interested in more than sense – is about enabling a text to mean all that it possibly can mean, in the sense of its reference, to exceed and extend the boundary between the expressible and the inexpressible, this is interpretation. (Ricoeur, 2013, p. 58)

Texts contain 'clues' and they form the starting point in this process. These clues guide us towards a specific construction, in the sense that they contain 'a permission and a prohibition' by which unsuitable constructions are excluded and constructions that give 'more' meaning to the same words are allowed:

> In both cases, one construction can be said to be more probable than another, but not more truthful. The more probable is that which, on the one hand, takes account of the greatest number of facts furnished by the text, including its potential connotations, and on the other hand, offers a qualitatively better convergence between the features it takes into account. A mediocre explanation can be called narrow or forced. (ibid.)

So interpretation is judicious. It is about asking questions of the text, seeking both the fine detail and the bigger picture. If the central task of hermeneutics is to understand a mystery, in the final analysis interpretation is a guess which must be validated by others and which has the aim of terminating in comprehension. Because interpretation is an argumentative practice we must offer reasons that are relevant and convincing if we are to determine which guesses are more plausible than others and demonstrate the relative superiority of one conflicting interpretation over another. This is not a linear progression from ignorance to understanding but is a circular process of endless enquiry that is subject to historical incompleteness. It is a reminder that human understanding is an ongoing work of contestation.

A hermeneutics of trust and suspicion

Guesswork, validation, probability and plenitude – none of this can proceed without our initial investment in the text as the site of the clues we need. But while we trust in the presence of something mysterious that demands to be understood, we must also remain suspicious, ever watchful for the ways in which our interpretation could be shown to be less valid than we thought it was. Give any 'text' of meaning to a group of people, and whether the object of interpretation is drawn from the world of letters or from the world of human action all around us, each individual will 'read' something different. This is because our response to a text results from a particular way of reading – a hermeneutic strategy. Our construction of a text is not a methodological 'truth' universally acknowledged. The conclusions we draw are tendentious by their very nature. So we proceed with caution; we must be determined to test against the highest standards of reason every claim we believe a text is making. Wise words come to us by way of Humpty Dumpty, who remarks to Alice,

> 'There's glory for you!'
> 'I don't know what you mean by "glory", Alice said.
> Humpty Dumpty smiled contemptuously. 'Of course you don't – till I tell you. I meant " 'there's a nice knock-down argument for you".
> 'But "glory" doesn't mean "a nice knock-down argument", Alice objected.
> 'When I use a word,' Humpty Dumpty said in a rather scornful tone, 'it means just what I choose it to mean – neither more nor less.'
> 'The question is,' said Alice, 'whether you can make words mean so many different things.'
> 'The question is,' said Humpty Dumpty, 'which is to be master – that's all.' (Carroll, 1999, p. 213)

In the sense that we control only our own imputations, neither the author nor the reader is the 'master' of the texts that we read. Since texts offer only a limited field of constructions, moreover, the possibility that a different interpretation will emerge to challenge the primacy of our reading is ever-present. As Ricoeur maintains, 'The logic of validation allows us to move between the two limits of dogmatism and scepticism. It is always possible to argue for or against an interpretation, to confront interpretations, to arbitrate between them and to seek agreement, even if this agreement remains beyond our immediate reach' (Ricoeur, 1976, p. 79).

Present in almost every act of reading and interpretation are two interlinked dispositions of 'trust' and 'suspicion' that animate both our imputation of meaning – our understanding *into* the world of the text – and our defence of the same. This dialectic, between trust and suspicion, dogmatism and scepticism, is about refusing objectivism, whereby we claim to forget ourselves, and absolute knowledge, by which we would claim to capture the world within a single horizon. This is an approach to interpretation based on mindfulness: of the tendentiousness of appropriation and the tentativeness that surrounds the interpretations we produce as a result. Benjamin's hermeneutic model advances a similar method. 'For successful excavation', he writes, 'a plan is needed':

> Yet no less indispensable is the cautious probing of the spade in the loam; it is to cheat oneself of the richest prize to preserve as a record merely the inventory of one's discoveries, and not this dark joy of the place of the finding itself. Fruitless searching is as much a part of this as succeeding, and consequently remembrance must not proceed in the manner of a narrative or still less of a report, but must . . . assay its spade in ever new places and in the old ones delve to ever deeper layers. (Benjamin, 1999, p. 611)

Kearney describes Benjamin's approach as above all one of open-endedness. When it comes to the construction of history, for example, Benjamin argued that every stage of history was neither complete nor predetermined and open to heterogeneous readings, subverting any presumption of certainty. In such an approach, Kearney observes, not only the past but also the present must be 'brushed against the grain' so as to explode the erroneous notion that history is a continuous and progressive march towards 'progress' (1994, p. 160).

When I think of this dialectic of trust and suspicion a particular image always comes to mind. It is of a poster that hangs in the office of fictional Special Agent Fox Mulder in the television series *The X-Files* (1993–2002). The poster shows a grainy photograph of a UFO flying over a patch of green woodland. At the foot of the poster bold white text reads simply, 'I want to believe'. From his tiny room in the basement of FBI headquarters Mulder investigates the 'X-Files' – mysterious cases and unexplained events that remain unsolved. Since the disappearance of his younger sister under strange circumstances it has been Mulder's lifelong goal to find out what happened to his sister and uncover the truth about what he believes to be a government conspiracy to deny the existence of extraterrestrial life. In the pilot episode Special Agent Dana Scully, a medical doctor and instructor in the FBI academy, is assigned to the X-Files unit as Mulder's partner. Rooted in the world of science, her character stands for reason and rationality and forms the sceptical counterpoint to Mulder's unwavering belief in the paranormal and the allure of the unknown. The poster is a powerful visual metaphor for the endless circle of trust and suspicion that both characterizes and sustains Mulder's quest. Simultaneously, it is a succinct statement of his lack of understanding vis-à-vis the existence of aliens and a government cover-up, which in turn feeds his lack of belief. But it is also an earnest statement of his investment in the possibility of a government conspiracy and the existence of extraterrestrial life – that there might indeed be something *to be understood*. In declaring his lack of belief he also signs himself up to the existence of something to believe *in*. In other words, it is precisely by addressing his lack of understanding that he creates his own object to be understood. For the episode "Closure" (*The X-Files*, 2000), in which Mulder finally learns the truth about his sister's disappearance, the series tagline, 'The truth is out there', which appeared on screen each week at the end of the opening credits, was changed to 'Believe to understand'. Like the poster, it is a reminder that when it comes to the quest for understanding that directs our investigative efforts, there is no independent 'truth' except that which is constructed through the methods of understanding by which it is derived. To understand a text, we must believe that it is more than the sum of its parts, while divesting ourselves simultaneously of our presumption of understanding. In so doing, we embrace both our lack of understanding and its very possibility. In Ricoeur's terms:

> You must believe in order to understand. No interpreter in fact will ever come close to what his text says if he does not live in the aura of the meaning that is sought. And yet it is only by understanding that we can believe. The second immediacy, the second naïveté that we are after, is accessible only in hermeneutics; we can believe only by interpreting. This is the 'modern' modality of belief in symbols; expressions of modernity's distress and cure for this distress. Such is the circle: hermeneutics proceeds from the preunderstanding of the very matter which through interpretation it is trying to understand. (Ricoeur, 2004, pp. 294–5)

We interpret because there is a mystery we do not understand. Because we do not understand what we interpret, we believe. By interpreting we confirm our belief both in our lack of understanding and in the possibility of achieving it by interpreting. We must understand in order to believe but we must also believe in order to understand.

'Read' thyself

The hermeneutic circle of belief and suspicion repudiates the immediacy of understanding. It challenges the notion that we might extend to texts and actions the same empathy we extend to others in face-to-face meetings – what Ricoeur describes as the 'romantic illusion of a direct link of congeniality between the two subjectivities implied by the work, that of the author and that of the reader' (2008, p. 18). Texts are not people, and actions, once decoupled from their agents, are open to be read and interpreted in ways beyond those envisaged by their owner. In the context of translation, this calls us to reject any notion of the text-*qua*-author. The author of a text for translation cannot be recovered through translation and the translation is not the same as the author's text or what the author intended for it. 'After' and 'away' from the time and place in which the text was produced and received, 'meaning' is no longer animated by the presence of the author. Because psychological intention and textual meaning no longer coincide, readers are at a distance from the text. The only course of action is to involve oneself directly in the process of meaning-making. Or, as Ricoeur suggests, 'I must quit the position, or better, the exile, of the remote and disinterested spectator in order to appropriate in each case an individual symbolism' (2004, p. 294). In other words, we must go from asking what is the meaning of a phenomenon – the symbol, the text, the action, the *other* – to asking what these things mean *to me*? Or, more accurately, how do I *make* them mean?

This insight sets into motion a fundamental reorientation of the task of interpretation. It suggests first and foremost that the answers to the mysteries of the world do not lie 'out there', with some*thing* or some*one* else, but in here, with me, the one doing the interpreting:

> If we can no longer define hermeneutics in terms of the search for the psychological intentions of another person which are concealed *behind* the text, and if we do not want to reduce interpretation to the dismantling of structures, then what remains to be interpreted? I shall say: to interpret is to explicate the type of being-in-the-world unfolded *in front of* the text. (Ricoeur, 2008, p. 82, original emphasis)

Rather than the revelation of mystery, the primary focus of Ricoeur's hermeneutic philosophy is the question of 'who': who is it that is interpreting, who says what, who does what, about whom and about what does one construct a narrative, who is morally responsible for what is interpreted? Hermeneutics remains a play of the distanciation that bears meaning apart from the intention of its author and the appropriative drive to make familiar what is far – spatially, temporally, geographically, linguistically and culturally. In the process, the text is decoupled from its own context of production and reception and is reconstituted in the time and place of the interpreter, transforming it irrevocably. But when it comes to appropriation something is also transformed in the person doing the appropriating. To understand, we must step off the interpretive precipice into the unknown. We make our best guess and take our chances. But we might misstep. The validity of our position vis-à-vis the object of interpretation could be challenged. Our interpretation could be shown to be less likely or less probable than another. Because we must defend our interpretation while also acknowledging that our interpretation could be invalidated, appropriation is not so much a possession of the world around us as a *dispossession* of the certainty with which we might presume to understand it. A conflict of interpretations is always inevitable because there is no such thing as absolute knowledge, and 'truth' is not a finality to be arrived at but a 'wager' to be asserted. It is a reminder that the interpretive ground from which we venture into the hermeneutic abyss is never secure. By placing ourselves under suspicion we remember that our own particular interpretive constellation is simply one in a whole galaxy of possibilities.

Consider what this means for the interpreter. If objects are not transparent unto themselves and understanding is always tentative, then reflection on the world is not simply a matter of intellectual intuition. It is, in Ricoeur's conceptualization, 'the making explicit of this ontological understanding, an understanding always inseparable from a being that has initially been thrown into the world' (2008, p. 14). Precisely by renouncing what Ricoeur describes as 'the dream of a total mediation', we expose the fallacy of the interpreting subject as 'first truth' (p. 17). It is not the fulcrum around which all things turn but a being-in-the-world engaged as much in the activity of interpreting others as it is in the activity of being interpreted by them in return. The consequences of this are profound. By challenging the idealist doctrine that the self is knowable to itself, Ricoeur's hermeneutic ontology rejects the temptation to reduce being to being-for-consciousness: I 'think', therefore I 'am'. Against the tradition of the *cogito* Ricoeur maintains that the self is not a priori but 'posited' (1995, p. 19). To achieve selfhood it is not enough merely to think; we only 'become' when we locate ourselves in the context of our existence as a being that exists with, alongside and in response to others:

> The first truth—*I think, I am*—remains as abstract and empty as it is unassailable. It must be 'mediated' by representations, actions, works, institutions, and monuments which objectify it; it is in these objects, in the largest sense of the word, that the *ego* must both lose itself and find itself. We can say that a philosophy of reflection is not a philosophy of consciousness if, by consciousness, we mean immediate self-consciousness. (Ricoeur, 2004, p. 323, original emphasis)

Like consciousness, which cannot conceive of itself by itself, and which does so only by going outside of itself to experience that which it is not, the self-before-others is not a given. It can only understand itself through the long detour across 'the signs of humanity deposited in cultural works' that lie outside our immediate consciousness (Ricoeur, 2008, p. 84). The journey from the self to the self across the significations of history and culture by which we constitute the world around us thus follows a circular motion, directing itself away from the self before arching back again. In this way, the self becomes so inextricably linked to the world that there *is* no cogito except a self that is 'mediated' through the texts, ideas, actions, works, institutions and monuments that construct it in return – the 'objectifications' of the world all around us. For Ricoeur, this final stage of distanciation 'is the ruin of the ego's pretension to constitute itself as ultimate origin' (2008, p. 35).

If self-understanding is postponed until the end, after the subject's long detour across the terrain of the other and back again, then to *know* oneself is to understand how one relates to others and what this relation means. Interpretation is therefore about *resisting* the self; it is about dissipating the 'illusion' of self-knowledge through intuition by forcing our self-understanding to pass first through the signs of the external world before coming to existence itself:

> That appropriation does not imply the secret return of the sovereign subject can be attested to in the following way: it if remains true that hermeneutics terminates in self-understanding, then the subjectivism of this proposition must be rectified by saying that to understand *oneself* is to understand oneself *in front of the text*. Consequently, what is appropriation from one point of view is disappropriation from another. To appropriate is to make what was alien become one's own. What is appropriated is indeed the matter of the text. But the matter of the text becomes my own only if I disappropriate myself, in order to let the matter of the text be. So I exchange the *me*, the *master* of itself, for the *self, disciple* of the text. The process could also be expressed as a *distanciation of self from itself* within the interior of appropriation. (Ricoeur, 2008, p. 35, original emphasis)

If appropriation is about understanding oneself in front of the text, the text is now the very *medium* through which we come to an understanding of ourselves. Distanciation and appropriation thus operate as two sides of the same interpretive coin, where multiple dialectics of containment and transformation, inclusion and exclusion, ensure that the terminal phase of interpretation is not to understand another but *ourselves*.

Holding a mirror up to nature

There is something transformational in this, as much for the interpreter as for the text that is being interpreted. By appropriating meanings that have been distanciated from our consciousness we expose ourselves to these other horizons. This has the effect of enabling us to transcend the limits of our own subjectivity, of the familiarity of the local and the security of the known, to open ourselves up to the possibility of others, to the existence of other modes and other worlds of thinking. Because meaning 'is never first and foremost *for me*', Ricoeur explains, we possess the other while dispossessing *ourselves* (In Kearney, 1994, p. 94). Appropriation is therefore not only one half of the dialectical partnership; it brings about a profound change in self-understanding:

> Far from saying that a subject already mastering his own way of being in the world projects the *a priori* of his self-understanding on the text and reads it into the text, I say that interpretation is the process by which disclosure of new modes of being – or if you prefer Wittgenstein to Heidegger, of new forms of life – gives to the subject a new capacity for knowing himself. If the reference of the text is the project of a world, then it is not the reader who primarily projects himself. The reader rather is enlarged in his capacity of self-projection by receiving a new mode of being from the text itself. (Ricoeur, 1976, p. 94)

For the reading subject, interpretation is above all a transformative experience in which we gain ourselves precisely by losing ourselves in the process. Through the long detour across the terrain of the other and back again we receive a 'truncated ontology' by which we come to see ourselves above all as beings-before-others. By seeing ourselves from the outside our consciousness becomes heightened. A 'second naïveté' reminds us that neither the subjectivity of the reader nor the author, neither the self nor the other, comes first:

> The first function of understanding is to orientate us in a situation. So understanding is not concerned with grasping a fact but with apprehending a possibility of being. We must not lose sight of this point when we draw the methodological consequences of this analysis: to understand a text, we shall say, is not to find a lifeless sense that is contained therein, but to unfold the possibility of being indicated by the text. (Ricoeur, 2008, p. 64)

By unseating the authority with which the cogito presumes to self-assert, the ego is made to 'assume for itself the "imaginative variations" by which it could *respond* to the "imaginative variations" on reality that literature and poetry, more than any other form of discourse, engender' (p. 35, original emphasis). Understanding is not about capturing these 'imaginative variations', therefore, but receiving from them the possibility of increased self-knowledge. Instead of asking, 'how and what do we know', the hermeneutic detour requires us to ask instead, what is the mode of being of the one who exists only in relation with others?'

This is theorization that seeks to shatter the subject's desire to set itself up as the measure of objectivity. It insists that it is only by reaching outwards to the external world that we discover who we are. In the encounter with other people, other ideas, other ways of thinking and acting, interpretation requires us not only to face up to the existence of other subjectivities, other modes of thought and other modes of expression but also to be changed by them in the process. By transforming the experience of the reader in the encounter with otherness, taking us out of our comfort zone, estranging us in the foreign terrain of the unknown, reading serves a critical function – what Kaplan describes in his study of Ricoeur as 'displacing the illusions of subjectivity'. In so doing, Kaplan maintains, Ricoeur combines a hermeneutics of trust and suspicion with a hermeneutics of the text, linking the power of the text to *reveal* with the critique of subjectivity by which the self is revealed to itself, and, in the revealing, is changed (2012, p. 36).

What does it mean to hold a mirror to nature in this way? In what sense is the self revealed to itself when we deploy interpretation beyond the realm of the text, to engage with the actions of human beings? With 'Britain Furst', which uses social media platforms to upload satirical images disguised as Islamophobic or anti-immigrant invective and designed to mock the social media strategy of the real 'Britain First', we see these claims in action. Britain First is a far-right movement led by former British National Party councillor Paul Golding and describes itself as a 'patriotic political party' (Britain First, n.d.). On the group's Facebook page, a statement of principles includes the following: 'Britain First is committed to preserving our ancestral ethnic and cultural heritage, traditions, customs and values. We oppose the colonisation of our homeland through immigration and support the maintenance of the indigenous British people as the demographic majority within our own homeland. Britain First is committed to maintaining and strengthening Christianity as the foundation of our society and culture' (Britain First, n.d.). The group is known for its direct action mosque invasions, protest marches and for its frequent use of the image of Lee Rigby, a twenty-five-year-old British Army Fusilier killed on 22 May 2013 near the Royal Artillery Barracks in southeast London by Michael Adebowale and Michael Adebolajo, who stated on video immediately after the attack that 'The only reason we have killed this man today is because Muslims are dying daily by British soldiers. And this British soldier is one. It is an eye for an eye and a tooth for a tooth. By Allah, we swear by the almighty Allah we will never stop fighting you until you leave us alone' (*The Telegraph*, 2013). Ahead of standing candidates in Wales for the European elections on 22 May 2014, Britain First registered its party description as 'Remember Lee Rigby'. This description was approved by the political registrations watchdog the Electoral Commission and printed on all ballot papers in Wales, a move for which the Commission has since apologized (Electoral Commission, 2014).

The group is also known for the reach and frequency of its viral marketing campaign strategy and use of social media to share emotive imagery and messages of a nationalist or anti-immigration nature across audiences on a massive scale. The group uses social media to raise funds and in July 2015 came first in the Electoral Commission's donations league table for smaller political parties in the United Kingdom (BBC, 2015). Its tweets and Facebook posts are visually arresting, often written in capital letters and tend to focus towards the histrionic, featuring 'share if you agree' calls to action superimposed over images of Winston Churchill, the knights of the Crusades and the British and English flags. With over one million 'likes', Britain First's Facebook page reaches a vast online audience and it has been reported that as many as two million people interact with its online content daily (Wheelan, 2014). A survey of posts by Britain First on 12 November 2015 includes a mocked-up *Sun* newspaper front page headline, 'Britain First declares war on Muslim extremists' (Britain First, 2015a); a link to an authentic *Daily Mail* article on the trial at Bradford Crown Court of thirteen men and a seventeen-year-old charged with twenty-eight sexual offences against a girl when she was thirteen and fourteen, which Britain First described in the attached status update as 'A BAD CASE OF MUSLIM GROOMING....' (Britain First, 2015b); and 'OBAMA, THE MUSLIM SOCIALIST, IS A FAILURE AS A PRESIDENT!' which appeared as a status update attached to an image of the words 'Like if you agree the Obama presidency is a disaster!' (Britain First, 2015c).

The 'Britain Furst' Facebook page, meanwhile, run by blogger Gareth Arnoult, shares posts of a similarly histrionic nature, but with a very different intention, for these posts are not made in earnest. They are designed to piggyback on Britain First's emotive content circulation strategy and are crafted deliberately to be as ridiculous, as melodramatic and as apparently xenophobic as possible, in a bid to lampoon the very people who support Britain First. Britain Furst's satirical posts have been covered by numerous media outlets, including the *Guardian*, the *Independent*, the *Daily Express*, the *Huffington Post* and *Vice*, as well as numerous online blogs. On 9 November 2015, for example, Britain Furst posted a mocked-up image of a vast queue of people waiting at 'UK Border Controls' overlaid with the words 'Immigrants are trying to force David Cameron to ban Christmas because it offends them. Share to tell David Cameron not to cancel Christmas. This is our country, not there's. Keep Christmas British'. The image was accompanied by a status message reading, 'KEEP CHRISTMAS BRITISH' (Britain Furst, 2015).

Recall that in Ricoeur's approach interpretation is about increasing self-knowledge through the journey outwards to the domain of the other, unseating the authority with which we assert our own existence and receiving from this journey the possibility of increased self-knowledge through the realisation that understanding is not a given. 'Meaning', in this sense, exists only in the relational interplay, in the 'imaginative variations' between a self and another. Interpretation causes us to reflect upon who we are in relation to others and, in so doing, to achieve a heightened sense of consciousness. What, then, do Arnoult's own 'imaginative variations' on the themes of Islamophobia and anti-immigration engender with regard to the agenda of Britain First? What mirror to nature do they hold? In an interview with *Vice* about the satirical news website 'British Fake News Network', his companion project to Britain Furst, Arnoult said:

> One of the things I don't like on the site is when you get people going, 'Can't believe this. Bloody Muslims.' Those things you expect from people who don't realise it's satire – fine. But it's the next guy going, 'You're an idiot, you don't get it do you?'. What good's that going to do? They might not be the most critically-thinking of people, but you're never going to get them back into the mainstream of politics if you're just going to belittle them. The people who are going, 'You people are bigots, you're racists, you're scum' are just satisfying their own egos. (Haynes, 2015)

The outworkings of this strategy – to encourage critical thinking, to bring to thoughtful reflection rather than foster marginalized entrenchment – can be seen in action on another Facebook timeline, that of the *Guardian* newspaper. On 20 June 2014 the *Guardian* posted a link to its own article on Britain Furst, with the status, 'In a few years, we'll all be wearing Muslamic Ray-Bans' (*Guardian*, 2014). The article covered a post by Britain Furst in which the image of a pair of Ray-Ban sunglasses with a halal sticker over one lens has been overlaid with the words 'Muslamic Ray-Bans/ Ray-Ban have been forced to make "halal" sunglasses. SHARE IF YOU THINK THIS IS A DISGRACE!!!!' (Walsh, 2014). The first comment from a Facebook user in response to the *Guardian*'s post promoting the Ray-Ban article summarizes incisively the effect and impact of Arnoult's own agenda:

> If media attention given to 'Britain Furst' highlights the ridiculousness of the ignorant and xenophobic posts from the actual 'Britain First' fascist page, then that is only a good thing in my opinion. Whether you think that the page itself is funny or not. […] 'Britain Furst' is the direct opposition to the real far-right 'Britain First' page. How is it not constructive to take their posts and make a mockery of them, pointing out their shortsightedness and the fallacies of their arguments in order to show people how wrong they are? It sounds very constructive to me. 'Britain Furst' is quite obviously a parody page since the idea of 'halal sunglasses' is quite obviously ludicrous.

> The more people point out the idiocy of the ideologies of pages like 'Britain First' the less likely people are to follow their page or to agree with the admin running it. (*Guardian*, 2014)

Viewed through a hermeneutic lens, this user's comments suggest that the satirical posts circulated by Britain Furst have functioned as interpretative journeys across the terrain of anti-Islamic sentiment that flourishes in the online environment. Riffing off the topics of greatest concern to the real Britain First, Britain Furst promulgates its own imaginative variations on these themes, using the devices of satire and parody to – in the words of the Facebook commenter – 'point out their short sightedness' and 'make a mockery of them'. As such, Britain Furst serves to 'highlight the ridiculousness' of Britain First by demonstrating that at a time of political and economic instability the worldview promoted by the latter is but one way of characterizing urgent questions of respect, tolerance, asylum, freedom of movement and border security. If the campaign work carried out by Britain First is shown to be just one hermeneutic guess among many, valid for some but 'short sighted' and 'fallacious' for others, something of the certainty with which Britain First presumes to speak for the people of the United Kingdom with regard to issues of immigration, among others, is diminished, and with it, the illusions of the party as both a speaking, and acting, subject.

Saving us from ourselves

How can interpretation's critique of the subject be operationalized in such a way that we might critique ideology itself? It is here that cultural translation makes its most significant contribution in three key domains. In its broadest terms, understanding always remains within the historical limits of the hermeneutic circle. By this, we mean that the work of alterity that hermeneutics addresses – the distanciation of a reader from the time and place in which a text was written and the distanciation of an author from the time and place in which the text is read – finds its echo in the work of alterity at the heart of our selfhood. Like the distanciation that separates a text from its reader, the other stands in contrast to the self. But just as the other stands before the self, the self also stands before the other. This other is another self and both are at a distance from one another. In the final analysis, each occupies the same position in this circle of distanciation and appropriation, as an 'othered' self in the face of another self engaged in the process of 'othering' the other self. When we interpret within this context we make a hermeneutic wager: that our self-comprehension will be enhanced rather than diminished as we make our way around the hermeneutic circle, reaching outwards to the world of the other before returning to the domain of the self. In so doing, our consciousness is heightened. The more we engage ourselves in the explanation of alien meanings, in other words, the better placed we are to understand our own inner meaning. Ricoeur's dictum, 'the shortest route from self to self is through the other' expresses his conviction that self-knowledge is achieved only in the encounter with otherness. The self can never be self-*sufficient* without the signs and signals of meaning that come from the other. As Kearney explains, because there can be no one true reading of a text, we find ourselves 'condemned' to a conflict of interpretations and for Ricoeur, this condemnation has a positive effect:

> Because my ontological self-understanding as a being-in-the-world can only be 'recovered by a detour of the decipherment of the documents of life' – that is, by means of a hermeneutic critique of the various 'signs' of existence – it always remains a *desire to be*, a project of interpretation that can never be completed in any total sense. Finding ourselves thus exposed to an inevitable plurality of interpretations, we learn that a philosophy of consciousness which holds to the hegemonic claims of the cogito is a philosophy of *false* consciousness. To reduce the *desire to be* to the immediacy of self-consciousness, removing it from the mediating detour of interpretation, is to hypostasise it. But the *desire to be* can never relinquish its role as a *being-interpreted*. (Kearney, 1994, p. 104, original emphasis)

By reaching outwards to the world of the other, we dispossess ourselves of the self-confidence with which we presume to understand. This has the effect of broadening our horizon of experience and transforming who we are and how we understand ourselves as living, acting, beings in the world (Kaplan, 2012, p. 36). To interpret others, in other words, is to become who we are. Though ostensibly directed towards understanding the world of the other, interpretation in fact has the effect of revealing the self to itself: 'The selfhood of oneself implies otherness to such an extent that one cannot be thought of without the other, one passes into the other. It is thus the growth of his own understanding of himself that he pursues through his understanding of the other. Every hermeneutics is thus, explicitly or implicitly, self-understanding by means of understanding others' (Ricoeur, 1995, p. 16).

As human beings we remain incomplete until we interpret others and are interpreted by them in return. We gain life by engaging in the conflict of interpretations. We *exist* insofar as we interpret. Rather than abandon speculation altogether, it is precisely the fallibility of our interpretation across a distance that invites us to think *more*, to think *differently* and to think *better*.

As we interpret, we learn, we develop, and we transform ourselves. Corresponding to the appropriation of proposed worlds offered by the text is the 'disappropriation' of the self. Interpretation implies self-interpretation, thus any discourse that challenges authority may also challenge one's self-understanding. Self-reflection turns into critical reflection when it identifies the limits of understanding in order to determine legitimate and illegitimate prejudices and authority. Any interpretation that exposes the illusions of the subject functions in the same way as a critique of ideology. (Kaplan, 2012, p. 39)

If discourse that challenges authority may also challenge one's self-understanding, and if critique follows the exposure of the illusions of the subject, how do we actually make use of interpretation to these ends? What might it look like to deploy interpretation in a strategic effort to critique ideology? The answer lies not just in using subversive discourse to challenge the authority of an agent or institution of ideology. If critique of ideology is only secured when a subject's illusions are exposed through the interpretive detour across the terrain of otherness, then the key to operationalizing interpretation for emancipatory purposes is to ensure that the agents and institutions of ideology *become interpreting subjects themselves*. That is, to *place* the subjects of power in a position whereby they are required both to undertake a journey of understanding across a distance, and, in doing so, to achieve a heightened sense of the fallibility of their own presumptions to knowledge as a result. In other words, by translating back to the agents and institutions of ideology their own ideologically marked translations of others. In this way, they are brought into a hermeneutic circle by which they are required to engage with a conflict of interpretations. Their interpretation is exposed as only one hermeneutic guess among many and they are required to build a case for support for the validity of theirs above all others. Whether their guess is proven to be less probable an interpretation or not, by facing the possibility of other perspectives, other possible ways of construing the world, something of their horizon is expanded and with it something of the certitude with which the agents and institutions of authority speak for the world is also transformed. In this, Ricoeur asserts, we start to achieve a critique of ideology.

Self-knowledge through interpretation

Let us consider two recent cases in which the refusal of a service had been justified on grounds of religious conscience and the different forms of opposition that were posed in response. What might it mean, for example, to deploy one's 'discourse' in order to challenge the 'authority' of Kentucky clerk Kim Davis to refuse same-sex marriage licenses in Rowan County? On 26 June 2015 same-sex marriages became legal across the United States, following a supreme court ruling that the constitution grants gay couples 'equal dignity under the law'. In the weeks following the ruling Davis refused to issue any marriage licenses and in July 2015 two same-sex and two opposite-sex couples brought legal proceedings against her. In the subsequent federal court hearing she said that the first amendment to the US constitution gave her the right not to issue marriage licenses to same-sex couples, because to do so would violate her religious beliefs. In a statement posted to the website of the Liberty Counsel, a Christian legal aid group that had been engaged in representing Davis, she said:

> I never imagined a day like this would come, where I would be asked to violate a central teaching of Scripture and of Jesus Himself regarding marriage. To issue a marriage license which conflicts with God's definition of marriage, with my name affixed to the certificate, would violate my conscience. It is not a light issue for me. It is a Heaven or Hell decision. For me it is a decision of obedience. I have no animosity toward anyone and harbor no ill will. To me this has never been a gay or lesbian issue. It is about marriage and God's Word. It is a matter of religious liberty, which is protected under the First Amendment, the Kentucky Constitution, and in the Kentucky Religious Freedom Restoration Act. Our history is filled with accommodations for people's religious freedom and conscience. I want to continue to perform my duties, but I also am requesting what our Founders envisioned – that conscience and religious freedom would be protected. (Ohlheiser, 2015)

After she defied the federal judge's order to process licenses she was taken into custody on 3 September 2015 and released on remand six days later, on the condition that she would not prevent her deputies from issuing marriage licenses. Challenges to Davis's refusal came in myriad guises, from direct confrontations with gay couples across the service counter in the clerk's office, to street protests and even the commissioning of a billboard in Davis's hometown of Morehead, Kentucky, which read: 'DEAR KIM DAVIS,/ The fact that/ you can't sell your daughter/ for three goats and a cow/ means we've already REDEFINED MARRIAGE' (Nichols, 2015). At the height of these events and as public interest in the case spiked, an anonymous Twitter account entitled 'Sitnexto Kim Davis' was set up, purporting to offer a series of insider reports on the stand-off from one of Davis's co-workers. The description for the account reads, 'I sit next to Kim Davis. This was supposed to just be a chill job. Goddamn it, Kim' (Sitnexto Kim Davis, 2014). As the tone of the description belies, this is a fictitious account of life as one of Davis's co-workers in the clerk's office. With nearly one hundred thousand followers, over four hundred satirical tweets have been posted through the account, including:

> 'I'm supposed to go to the lake on Friday, but I just realized I won't be able to get the jet ski trailer in the parking lot. #KimDavis' (Sitnexto Kim Davis, 2015a);
> '#IStandWithKimDavis – her brave stand to go to jail has made this the best BBQ in years!' (Sitnexto Kim Davis, 2015b);
> 'Todd changed the marriage forms this morning. #KimDavis name is now in 72pt font, SO EVERYONE KNOWS IT'S HER (Sitnexto Kim Davis, 2015c).

These tweets not only bemoan the media circus caused by Davis's actions, they also mock the principles on which she made her stand and question her rationale for distancing herself from same-sex marriage. According to Ricoeur's framework, however, they achieve something more. By challenging the moral authority with which Davis refused to issue marriage licenses to gay people, these four hundred satirical tweets also challenge how *we ourselves view these events*. They ask us to consider our own moral platforms vis-à-vis not only same-sex marriage but also the potentially competing interests of equality of opportunity and conscientious objection. By exposing ourselves to Davis's actions and the discursive challenges it has activated, we come to greater knowledge about where we stand as regards the legitimacy or prejudice of her actions, exposing our own moral position by tracing the contours of debate and identifying the limits of our own understanding. To engage in interpreting the Davis case is also to set about a work of interpreting *ourselves*.

When it comes to the self-improvement work of interpretation, then, it is only by engaging with ideology, by entering into interpretive debate across the terrain of difference that we acquire knowledge of our own position in the world. From the perspective of the distanciated consciousness, when it comes to challenging ideology through the interpretive devices of appropriation, therefore, the aim is not to *undo* the distance but in fact to *preserve* it, precisely so that we can achieve the critical perspective on oneself and one's culture that we need in order to evaluate them both critically:

> [Appropriation] does not purport, as in Romantic hermeneutics, to rejoin the original subjectivity that would support the meaning of the text. Rather it *responds* to the matter of the text, and hence to the proposals of meaning the text unfolds. It is thus the counterpart of the distanciation that establishes the autonomy of the text with respect to its author, its situation, and its original addressee. It is also the counterpart of that other

> distanciation by which a new being-in-the-world, projected by the text, is freed from the false evidences of everyday reality. Appropriation is the *response* to this double distanciation, which is linked to the matter of the text, as regards its sense and as regards its reference. (Ricoeur, 2008, pp. 34–5, original emphasis)

This is about conceptualizing appropriation as part and parcel of a productive relationship with difference – of opinion, idea, ideology, language, culture, history and politics – by which we would acknowledge that the very gap that separates us from the objects of our understanding is also that which opens up the possibility for fruitful debate. We need to be challenged by the difference of others precisely because it is only by entering into interpretive debate that we discover for ourselves who we are and where we stand – I interpret, therefore I exist; I exist in order to interpret. As with textual interpretation, there is no transcendental vantage point from which to ascertain if the traditions by which we live are ideologically biased. As collectivities of human endeavour, society and culture, we achieve existence only by retrieving meanings that exist first 'outside' the sociocultural phenomena by which human life is objectified. Critique can be raised in this hermeneutic circle precisely because the distance between us, between traditions, institutions and ways of living that are foreign to one another, is never fully overcome. Just as the text is always distanced both from its author and from its reader, human existence is not transparent onto itself:

> We exist neither in closed horizons nor within a horizon that is unique. No horizon is closed, since it is possible to place oneself in another point of view and in another culture. It would be reminiscent of Robinson Crusoe to claim that the other is inaccessible. But no horizon is unique, since the tension between the other and oneself is unsurpassable. (Ricoeur, 2008, p. 275)

It is for this reason that we must not shy away from bringing together parties separated by an ideological distance, as appears to be a catching trend with regard to the cancellation of guest lectures by contentious speakers on university campuses. All phenomena *can* and *should* be subjected to critique of this nature just as textual theory *can* and *should* be used to tackle the hardest questions and most difficult issues of our age. 'Distance', Kaplan explains, 'opens the possibility for critique within hermeneutics. We never belong to our horizon and tradition to the extent that we cannot reflect on the limits of our own understanding' (2012, p. 38). We must respond because we can respond – productively, imaginatively – so that we can establish our own position as opposed. Without the opportunity to enter into interpretive debate across the terrain of difference we cannot identify the contours of our own position with regard to ideology, much less seek to challenge it. Unless we respond to those who challenge us – in other words, by *participating* in the conflict of interpretations – we cannot take up a position opposed to them.

Translating ideology back to itself

We have moved from the critique of the subject towards its own transformation, through thoughtful engagement with ideology. To go from here to a place where real opposition to ideology can be effected, we must remember that it is only when a subject's illusions are exposed through the interpretive detour across the terrain of otherness that the fallibility of their own presumptions to knowledge can be exposed as a result. By translating *back* to the agents and institutions of ideology their own ideologically marked translations of others, in other words, by placing them in the position of interpreting *subjects*, enmeshed within a circle of conflicting interpretations in which their hermeneutic guesses must be articulated, defended and validated, we take the first steps towards operationalizing interpretation for emancipatory purposes in the domain of the real. On hermeneutics and the critique of ideology, Kaplan writes:

> Any critique is raised from someplace and must be expressed in language, that is, in terms of a concrete, historical context. The critique of ideology is made on the basis of a creative interpretation of a cultural heritage. It is an interpretation prejudiced by the idea that domination and exploitation are unacceptable. Hermeneutics presupposes something different and better in terms of which the object of interpretation is explained and understood. (Kaplan, 2012, p. 40)

Kaplan writes that the critique of ideology proceeds from a particular 'creative interpretation' that takes place within a concrete historical context and which starts from the presupposition that something 'different and better' exists to challenge 'domination and exploitation'. In the context of the DUP 'conscience clause', what assumptions of domination and exploitation would a critique of ideology seek to expose? What would a hermeneutics-based critique of ideology actually look like and how would it pose something different and better?

If, as Ricoeur claims, the dialectic of distanciation and appropriation is the 'last word in the absence of absolute knowledge' (1976, p. 44), then the answers lie in a return to the mechanics of interpretation itself. Remember that interpretation is predicated on an act of judgement. Once a distance of time and space opens up between the object of interpretation and the interpreter herself, 'meaning' no longer coincides with the intentions of the object's originator. The interpreter must make a stand vis-à-vis the object of interpretation and engineer its meaning for herself. In effect, interpretation represents our best 'guess' at the opportunities for meaning the object presents to us. But this does not give us free rein over the object for interpretation. Our guesses should be based on solid detective work and not all guesses are equal. They should follow thoughtful engagement with and detailed analysis of all the available information. They should stand up to scrutiny. It is the interpreter's job to show that her guess is the most likely, the most probable, the most solid case that can possibly be built in the light of everything that is known about the object of interpretation. The interpreter must therefore offer an evidence-based argument for the interpretation and they must defend it against alternative views. In short, our guesses must be submitted to a process of validation and it is a process that they must pass.

In the case of the DUP 'conscience clause', two competing interpretations appear to be in force – on the one hand, that of the DUP and Ashers Baking Company; on the other, the Northern Ireland Equality Commission on behalf of Gareth Lee. On 6 November 2014 the Commission issued a press release in which it confirmed that it had written to solicitors acting for Ashers to set out the grounds on which unlawful discrimination had been alleged. The press release noted: 'This case raises issues of public importance regarding the extent to which suppliers of goods and services can refuse service on grounds of sexual orientation, religious belief and political opinion. The Commission has issued a civil bill in this case and a decision as to whether or not discrimination has occurred will be a matter for the court' (Equality Commission, 2014). Following the judgement that the company had discriminated against Lee on the grounds of sexual orientation, meanwhile, the general manager of Ashers, Daniel McArthur said:

> We've said from the start that our issue was with the message on the cake, not the customer and we didn't know what the sexual orientation of Mr Lee was, and it wasn't relevant either. We've always been happy to serve any customers that come into our shops. The ruling suggests that all business owners will have to be willing to promote any cause or campaign no matter how much they disagree with it. Or as the Equality Commission has suggested, they should perhaps just close down, and that can't be right. But we won't be closing down, we certainly don't think we've done anything wrong and we will be taking legal advice to consider our options for appeal. (Christian Institute, 2015)

Where the translational model becomes properly critical, therefore, is in the sense of interrogating the argumentational platform on which these hermeneutic guesses are predicated.

To view as guesses both the 'conscience clause' and the claim that the refusal to fulfil the order for a cake with a message 'support gay marriage' was an act of discrimination places the translator in the role of *validator* and the DUP and Equality Commission in the role of *interpreters* – of issues of tolerance, religious and moral freedom, human rights and equality of opportunity in general and the gay cake case in particular. We therefore activate a critique of ideology on two levels. First, by conceiving of both the conscience clause and the case against Ashers as but two approaches to constructing this landscape out of many, we open up the possibility for a critique of the illusions of the subject. Second, precisely by construing the conscience clause as a hermeneutic guess we require each interpreter to submit a case for support by which its own particular view could be tested and validated. One might claim, for example, that the refusal of goods or services within this terrain could be construed not as an act of discrimination against a gay *person* but as a lack of endorsement for homosexuality as an *idea*. In this sense, the refusal to provide goods or services could be viewed as the exercise of private conscience, and, in this sense, any legal requirement to provide goods or services in contravention of one's deeply-held beliefs would be an illiberal intrusion into the Christian business-owner's right to a private life. As commentator Fionola Meredith wrote in the *Belfast Telegraph* at the time:

> If Ashers had refused to serve Gareth Lee, the LGBT activist who ordered the cake, because he was gay, then that would have been a clear act of discrimination, and the bakery's owners would have deserved to be prosecuted and fined. But that's not what happened. The message, not the customer, was the problem for Ashers. (Meredith, 2015)

By this view, what is packaged ostensibly as the enforcement of equality of opportunity law confuses actual discrimination with the exercise of one's right not to be forced to express approval for a political position with which one does not agree. The concern here is with the limitation of personal freedoms and the risk that with the pursuit of equality sometimes comes the limitation of freedom of belief. This view holds that what is intended as an attempt on the part of the Equality Commission to defend values of tolerance, justice and freedom of expression, in reality has the effect of limiting the freedom to disagree politically with positions that are at base political. This would reduce all diversity of opinion to a singular model, no less ideological, but which, even worse, is packaged as neutral and 'right'. It is on this basis that the DUP's bill was formed. Some equality legislation, Givan notes in the consultation document, 'passed with the intention of protecting minorities, is having an adverse effect on those with religious belief when it comes to the provision of goods and services. I believe that this is wrong and that there should be legislation in place that strikes a balance between the rights of people not to be discriminated against and the rights of conscience of religious believers' (Givan, 2014, p. 1).

What would a counter-claim to the DUP's position look like? What would happen, in other words, when we test the DUP's claim by bringing under hermeneutic scrutiny the 'validity' of its interpretation and its understanding of the situation? One might view the case not as a matter of religious conscience, for example, but as one where the exercise of conscience appears to conflict with the provision of goods and services which, according to the law, must be provided to all people, regardless of their sexuality. Under the provisions of the DUP's bill, Christian-run catering outlets, banks and hotels could lawfully deny a same-sex couple any service that could be perceived as endorsing or facilitating same-sex relations. A bill purporting to support the rights of a religious group could in turn restrict the rights of another group on the basis of their sexuality. But remember that the language of the bill is more generalized than this:

> Nothing in these Regulations shall make it unlawful (a) to restrict the provision of goods, facilities and services; or (b) to restrict the use or disposal of premises, so as to avoid endorsing, promoting or facilitating behaviour or beliefs which conflict with the strongly held religious convictions of A or, as the case may be, those holding the controlling interest in A. (p. 11)

By this measure, the same bill that could also allow catering outlets, banks and hotels to deny any service that could be construed as supporting same-sex relations could also be used to lawfully restrict the provision of goods and services to *anyone* exercising 'behaviour or beliefs' felt to conflict with the unspecified but 'strongly held religious convictions' of a particular business. Another view on this case questions whether the exercise of conscience should have any role in the provision of goods and services, which must be provided to all people regardless of sexuality. By this measure, the provision of goods and services need not be confused for endorsement of political opinion. One might claim, for example, that plenty of alternatives are available to Christian business owners faced with the prospect of providing goods or services in ways that are contrary to their religious beliefs. Other options could include continuing to provide the service while reserving the right not to reproduce wording deemed 'offensive'; forwarding the delivery of a service to an internal colleague not offended by the wording or outsourcing the service entirely; or advertising clearly the business's Christian values or displaying clear public notices that the provision of a particular service does not imply endorsement. Moreover, if the only way to validate a hermeneutic guess is through argumentation and if the eventual ruling by Judge Brownlie is construed as a form of hermeneutic judgement over the merits of two competing interpretations of questions of equality of opportunity, access to equitable provision of goods and services, religious conscience, homosexuality and same-sex marriage, then every interpreting party itself, as the interpreting subject engaged in witnessing, *and responding imaginatively* to the phenomenon of the gay cake court case, must be required to argue for the validity of its interpretation. According to the judge's ruling, which is subject to appeal, the refusal to fulfil the order for the cake was unlawful. If, as Ricoeur says, hermeneutics can offer a critique of ideology because 'the subject of which it speaks is always open to the efficacy of history' (2008, p. 33), then to place the conscience clause within this wider context of competing interpretations is to construe it as only *one* possible way of responding to the case among many. The validation process has the effect of placing every interpreter's position among a galaxy of other selves, each taking a different position on the same social phenomena.

Ricoeur's view of the critique of ideology is that the self can only retrieve itself 'through the exodus of oneself-as-another' and that 'this return of self (*moi*) to itself (*soi-même*) carries with it an additional charge: a call to *action*' (Kearney, 1996, p. 1, original emphasis). With this a third level of critique begins to crystallize and it is based on a return to the transformative potential interpretation brings for the interpreting subject. Ricoeur notes that if every text contains its own possibility of escape from the finite intentional horizon of its original author through its recontextualization in the new world of the reader then 'thanks to writing, the "world" of the *text* may explode the world of the *author*' (2008, p. 80, original emphasis). Remember, further, that one of the key lessons from the practice of interlingual translation is of the purposefulness and directionality that characterizes the work of the translator. Though predicated on an act of appropriation across a distance, releasing any number of interpretive possibilities to be read into the text-for-translation, the direction of travel is always towards an imagined audience, an implied reader who will receive the translation. Simultaneously, then, that which starts out as the opening up and expansion of horizons terminates in the closing down of interpretive possibilities and the eventual fixing of just one way of looking among many. A translation is therefore as hermeneutic a guess as any interpretation, but it is also a hermeneutic guess which is designed deliberately in order to fulfil a particular purpose and to address a particular need on the part of an audience. What, then, would it mean to place the DUP and Equality Commission in the position of 'author'– to face, in other words, the interpretations of others as they engage in 'reading' them? What would it mean, in other words, to translate *back* to the interpreter the interpreter's own translations of others? Such back-translations might include signing a petition alongside over 285,000 others calling for the amendment to be dropped and to share the petition on social media; joining the over 11,000 'likes' for a Facebook campaign group against the bill; hiring a no-conscience clause billboard to go on tour across Northern Ireland, as the All-Out group had done following a successful crowd funding effort; tweeting to over eleven million followers that the bill is 'sick', as Stephen Fry had done; or holding a demonstration march against the conscience clause, as the Rainbow Project had done, using a poster with the slogan, 'No dogs, no blacks, no Irish, no gays?', condemning the denial of goods and services on the basis of sexuality by satirizing the historical refusal of goods and services to people on the basis of race and ethnicity. To present the interpreter with a subversive, oppositional, resistant interpretation *of itself* is to enter into a conflict of interpretations by which translators such as Stephen Fry, the Rainbow Project and others not only view the DUP's actions as a text-for-interpretation, but also *return* the self-same interpretation *back* to the interpreter through the power of social media. By bringing the interpreter into the hermeneutic circle in this way, it is made to become an interpreting subject – as much of its *own* actions and interpretations as it ever was of the actions of others.

This kind of cultural translation – where ideologically motivated interpretations are interpreted for subversive reasons, and these, in turn, are returned to the authors of ideologically marked interpretation as subversive and oppositional interpretations-of-interpretations – ushers in what Steiner terms an 'alternate existence, a "might have been" or "is yet to come" into the substance and historical condition of one's own language, literature, and legacy of sensibility' (1998, p. 351). By requiring the authors of ideology to confront themselves through the very interpretations with which they confront the world, they too are placed at a distance from these 'texts' of their own making and must take an appropriative stand before their own interpretations. By glimpsing something of the tentativeness of their own claims to understand, they must also relinquish something of the certainty with which they view themselves and others. To place the author of an ideologically motivated interpretation of the world in the position of interpreter in this way is, in Steiner's terms:

> To experience difference, to feel the characteristic resistance and 'materiality', of that which differs, is to re-experience identity. One's own space is mapped by what lies outside; it derives coherence, tactile configuration, from the pressure of the external. 'Otherness', particularly when it has the wealth and penetration of language, compels 'presentness' to stand clear. Working at the point of maximal exposure to embodied

difference, the translator is forced to realize, to make visible, the perimeters, either spacious or confined, of his own tongue, of his own culture, of his own reserves of sensibility and intellect. (Steiner, 1998, p. 381)

It is this quality that gives cultural translation its resistant potential, for if the others that we wish to resist are, in turn, required to become interpreting selves in the face of their own ideologically marked interpretations, there is the possibility that they too can be humbled by the hermeneutic journey outwards. Through the mechanics of interpretation, resistant cultural translation of this nature places powerful institutions, the promoters of ideology, in the position of selves-being-interpreted. In this position, they must not only read themselves; they must meet themselves coming back through the hermeneutic detour across the terrain of reading. By operationalizing translation's purposeful, targeted, audience-driven gestures for oppositional ends, translation becomes 'critical' not only in the sense that it offers an incisive running commentary on what it sees but also in the sense that it requires its objects of opposition to question the very authority with which their own particular stance is thought to represent the situation to which it relates.

What would it mean to make similar instances of ideology subject to hermeneutic critique in this way? We need only look to other examples where protests, counter-movements and online activism start from the presumption that the ideologically marked interpretations of certain agents and institutions constitute vehicles of domination and exploitation. As a critique of ideology, cultural translation presumes in turn to pose something different and better; a different way of viewing things; a contrapuntal construction of events; a different characterization of the lead characters; a different presumption of authority with which to represent the views of others. To do this, cultural translators view the ideologically marked interpretations of others as 'source texts', that is, as examples of conflicting interpretations to be engaged with and interrogated. By interpreting *back* to the agents and institutions of ideologically marked interpretation, cultural translation places them in the position, above all, as interpreters *of themselves*. As Kaplan notes:

> A new kind of critical theory is taking shape that is less concerned with allegiances to any particular philosophical tradition than with examining and criticizing power, authority, gender, race, culture, ethnicity, the political economy, the environment, and other issues having to do with social justice. Critical theory challenges power and authority everywhere it resides, especially in public policy, mass media, the law, multinational corporations, and global economic and political organizations. It is interdisciplinary, empirical, normative, practical, and emancipatory. It is practiced not only

by academics but journalists, social scientists, public advocates, grassroots organizers and activists, and others connected with social movements. (Kaplan, 2012, pp. 153–4)

By translating for political reasons we can put critical theory into practice and it becomes a practice that anyone can take up: from the University of Syracuse student, who, on seeing a woman standing on a street corner at the university campus holding a sign that read, 'Homosexuality is a sin, Christ can set you free!', took action by constructing his own sign, 'Corduroy skirts are a sin', and standing next to the same woman (Fbomb, 2009) to the decision by non-profit organisation Planting Peace to site their rainbow-painted headquarters, Equality House, directly opposite the headquarters of Westboro Baptist Church in Topeka, Kansas (Erbentraut, 2015) or to the erection of a so-called equality bakery in the same neighbourhood as an Oregon bakery that refused to make a wedding cake for a same-sex couple (Wong, 2015). When translation enables the ideologically marked interpretations of others to be viewed as 'texts' to be interpreted, the possibility for critique is opened. By placing the agents and institutions of ideology within the hermeneutic circle in this way, that is, by 'othering' their very interpretations of otherness, the same authors of ideology *become interpreting subjects themselves*. Confronted with a range of competing views translation requires them to undertake an interpretive detour across the terrain of otherness. In so doing, translation functions as a reminder of the fallibility of the presumption to knowledge, for an ideologically marked interpretation is only one interpretation among many. To bring the agents and institutions of ideology into dialogue with the conflict of interpretations, in this way, is to interpret-*back*, through purposeful, directed translation, the possibility of a new and different way of understanding the world around us. By bringing to awareness of the existence of such a way, and with it the expansion of the horizons of the ideological subject, translation encourages the first steps towards a critique of the self, and with it, ideology.

Conclusion

Cultural translation: Saving us from ourselves?

In the domain of the real, cultural translation is the manifestation of interpretive gestures of distanciation, incorporation, transformation and emancipation we associate most closely with the practice of interlingual translation, and as such, it is a hermeneutic enterprise par excellence. But it is also so much *more*. With hermeneutics, Ricoeur's ultimate project was to find a way to address some of the most vexing problems of our time. In an age of violence, his was an ethics of responsibility, concerned primarily with the ethical and political dimensions of human action, animated by a belief in the power of discourse over violence. He believed that reflection was the *point de départ* for the renovation of our political imagination. The guiding principle throughout this book has been that interlingual translation, as both a creative process and a cultural product, is at its most insightful when construed as a locus of intercultural encounter: between a translator, the text-for-translation and an audience. As thinking, feeling, beings in the world, embedded socially, culturally, politically and historically, the subjectivity of translators means that the process of translation is above all one of cognitive outreach. It is a thoughtful journey outwards, across the terrain of otherness and back again. Always at a distance from the objects of interpretation, translators must make imaginative leaps into the unknown. When pen meets page, the resulting translation reveals more about the translator's own subjectivity than the reality of translation's object itself. Underlying each of these chapters is the insistence that as an interpretive regime, translation means *transformation*. It means mediation. It means *change*. In effect, and in answer to those who would force a separation of interlingual translation from its cultural pretentions, *all* translation is cultural translation, since no act of interlingual translation remains outside the hermeneutics of variance and contingency that radically alter the form and function of texts when they are translated. Mediated through the subjective 'gaze' of the translator, the hermeneutics of translation issues a challenge to protectionist claims to the interlingual sovereignty of the discipline, precisely because regimes of cultural translation are implied in the very thing such claims seek to protect. To embrace the transformative nature of translation is to take the first steps towards the ethical project that exists at the heart of cultural translation.

For Ricoeur, the hermeneutic dimension of human life means that, as with the text-for-translation, the world is a mystery to be engaged with and understood. And, as with the text-for-translation, the psychological intentions of the world of others remain forever out of reach. It is in the dialectical relation through which we engage with the other and the incommensurable mystery for which they stand that we unfold an understanding of ourselves. By bringing into our horizons of understanding meanings that are not our own and which we cannot fully understand, we expose ourselves to these other horizons and transcend something of our own limitations. Crossing the borders of the familiar, we open ourselves up to the world of others – other people, other ideas, other ways of living and acting in the world. It is in the journey outwards that we come to understand not only something about the world but also something about our own place within it. Through this circular hermeneutics, the point of the journey from the self to the other and back again is to arrive at self-understanding. Reflection is therefore critical to our existence because it is only through an active, critical, engagement with the mysteries of other people that we grasp the activity of existence in the first place. In the language of hermeneutics, we achieve selfhood only in the hermeneutic detour, through the fact of being distanced and through the process of appropriating.

Interpretation is therefore so much more than the means by which we interact with and create the world. It is through interpretation that every social actor makes sense of the world and it is through our expressions of life that we seek to understand ourselves, for the desire to understand is a basic human impulse. It is a key dimension of human existence. If it is the contingency of the translator's interpretation that impedes translation from reaching a full understanding of the texts it attempts to approximate, then it is the self-same contingency that reminds us not just of translation's fallibility to understand across a distance, but also of the resistance that our objects of interpretation project in the face of interpretation. Precisely because the possibility of a 'perfect' translation is forever suspended, it is the interpretive mechanics of translation responsible for distanciation that offers a solution to the very problems it creates. If every translation is contingent upon the subjectivity of the translator behind it – a hermeneutic guess – then no translation can stand as final. A resistant veil will always separate the translator and the text-for-translation. Because the guesswork of interpretation reminds us of the fallibility of our capacity to perceive, we suspend judgement about what we can understand about the world through direct perception.

It is this resistance to the certitude with which we might presume to understand in the world that is the first step towards a critique of ideology, for it is through hermeneutic doubt and the fact that we can only ever *posit* – the fact that we may be wrong! – that we take the first steps towards saving ourselves from the totalism that accompanies our own attempts at understanding. Hermeneutics, then, is less about understanding than it is about ontology, for the quest for understanding and the acquisition of being correspond dialectically. It is only by stepping outside of ourselves, to place our knowledge within the context of the knowledge of others that we find our being transformed, enriched and enlarged by the journey. Hermeneutics teaches that we displace ourselves in the appropriation of the text. By displacing ourselves we take the first steps towards critique, removing something of the certitude with which we attempt to construct the world. If we do not understand the world directly except through the engagement with the texts and human actions of the world around us, then we *must* employ cultural translation if only to learn something about who it is that we are and what it is that we know and understand.

In *Leviathan*, Thomas Hobbes famously translated the ancient Greek aphorism, 'know thyself', transliterated into Latin as *nosce teipsum*, as 'read thyself'. In the language of hermeneutics, this injunction might be better expressed in more cyclical terms – 'read others, read thyself, know thyself'. Before cultural translation can be operationalized for resistant ends, we must enter into thoughtful, reflective engagement with the phenomena of the world around us, not just to foster debate, to satirize, to parody, to mock, to resist or to otherwise oppose, but to discover first and foremost who we ourselves are. The lesson for cultural translation is not just that the translator's distanciation from the object of interpretation means a certain transformative dimension will always abound; or even that this transformative dimension can be harnessed for political, resistant or oppositional reasons. It is that we *must* translate – to learn something about where we stand, to locate for ourselves a position in the world, without which emancipation cannot be achieved. This is the first step towards a critique of ideology and the last word in absolute knowledge.

Bibliography

American Hustle (2013) [Film]. David O. Russell (dir.), USA: Columbia Pictures.
American University of Paris (n.d.), 'Master of Arts in Cultural Translation', American University of Paris. Available online: https://www.aup.edu/academics/graduate/cultural-translation (accessed 25 November 2015).
Armageddon (1998) [Film]. Michael Bay (dir.), USA: Buena Vista Pictures.
Anderson, B. (2006), *Imagined Communities: Reflections on the Origin and Spread of Nationalism*, London: Verso.
Arendt, H. (1999), 'Introduction: Walter Benjamin 1892–1940', in W. Benjamin, *Illuminations*. Trans. H. Zorn, Random House: London.
Aristotle (1999), *Physics*. Trans. Robin Waterfield, Oxford: Oxford University Press.
Asad, T. (1986), 'The Concept of Cultural Translation in British Social Anthropology', in J. Clifford and G. E. Marcus (eds), *Writing Culture: The Poetics and Ethics of Ethnography*, Berkeley and Los Angeles: University of California Press.
Bachmann-Medick, D. (2006), 'Meanings of Translation in Cultural Anthropology', in T. Hermans (ed.), *Translating Others: Volume 1*, Manchester: St Jerome.
Bachmann-Medick, D. (2009), 'Introduction: The Translational Turn', *Translation Studies*, 2 (1): 2–16.
Battersby, M. (2013), 'Not Just Mona Lisa's Smile? Da Vinci's La Bella Principessa Also Has "Uncatchable" Expression', *The Independent*. Available online: http://www.independent.co.uk/arts-entertainment/art/news/not-just-mona-lisas-smile-da-vincis-la-bella-principessa-also-has-uncatchable-expression-8460302.html (accessed 25 November 2015).
Baker, M. and G. Saldanha (eds) (2009), *Routledge Encyclopedia of Translation Studies*, London: Routledge.
BBC. (2015), 'Britain First Best-Funded Small Party – Electoral Commission', BBC. Available online: http://www.bbc.com/news/uk-politics-33367673 (accessed 25 November 2015).
Belzoni, G. (1820), *Narrative of the Operations and Recent Discoveries Within the Pyramids, Temples, Tombs and Excavations in Egypt and Nubia; and of a Journey to the Coast of the Red Sea, in Search of the Ancient Berenice and Another to the Oasis of Jupiter, Ammon*, London: John Murray.
Benjamin, W. (1994), 'The Work of Art in the Age of Its Technical Reproducibility', in S. D. Ross (ed.), *Art and Its Significance: An Anthology of Aesthetic Theory, Third Edition*, New York: State University of New York Press.
Benjamin, W. (1996), *Selected Writings: 1913–1926, Volume 1*, Harvard: Harvard University Press.
Benjamin, W. (1997), 'The Translator's Task', Trans. S. Rendall, *TTR: Traduction, Terminologie, Rédaction*, 10 (2): 151–65.

Benjamin, W. (1999), *Illuminations*, Trans. H. Zorn. Random House: London.
Benjamin, W. (2005), 'The Work of Art in the Age of Mechanical Reproduction', in R. Guins and O. Zaragoza Cruz (eds), *Popular Culture: A Reader*, London: SAGE Publications.
Bery, A. (2009), 'Response', *Translation Studies*, 2 (2): 213–16.
Bhabha, H. (1990), 'The Third Space', in J. Rutherford (ed.), *Identity: Community, Culture, Difference*, London: Lawrence & Wishart.
Bhabha, H. K. (1994), *The Location of Culture*, London: Routledge.
Bland, A. (2014), 'Camera Phones at the National Gallery Stoke Fears that Technology Is Leaving Us Incapable of Deep Engagement with Anything', *The Independent*. Available online: http://www.independent.co.uk/arts-entertainment/art/news/cameraphones-at-the-national-gallery-stoke-fears-that-technology-is-leaving-us-incapable-of-deep-9673776.html (accessed 25 November 2015).
Borges, J. L. (1964) *Dreamtigers*. Trans. M. Boyer and H. Morland, Austin: University of Texas Press.
Britain First. (n.d.), 'About Britain First: Page Info', *Facebook*. Available online: https://www.facebook.com/OfficialBritainFirst/info/?tab=page_info (accessed 25 November 2015).
Britain First. (2015a), 'Timeline Photos', *Facebook*. Available online: https://www.facebook.com/OfficialBritainFirst/photos/a.346633882148546.1073741826.300455573433044/907782406033688/?type=3&theater (accessed 25 November 2015).
Britain First. (2015b), 'A Bad Case of Muslim Grooming . . .', *Facebook*, Available online: https://www.facebook.com/OfficialBritainFirst/posts/907587852719810 (accessed 25 November 2015).
Britain First. (2015c), 'Timeline Photos', *Facebook*. Available online: https://www.facebook.com/OfficialBritainFirst/photos/a.346633882148546.1073741826.300455573433044/907585329386729/?type=3 (accessed 25 November 2015).
Britain Furst. (2015), 'Timeline Photos', *Facebook*. Available online: https://www.facebook.com/BritiainFurst/photos/a.722782891130445.1073741828.722772297798171/1012821702126561/?type=3&theater (accessed 25 November 2015).
British Pathé. (1965), 'Map Survey 1965', *British* Pathé. Available online: http://www.britishpathe.com/video/map-survey/query/cartography (accessed 25 November 2015).
Brown, D. (2003), *The Da Vinci Code*, New York: Doubleday.
Buden, B. and S. Nowotny (2009), 'Cultural Translation: An Introduction to the Problem', *Translation Studies*, 2 (2): 196–208.
Burke, P. (2007), 'Cultures of Translation in Early Modern Europe', in P. Burke and H. P. Hsia (eds), *Cultural Translation in Early Modern Europe*, Cambridge: Cambridge University Press.
Burns, L. (2014), 'Asked to Cover Up with this Ridiculous Shroud while #breastfeeding so not to Cause Offence @ClaridgesHotel today.', *Twitter*, 1 December. Available online: https://twitter.com/andysrelation/status/539522173380333569 (accessed 25 November 2015).
Buttimer, A. and D. Seamon (1980), *The Human Experience of Space and Place*, London: Taylor & Francis.

Cakeadoodledo. (2014), 'We're Causing a Bit of a Stir. Love It. #Exeter #cakeadoodledo #getagrip', *Twitter*, 9 December. Available online: https://twitter.com/kateshirazi/status/542340889520390145 (accessed 25 November 2015).

Carroll, L. (1869), *Alice's Adventures in Wonderland*, Boston: Lee and Shephard.

Carroll, L. (1999), *The Annotated Alice: The Definitive Edition*, New York: W. W. Norton.

Chesterman, A. (2010), 'Response', *Translation Studies*, 3 (1): 103–6.

Christian Institute. (2015), 'Ashers Baking Company Deeply Disappointed after Losing 'Gay Cake' Case – Family Consider Appeal'. Available online: http://www.christian.org.uk/press-releases/ashers-baking-company-deeply-disappointed-after-losing-gay-cake-case-%E2%80%93-family-consider-appeal/ (accessed 25 November 2015).

Crapanzano, V. (1986), 'Hermes' Dilemma: The Masking of Subversion in Ethnographic Description', in J. Clifford and G. E. Marcus (eds), *Writing Culture: The Poetics and Ethics of Ethnography*. Berkeley and Los Angeles: University of California Press.

Cloverfield (2008) [Film]. Matt Reeves (dir.), USA: Paramount Pictures.

Colley, L. (2010), *Captives: Britain, Empire and the World 1600–1850*, London: Random House.

Compton, S. (2014), 'Why You Shouldn't Take Photos in Galleries', *The Daily Telegraph*. Available online: http://www.telegraph.co.uk/culture/art/art-news/11030975/Why-you-shouldnt-take-photos-in-galleries.html (accessed 25 November 2015).

Conway, K. (2010a), 'News Translation and Cultural Resistance', *Journal of International and Intercultural Communication*, 3 (3): 187–205.

Conway, K. (2010b), 'Paradoxes of Translation in Television News', *Media, Culture & Society November*, 32: 979–96.

Conway, K. (2012), 'A Conceptual and Empirical Approach to Cultural Translation', *Translation Studies*, 5 (3): 264–79.

Cresswell, T. (2004), *Place: A Short Introduction*, Oxford: Wiley-Blackwell.

The Da Vinci Code (2006) [Film]. Ron Howard (dir.), USA: Columbia Pictures.

Dargis, M. (2009), 'A Franchise Goes Boldly Backward', *New York Times*. Available online: http://www.nytimes.com/2009/05/08/movies/08trek.html (accessed 25 November 2015).

Dawkins, R. (2006), *The Selfish Gene*, Oxford: Oxford University Press.

Diodorus Siculus (1933), *Library of History, Volume I: Books 1–2.34*. Trans. C. H. Oldfather, Harvard: Harvard University Press.

Don't Panic. (n.d.), 'Everything Is NOT Awesome', *Don't Panic*. Available online: https://www.dontpaniclondon.com/portfolio/greenpeace-lego/ (accessed 25 November 2015).

D'hulst, L. (2010), 'Response', *Translation Studies*, 3 (3): 353–6.

DUP. (2014), 'Consultation on the Northern Ireland freedom of conscience amendment bill', *DUP*. Available online: http://www.mydup.com/publications/view/consultation-on-the-northern-ireland-freedom-of-conscience-amendment-bill (accessed 25 November 2015).

Electoral Commission. (2014), 'Outcome of Independent Investigation into Registration of Party Description', *Electoral Commission*. Available online: http://www.electoralcommission.org.uk/i-am-a/journalist/

electoral-commission-media-centre/news-releases-corporate/outcome-of-independent-investigation-into-registration-of-party-description (accessed 25 November 2015).

Elle. (2015), 'Charlize Theron Is ELLE's New Cover Star', *Elle*. Available online: http://www.elleuk.com/now-trending/charlize-theron-elle-cover-june-2015 (accessed 25 November 2015).

Equality Commission. (2014), 'Commission to Proceed with Bakery Case', *Equality Commission for Northern Ireland*. Available online: http://www.equalityni.org/Footer-Links/News/Delivering-Equality/Statement-from-The-Equality-Commission (accessed 25 November 2015).

Erbentraut, J. (2015), 'What the Equality House Can Teach Us about Making Societal Change', *Huffington Post*. Available online: http://www.huffingtonpost.com/entry/equality-house-aaron-jackson-planting-peace_562e9080e4b06317990eff22 (accessed 25 November 2015).

Etzler, T. (2014), 'Wrecks, Rats and Roaches: Standoff in the South China Sea', *CNN*. Available online: http://edition.cnn.com/interactive/2014/07/world/south-china-sea-dispute/ (accessed 25 November 2015).

Exodus: Gods and Kings (2014) [Film]. Ridley Scott (dir.), USA, UK and Spain: 20th Century Fox.

Fbomb. (2009), 'Corduroy Skirts Are a Sin', *Fbomb*. Available online: http://thefbomb.org/2009/11/corduroy-skirts-are-a-sin/ (accessed 25 November 2015).

Fels, J. and J. Wood (1986), 'Designs on Signs/Myth and Meaning in Maps', *Marxist Perspectives*, 23 (3): 54–103.

Furness, H. (2014), 'National Gallery Relents Over Mobile Phones', *The Daily Telegraph*. Available online: http://www.telegraph.co.uk/culture/art/art-news/11028015/National-Gallery-relents-over-mobile-phones.html (accessed 25 November 2015).

Gambier, Y. and L. van Doorslaer (eds) (2012), *Handbook of Translation Studies: Volume 3*, Amsterdam: John Benjamins Publishing.

Gareth Lee v Ashers Baking Co Ltd and Colin McArthur and Karen McArthur [2015]. (2015), *Northern Ireland Court Service*. Available online: https://www.courtsni.gov.uk/en-GB/Judicial%20Decisions/PublishedByYear/Documents/2015/%5B2015%5D%20NICty%202/j_j_2015NICty2Final.htm (accessed 25 November 2015).

Gateshead Council (n.d.), 'Background & History', *Gateshead Council*. Available online: http://www.gateshead.gov.uk/Leisure%20and%20Culture/attractions/Angel/Background/Background2.aspx (accessed 25 November 2015).

Geertz, C. (1973), *The Interpretation of Cultures: Selected Essays*, New York: Basic Books.

Givan, P. (2014), 'Consultation on the Northern Ireland Freedom of Conscience Amendment Bill: Consultation Paper', *DUP*. Available online: http://dev.mydup.com/images/uploads/publications/Freedom_of_Conscience_Consultation_Document_Final.pdf (accessed 25 November 2015).

The Godfather (1972) [Film]. Francis Ford Coppola (dir.), USA: Paramount Pictures.

Grease (1978) [Film]. Randal. Kleiser (dir.), USA: Paramount Pictures.

Greenpeace. (2014), 'LEGO Putting Cash before Kids, Says Greenpeace as It Kicks Off Global Campaign', *Greenpeace*. Available online: http://www.

greenpeace.org/international/en/press/releases/LEGO-putting-cash-before-kids-says-Greenpeace-as-it-kicks-off-global-campaign/ (accessed 25 November 2015).
GreenpeaceVideo. (2014), 'LEGO: Everything is NOT Awesome', *YouTube*. Available online: https://www.youtube.com/watch?v=qhbliUq0_r4 (accessed 25 November 2015).
Guardian (2014), 'In a Few Years, We'll all be Wearing Muslamic Ray-Bans', *Facebook*. Available online: https://www.facebook.com/theguardian/posts/10152505551086323 (accessed 25 November 2015).
Ha, K. N. (2010), 'Response', *Translation Studies*, 3 (3): 349–53.
Hamada, J. (2011), 'Remake/Photo Project', *Booooooom*. Available online: http://www.booooooom.com/2011/09/27/remake-a-project-by-booooooom-and-adobe/ (accessed 25 November 2015).
Hardman, I. (2014), 'Not a Mother but what Is "Ostentatious Breastfeeding?" Does It Involve a Small Brass Band and a Neon Sign?' *Twitter*, 5 December. . Available online: https://twitter.com/IsabelHardman/status/540824692559716352 (accessed 25 November 2015).
Haynes, G. (2015), 'This British Satirical News Network Is at War with the Far-Right and Far-Left', *VICE*. Available online: http://www.vice.com/en_uk/read/gavin-haynes-british-fake-news-network-521 (accessed 25 November 2015).
Herodotus (1996), *Histories*, Ware: Wordsworth Editions.
Huggan, G. (1994). *Territorial Disputes: Maps and Mapping Strategies in Contemporary Canadian and Australian Fiction*, Toronto: University of Toronto Press.
The Interview (2014) [Film]. Seth Rogan and Evan Goldberg (dirs.), USA: Columbia Pictures.
Iser, W. (2000), *The Range of Interpretation*, New York: Columbia University Press.
Jakobson, R. (1959), 'On Linguistic Aspects of Translation', in R. A. Brower (ed.), *On Translation*. Cambridge Mass.: Harvard University Press. Reprinted in L. Venuti, (ed.) *The Translation Studies Reader*. London & New York: Routledge, 2000. 113–18.
July, M. (2009), 'Dear Julie', *VICE*. Available online: http://www.vice.com/en_uk/read/photos-miranda-july-136-v16n9 (accessed 25 November 2015).
Kaplan, D. (2012), *Ricoeur's Critical Theory*, Albany: State University of New York Press.
Kearney, R. (1994), *Modern Movements in European Philosophy: Phenomenology, Critical Theory, Structuralism*, Manchester: Manchester University Press.
Kearney, R. (1996), 'Introduction', in R. Kearney (ed.), *Paul Ricoeur: The Hermeneutics of Action*, London: SAGE.
Kramer vs. Kramer (1979) [Film]. Robert Benton (dir.), USA: Columbia Pictures.
LBC. (2014), 'Farage: Mums "Could Breastfeed in the Corner"', *LBC*. Available online: http://www.lbc.co.uk/breastfeeding-mums-could-sit-in-corner-says-farage-101487 (accessed 25 November 2015).
The Lego Movie (2014) [Film]. Phil Lord and Christopher Miller (dirs), USA, Australia and Denmark: Warner Bros. Pictures.
Levit, B. (2009), 'Sm[art]: Miranda July Brings the Background to Foreground', *Bitch*. Available online: https://bitchmedia.org/post/smart-miranda-july-brings-the-background-to-foreground (accessed 25 November 2015).

The Lord of the Rings: The Fellowship of the Ring (2001) [Film]. Peter Jackson (dir.), New Zealand and USA: New Line Cinema.

Louvre. (n.d.), 'Mona Lisa – Portrait of Lisa Gherardini, Wife of Francesco del Giocondo', *Louvre*. Available online: http://www.louvre.fr/en/oeuvre-notices/mona-lisa-portrait-lisa-gherardini-wife-francesco-del-giocondo (accessed 25 November 2015).

Luippold, R. (2014), 'Bruce Springsteen & Jimmy Fallon Update "Born To Run" to Parody Chris Christie's Bridgegate', *The Huffington Post*. Available online: http://www.huffingtonpost.com/2014/01/15/bruce-springsteen-jimmy-fallon-christie-born-to-run_n_4601845.html (accessed 25 November 2015).

Masters, K. (2015), 'Jennifer Lawrence and Chris Pratt's Sci-Fi "Passengers" Nears Greenlight After Sony Behind-the-Scenes Drama', *Hollywood Reporter*. Available online: http://www.hollywoodreporter.com/heat-vision/jennifer-lawrence-chris-pratts-sci-802876 (accessed 25 November 2015).

MacGregor, N. (2010), *'Statue of Ramesses II'*, BBC, 13 February. Available online: http://www.bbc.co.uk/programmes/b00qg5mk (accessed 25 November 2015).

Meredith, F. (2015), 'Ashers "Gay Cake" Decision is a Threat to Our Freedom of Conscience', *Belfast Telegraph*. Available online: http://www.belfasttelegraph.co.uk/opinion/debateni/fionola-meredith/ashers-gay-cake-decision-is-a-threat-to-our-freedom-of-conscience-31237523.html (accessed 25 November 2015).

Ministry of Foreign Affairs of the People's Republic of China. (2014), 'Position Paper of the Government of the People's Republic of China on the Matter of Jurisdiction in the South China Sea Arbitration Initiated by the Republic of the Philippines', *Ministry of Foreign Affairs of the People's Republic of China*. Available online: http://www.fmprc.gov.cn/mfa_eng/zxxx_662805/t1217147.shtml (accessed 25 November 2015).

Mona Lisa Smile (2003) [Film]. Mike Newell (dir.), USA: Columbia Pictures.

Monty Python's Flying Circus, Season 2, Episode 14. (1970), BBC. 15 September.

Moore, A. (2008), *Watchmen*, Burbank: DC Comics.

Nancy, J. (1991), *The Inoperative Community*. Trans. P. Connor, L. Garbus, M. Holland and S. Sawhney, Minneapolis: University of Minnesota Press.

National Gallery. (2014), 'The National Gallery Introduces Free Wi-Fi', *National Gallery*. Available online: http://www.nationalgallery.org.uk/about-us/press-and-media/press-releases/the-national-gallery-introduces-free-wi-fi (accessed 25 November 2015).

New Internationalist (2003), 'Obituary', *New Internationalist*. Available online: http://newint.org/columns/2003/01/01/arno-peters (accessed 25 November 2015).

New York Times (2015), 'A Timeline for the George Washington Bridge Scandal', *New York Times*. Available online: http://www.nytimes.com/interactive/2014/02/04/nyregion/Timeline-George-Washington-Bridge-Scandal.html#/#time302_8368 (accessed 25 November 2015).

Nichols, J. M. (2015), 'Kim Davis Is about to Get a BIG Surprise In Her Hometown', *The Huffington Post*. Available online: http://www.huffingtonpost.com/entry/kim-davis_55f33486e4b042295e3653f0?ncid=fcbklnkushpmg00000050 (accessed 25 November 2015).

Ohlheiser, A. (2015), 'Kentucky Clerk Kim Davis on Gay Marriage Licenses: "It Is a Heaven or Hell Decision"', *Washington Post*. Available online: https://www.

washingtonpost.com/news/acts-of-faith/wp/2015/09/01/kentucky-clerk-kim-davis-on-gay-marriage-licenses-it-is-a-heaven-or-hell-decision/ (accessed 25 November 2015).

Patterson, S., J. Bartholomew, L. Harriton, A. Samberg, A. Schaffer and J. Taccone (2014), "Everything is Awesome!!!" Tegan and Sara featuring 'The Lonely Island', *The Lego Movie: Original Motion Picture Soundtrack*. [CD]. Sydney: WaterTower Music.

Polisano, E. (2014), 'Behind the Scenes at Greenpeace's Lego and Shell Protest Viral Video', *The Guardian*. Available online: http://www.theguardian.com/voluntary-sector-network/2014/jul/22/greenpeace-shell-lego-viral-video (accessed 25 November 2015).

Pratt, M. L. (2010), 'Response', *Translation Studies*, 3 (1): 94–6.

The Prince of Egypt (1998) [Film]. Simon Wells, Brenda Chapman and Steve Hickner (dirs), USA: DreamWorks Pictures.

Pym, A. (2009), *Exploring Translation Theories*, London: Routledge.

Pym, A. (2010), 'On Empiricism and Bad Philosophy in Translation Studies', *Intercultural Studies Group*. Available online: http://usuaris.tinet.cat/apym/on-line/research_methods/2009_lille.pdf (accessed 25 November 2015).

Reid, R. (2014), 'I'm going to Have Children so I Can Indulge in "Ostentatious Breast Feeding". I'm Imaging the Be Our Guest Scene from Beauty & the Beast', *Twitter*, 5 December. Available online: https://twitter.com/RebeccaCNReid/status/540826378451824640 (accessed 25 November 2015).

Reuters (2015), 'Philippines Reinforces Its Claim to South China Sea Outpost', *Guardian*. Available online:http://www.theguardian.com/world/2015/jul/14/philippines-reinforces-its-claim-to-south-china-sea-outpost-according-to-reports (accessed 25 November 2015).

Rice, A. (1989), *The Mummy, or Ramses the Damned*, Topeka: Tandem Library.

Ricoeur, P. (1976), *Interpretation Theory: Discourse and the Surplus of Meaning*. Trans. D. Pellauer, Fort Worth: TCU Press.

Ricoeur, P. (1995), *Oneself as Another*. Trans. K. Blamey, Chicago: University of Chicago Press.

Ricoeur, P. (1996), 'Reflections on a new ethos for Europe', in R. Kearney (ed), *Paul Ricoeur: The Hermeneutics of Action*, London: SAGE.Ricoeur, P. (2004), *The Conflict of Interpretations*. Trans. W. Domingo, C. Frielich, P. McCormick, K. McLaughlin, D. Savage and R. Sweeney, London: Continuum.

Ricoeur, P. (2008), *From Text to Action*. Trans. K. Blamey, London: Continuum.

Ricoeur, P. (2013), Hermeneutics: Writings and Lectures, Volume 2. Trans. D. Pellauer, Cambridge: Polity.

Roose, K. (2014), 'Hacked Documents Reveal a Hollywood Studio's Stunning Gender and Race Gap', *Fusion*. Available online:http://fusion.net/story/30789/hacked-documents-reveal-a-hollywood-studios-stunning-gender-and-race-gap/ (accessed 25 November 2015).

Rorty, R. (1989), *Contingency, Irony, and Solidarity*, Cambridge: Cambridge University Press.

Rose, S. (2009), 'J. J. Abrams: "I Never Got Star Trek"', *The Guardian*. Available online: http://www.theguardian.com/film/2009/may/07/jj-abrams-interview-star-trek (accessed 25 November 2015).

Ryle, G. (2009), *Collected Essays 1929–1968: Collected Papers, Volume 2*, London: Taylor & Francis.

Rushdie, S. (1988), *The Satanic Verses*, London: Vintage.
Sassoon, D. (2001), 'Mona Lisa: the best-known girl in the whole wide world', *History Workshop Journal*, 51: 1–18.
Shelley, P. B. (1819), *Rosalind and Helen, A Modern Eclogue; with Other Poems*, London: Printed for C. and J. Ollier.
Shoard, C. (2015), 'The Real Hollywood Scandal: why Jennifer Lawrence, Angelina Jolie and Other Female Stars Get Ripped Off', *Guardian*. Available online:http://www.theguardian.com/film/2015/jul/28/american-hustle-how-hollywood-rips-off-women-actors-sexism (accessed 25 November 2015).
Simms, K. (2003), *Paul Ricoeur*, London: Routledge.
Simon, N. (2010), *The Participatory Museum*, Santa Cruz: Museum 2.0.
Simon, S. (2009), 'Response', *Translation Studies*, 2 (2): 208–13.
Sitnexto Kim Davis (2015a), 'I'm supposed to go to the Lake on Friday, But I Just Realized I Won't Be Able to Get the Jet Ski Trailer in the Parking Lot. #KimDavis', *Twitter*, 2 September. Available online: https://twitter.com/nexttokimdavis/status/639204569197768708 (accessed 25 November 2015).
Sitnexto Kim Davis (2015b), '#IStandWithKimDavis – Her Brave Stand to go to Jail Has Made this the Best BBQ in Years!', *Twitter*, 7 September Available online: https://twitter.com/nexttokimdavis/status/640939474638123012 (accessed 25 November 2015).
Sitnexto Kim Davis (2015c), 'Todd Changed the Marriage Forms This Morning. #KimDavis Name Is Now In 72pt Font, SO EVERYONE KNOWS IT'S HER', *Twitter*, 8 September. Available online: https://twitter.com/nexttokimdavis/status/641267856894656512 (accessed 25 November 2015).
Spivak, G. C. (2008), 'More Thoughts on Cultural Translation', *EIPCP*. Available online: http://eipcp.net/transversal/0608/spivak/en (accessed 25 November 2015).
Springsteen, B. (1975). 'Born to Run', [Vinyl], New York: Columbia.
Star Trek (2009) [Film]. J. J. Abrams (dir.), USA: Paramount Pictures.
Star Trek into Darkness (2013) [Film]. J. J. Abrams (dir.), USA: Paramount Pictures.
Steiner, G. (1998), *After Babel: Aspects of Language and Translation*, Oxford: Oxford University Press.
Sturge, K. (2007), *Representing Others: Translation, Ethnography and the Museum*, Manchester: St Jerome.
Sturge, K. (2009), 'Cultural Translation', in M. Baker and G. Saldanha (eds). *Routledge Encyclopedia of Translation Studies*, London: Routledge.
Telegraph (2013), 'Woolwich Attack: The Terrorist's Rant', *The Telegraph*. Available online: http://www.telegraph.co.uk/news/uknews/terrorism-in-the-uk/10075488/Woolwich-attack-the-terrorists-rant.html (accessed 25 November 2015).
Tate London. (n.d.), 'Lichtenstein: A Retrospective Exhibition Guide: Room 4: War and Romance', *Tate London*. Available online: http://www.tate.org.uk/whats-on/tate-modern/exhibition/lichtenstein/lichtenstein-retrospective-room-guide-introduction-3 (accessed 25 November 2015).
The Ten Commandments (1956) [Film]. Cecil B. DeMille (dir.), USA: Paramount Pictures.

Thompson, N. (1996), *Herodotus and the Origins of the Political Community: Arion's Leap*, New Haven: Yale University Press.
Tindale, J. (2014), 'What Exactly Does "Ostentatious Breastfeeding" Involve Exactly? Doing It as a Landmark Exhibition at the British Museum?' *Twitter*, 5 December. Available online: https://twitter.com/JackTindale/status/540828188176580608 (accessed 25 November 2015).
The Tonight Show Starring Jimmy Fallon (2014), 'Bruce Springsteen & Jimmy Fallon: "Gov. Christie Traffic Jam" ("Born To Run" Parody)', *The Tonight Show Starring Jimmy Fallon*. Available online: https://www.youtube.com/watch?v=VKHV0LLvhXM (accessed 25 November 2015).
Trivedi, H. (2007), 'Translating Culture vs. Cultural Translation', in P. St-Pierre and P. C. Kar (eds), *In Translation: Reflections, Refractions, Transformations*, Amsterdam: John Benjamins Publishing.
Tymoczko, M. (2010), 'Response', *Translation Studies*, 3 (1): 106–10.
Tuan, Y. (1977), *Space and Place: The Perspective of Experience*, Minneapolis: University of Minnesota Press.
The Two Ronnies, Season 5, Episode 3 (1976), BBC. 18 September.
UNHCR (2015), 'UNHCR Media Page for Southern Europe Report', UNHRC. Available online: http://unhcr.org/medsea15/ (accessed 25 November 2015).
Van Gogh, V. (1888), 'Sunflowers' [Oil on canvas]. At: London: National Gallery.
Vermeer, J. (c.1665), 'Girl with a Pearl Earring' [Oil on canvas]. At: The Hague: Mauritshuis.
VO CS (2012), 'Charlie Bit My Finger (original full version)', *YouTube*. Available online: https://www.youtube.com/watch?v=bnRVheEpJG4 (accessed 25 November 2015).
Wagner, B. (2010), 'Response', *Translation Studies*, 3 (1): 97–9.
Walsh, J. (2014), 'Britain Furst: The Halal Ray-Ban-Wearing Far Right Facebook Mockers', *Guardian*. Available online: http://www.theguardian.com/media/2014/jun/20/britain-furst-the-halal-ray-ban-wearing-far-right-facebook-mockers (accessed 25 November 2015).
Wheelan, B. (2014), 'Britain First: Inside the Extremist Group Targeting Mosques', *Channel 4 News*. Available online: http://www.channel4.com/news/britain-first-far-right-anti-muslim-extremists-mosques (accessed 25 November 2015).
Williamson, C., D. McAleese and L. McKeown (2015), 'Ashers Bakery Lose "Gay Cake" Case: "We Will Not Be Closing Down, We Have Not Done Anything Wrong" Says Boss', *Belfast Telegraph*. Available online: http://www.belfasttelegraph.co.uk/news/northern-ireland/ashers-bakery-lose-gay-cake-case-we-will-not-be-closing-down-we-have-not-done-anything-wrong-says-boss-31233797.html (accessed 25 November 2015).
Winichakul, T. (1997), *Siam Mapped: A History of the Geo-body of a Nation*, Honolulu: University of Hawaii Press.
Wintour, P. and R. Mason (2014), 'Nigel Farage Says Breastfeeding Women Should Sit in a Corner', *Guardian*. Available online: http://www.theguardian.com/politics/2014/dec/05/nigel-farage-ukip-claridges-breastfeeding-mothers (accessed 25 November 2015).
Wolf, M. (2009), 'The Implications of a Sociological Turn. Methodological and Disciplinary Questions', in A. Pym and A. Perekrestenko (eds), *Translation Research Projects 2*, Tarragona: Intercultural Studies Group.

Wong, C. M. (2015) '"Sweet Equality Cakes" Created as a Counter-Effort to Anti-Gay Bakery', *Huffington Post*. Available online: http://www.huffingtonpost.com/entry/sweet-equality-cakesfundraiser_55b8e509e4b0224d88349568 (accessed 25 November 2015).

The X-Files, Season 7, Episode 11, Closure (2000), *Fox*. 13 February.

Young, R. (2010), 'Response', *Translation Studies*, 3 (3): 349–60.

Zernike, K. (2014), 'Christie Faces Scandal on Traffic Jam Aides Ordered', *New York Times*. Available online: http://www.nytimes.com/2014/01/09/nyregion/christie-aide-tied-to-bridge-lane-closings.html?_r=1 (accessed 25 November 2015).

Zernike, K. and M. Santora (2015), '2 Indicted in George Washington Bridge Case; Ally of Christie Pleads Guilty', *New York Times*. Available online: www.nytimes.com/2015/05/02/nyregion/christie-ally-expected-to-plead-guilty-in-george-washington-bridge-lane-closing-case.html (accessed 25 November 2015).

Index

A History of the World in 100 Objects (2010) 69, 71
Abrams, J. J. 108–9
Achilles and the Tortoise, paradox of 80–1
Adam 37
Adams, Amy 73
Alice's Adventures in Wonderland (1869) 44–5, 135
All American Men of War 105, 124
allegory 37
ambiguity 16, 36, 45
American Hustle (2013) 73–4
amplification 6, 38
Angel of the North 71
anthropology 11–12
anti-immigration 142–5
anti-metaphor argument 21, 22–4
appropriation 76–81, 85
  art-selfie as 118–23
  as containment 98–100
  as counterpart of distanciation 76–81, 85–8
  over time 112
  reader-focused emphasis 88–90
  and self-understanding 137–41, 145–7
  subjectivity of 90–1
Arendt, H. 110–11
Aristotle 81
Arnoult, Gareth 143–5
Arquette, Patricia 74
art-selfie 118–23
artworks
  art-selfies as appropriation 76–81, 85
  photography of 118–19
  're-enactments' of 114–17, 125–7
  reproduction of 120–1
Asad, Talal 11–12, 14, 18

Ashers Baking Company 131–3, 152–6
audience 51–3, 107–9, 155, 157
  of human action 74–5
  needs of 9–10
  online 143
  reboot 108–9
  of re-enactments 117, 125–6, 128–9
  unclear 17
  of written discourse 61–3, 85–7
author, posthumous 'fame' of 111

Babel 45
Bachmann-Medick, D. 14, 19
Belzoni, G. 68–71
Benjamin, W. 6–7, 12, 15, 29, 35–6, 43–5, 66–7, 92–3, 110–27, 136
Bery, A. 23
Bhabha, H. 12–15, 18, 20, 24
Bibliotheca historica 69–70
Bland, A. 120
Boooooooom blog 114–15
Borges, Jorge Luis 96–7
breastfeeding 64–5
Britain First 142–5
Britain Furst 142–5
British Museum 68–9
'Bruce Springsteen & Jimmy Fallon: "Gov. Christie Traffic Jam" ("Born To Run" Parody)' 125–7
Buden, B. 15–16

Cambyses 66–7
camera phone technology 118–20
cartography 93–8
Chesterman, A. 16, 19–20, 23
Christie, Chris (Governor) 125–7
citizenship test 15–16
clues, in text 102, 134–5
colonial encounter, with cultural difference 13

Compton, Sarah 119–20
'Concept of Cultural Translation in British Social Anthropology, The' 11
conscience clause 132–3, 151–6
'Consultation on the Northern Ireland Freedom of Conscience Amendment Bill' 132–3, 154–6
Contingency, Irony and Solidarity (1989) 2–4
'Conventional Metaphors and Anthropological Metaphysics: The Problematic of Cultural Translation' 11
Conway, K. 14–17
Crapanzano, V. 34
'creative interpretation' 151
criticism, of translation 16, 18–27
  anti-metaphor argument 21, 22–4
  ethical perspective 23–4
critique of ideology 147, 151, 153, 155, 157, 161
  translation's role in 151–3, 155–8, 160–1
cultural translation, defined 8–10, 27–9, 50–3
'Cultural Translation: An Introduction to the Problem' 15
cyber attack 73–4

da Vinci, Leonardo 112–3
Davis, K. 148–9
Dawkins 38
Democratic Unionist Party (DUP) 132–3, 151–6
de-psychologization, of meaning 73, 75, 77–9
detractors 16
dialogue, *see* 'discourse', spoken
'discourse', spoken 51–2
  'eventful' dialogue 58
  interlocutors 42, 56–61
  referential co-dependency 57
  resolution of mystery in 59–60
  spatiotemporal co-situation 58
  subjectivity of speaker 58
  tripartite structure 57
  see also 'discourse', written
'discourse', written
  audience of 62
  'double historical reference' 62
  freedom from authorial intention 63–6
  freedom from historical context 66–72
  human action 47–8
  problem of interpretation 65
  semantic autonomy of 62–3
  speculation 61
  see also 'discourse', spoken
discrimination, on grounds of sexual orientation 131–3, 152–6
distanciation
  and appropriation 76–81, 85–8
  in cartography 94–5
  condition of 75
  consequences of reader's 88–9
  of self from itself 139–40
  and self- understanding 137–40, 145–7
Dreamtigers (1964) 96–7
Duchamp, M. 113
DUP, *see* Democratic Unionist Party (DUP)

Egypt 66–72
Egyptian Sculpture Gallery 68–9
Equality Act (Sexual Orientation) Regulations 132–3
Equality Commission for Northern Ireland 131–3, 152–6
ethnographer, and Hermes 34
Europe, refugee immigration 1–2
Eve 37
exposure, 8–9

Facebook 121–2, 129, 142–5
Fallon, Jimmy 125–8
'fallacy of the absolute text' 78
'familiar', being 85
familiaris 85
Farage, Nigel 63–5
film, as translation 93
Fry, Stephen 156

Gall, James (Reverend) 95
galleries 118–22
Garden of Eden 37
Geertz, C. 76–7

INDEX

gender, differentials in pay 73–4
George Washington Bridge (GWB) 125–7
Germany, citizenship test 15–16
Girl With a Pearl Earring (c. 1665) 118–19
Givan, P. 132–3, 153–4
Golding, Paul 142
Gormley, Anthony 71
Grease 86–7
Greenpeace 127–9
Guardians of Peace 73
GWB, *see* George Washington Bridge

Ha, K. N. 14, 23
Habermas 2
hack 73–4
Handbook of Translation Studies (2012) 16–17
Heidegger 2
hermeneutics 33–5
   as theory of text 48–9
   thought involved in 37–8
Hermes 33–5
   and ethnographer 34
   etymology of 34
Herodotus 66–7
Histories 66–7
homosexuality 131–3, 152–6
Huggan, G. 95–7
human action
   autonomy 72–5
   and text 47–8
human behavior, 'imaginative acts' of 77
human life, meaning of 49–50

'imaginative variations' 141–2
imitation 38–40
immigration, of refugees 1–2
Instagram 121–2
interlocutors 56–60
interpretations 6–8
   conflict of 146–7
   'creative' 151
   judicious 133–4
   self-knowledge through 147–51
Interview, The (2014) 73
Islamophobia 143–5

judges, discretionary powers 133–4
July, Miranda 115–17

Kaplan D. 75, 142, 146–7, 150–1, 157–8
Keesing, Roger 11
Kierkegaard 2
Kim Jong-un 73
knowledge-creation 35

'landmarks', of place 101–2
language
   concealment of meaning in 40–9
   and metaphor 41–2
Larsson, Stieg 111
Late Night programme 125–7
Lawrence, Jennifer 73, 74
Lee, Gareth 131–3
'LEGO: Everything is NOT Awesome' 127–9
'liberal ironist' 2–3
Lichtenstein 105–6, 124
'linguistic function' 45
Location of Culture, The (1994) 13
Lord of the Rings: The Fellowship of the Ring, The (2001) 39–40

MacGregor, Neil 69, 71
maps 93–8
Marx 2
McArthur, Daniel 152
meaning 84
   attribution to other languages 11–12
   and communication 4
   construction of 9–10
   de-psychologization 73, 75, 77–9
   of human life 49–50
   multiplicity of 35–8, 42
   surplus of 38, 39
memes 38–40
Mercator, Gerardus 95–6
Meredith, Fionola 153
'messy' theorization 16
metaphor 41–2
   translation as 21, 22–4
'middle', between the text and the reader 84–5
Milliennium series (2005–7) 111

INDEX

mindfulness 136
'Ministry of Silly Walks, The' 40
minorities, protection of 133
'Mischief Reef' 101
Mona Lisa (c. 1503-9) 112-13
Monty Python's Flying Circus (1970) 40
museums 118-22
myth 37

Nancy 8-9
narrative 5-7
National Gallery 119-20
Nietzsche 2
'non-substantive translation' 24
Northern Ireland 131-56
Nowotny, S. 15-16

'On Empiricism and Bad Philosophy in Translation Studies' (2010) 16
'On Language as Such and on the Language of Man' 43-4
'On Rigor in Science' 96-7
'One does not simply walk into Mordor' 39-40
Ordnance Survey 93-8
otherness, encounter with 145-7

parody, viral video 125-9
   'Bruce Springsteen & Jimmy Fallon: "Gov. Christie Traffi c Jam" ("Born To Run" Parody)' 125-7
   'LEGO: Everything is NOT Awesome' 127-9
Participatory Museum, The (2010) 121-2
pastiche, translational 113
Pathé News
pay, gender differentials in 73-4
Peters, Arno (Dr) 95-6
'petition of concern' facility 133
Physics 81
places, as 'translations' 100-4
Pratt, M. L. 14-16, 24, 26
Psammenitus 66-7
Pym, A. 16, 27
   survey 17

Rainbow Project 156
Ramesses II 55-6, 68, 71-2

Ramesseum 68
Rawls 2
reading
   act of *judgement* 133-4, 151-2
   consequences of distanciation from text 88-9
   dialectic between trust and suspicion 135-7
   dimensions of 79-81, 84
   self-understanding 137-40, 145-7
   ways of approaching text 90-1
'reboot' 108
'reciprocity of intentions' 57
're-enactments', art 114-17, 125-7
'Remember Lee Rigby' 142-3
renovation, translation as 117-25
reproduction, of art work 120-1
resistant potential, of cultural translation 156-7
revolution, translation as 125-9
rewriting, translation as 17
Ricoeur, P. 5-11, 18, 27, 29, 35-53, 56-66, 72-5, 78-80, 84-92, 98-9, 110, 117-18, 133-43, 146-51, 155, 159-60
Rigby, Lee 142-3
Romantic view 65
Romney, Mitt 65
Rorty, R. 2-4, 8-9, 18, 26
Routledge Encyclopedia of Translation Studies (2009) 16-17, 19
Rushdie, Salman 13, 18

Salt, Henry 69
Satanic Verses, The (1988) 13
sculpture
   transience of 70-2
   wonderment of 68-70
'second naiveté' 141
Second World War 1
Selfish Gene, The (2006) 38
self-understanding 137-47
   encounter with otherness 145-7
   through interpretation 147-51
semantic autonomy of written 'discourse'
   freedom from authorial intention 63-6
   freedom from historical context 66-72

INDEX

sexual orientation, discrimination on grounds of 131–3, 152–6
Shell 127–9
Shelley 55, 68, 70–1
Siculus, Diodorus 69–70
signs 40–1
  as negative truth 42
Simms, K. 7, 41
Simon, Nina 121–2
Sinn Fein 133
'snowclone' 39–40
solidarity, human 3–4
Sony Pictures Entertainment 73
sovereign authority, translation as exercise of 100–4
Spivak 14
Spratly Islands 100–4
Springsteen, Bruce 125–7
Star Trek 108–9
Steiner 34–5, 44–5, 78, 84–5, 87–8, 93, 98–100, 103, 106–10, 114, 118, 129, 156–7
storytelling 5–7
Sturge, K. 14, 17, 19
subjectivity, displacing 141–5
Sunflowers (1888) 118–19, 122
surveys of cultural translation 14–17
'suspicion', and 'trust' 135–9
symbols 36–8, 40–9
  allegory 37
  memes 38–40
  plurivocity of 37, 46
Synchronoptische Weltgeschichte – Sychronoptic World History 95–6

tangent, of translation 116, 124
'territorial sea' 100
text
  clues in 134–5
  consequences of distanciation from 88–9
  'fallacy of the absolute text' 78
  hermeneutics as theory of 48–9
  human action and 47–8
  ways of approaching 90–1
Theron, Charlize 74
transformation, translation as 111–17
translatability 77–8
translation
  as change in form 21–2

  as exercise of sovereign authority 100–4
  film as 93
  as metaphor 21, 22–4
  'non-substantive' 24
  pastiche 113
  places as 100–4
  power to illuminate 113–14
  'proper' 20
  as renovation 117–25
  as revolution 125–9
  'as total counterpart' 106–11
  as transformation 111–17
  transportational etymology of 18–19
  as 'transposition' 17
  validity as theory 24–5
translator 9–10
  role of 25
Travolta, John 86
Trivedi, H. 20–1, 23–5
'truncated ontology' 141
'trust', and 'suspicion' 135–9
Twitter 129
Tymoczko, M. 20–1

UK Independence Party 63–5
UKIP, *see* UK Independence Party
understanding, human
  border-limits of 34–5
  object of 77–8, 87–8
  quest for 50–1
United Nations Convention on the Law of the Sea 100

validation 133–6
validity, as theory of translation 24–5
Van Gogh 118–19, 122
Vermeer 118–19

Whaam! 105, 124
'Work of Art in the Age of Mechanical Reproduction, The' 120
writing 2–4

X- Files, The (1993–2002) 136–7

Young, R. 14–15, 21–2, 25, 27
Younger Memnon 68–70, 71–2
YouTube 129

www.ingramcontent.com/pod-product-compliance
Lightning Source LLC
Chambersburg PA
CBHW070640300426
44111CB00013B/2188